By the same author

Siam: Land of Temples

915.93

SIAM

———————✦———————

JOHN AUDRIC

19287

SOUTH BRUNSWICK
NEW YORK: A. S. BARNES AND COMPANY

SIAM.
© John Audric 1969.
First American edition published 1970
by A. S. Barnes and Company, Inc.,
Cranbury, New Jersey 08512

Library of Congress Catalogue Card Number: 76-114613

ISBN: 0-498-07638-5
Printed in the United States of America

To
Marian, Hilary and Jacqueline

Contents

·✠··

1 Bangkok to Chiengmai and Misser Louis   11
2 Capitals of Siam   26
3 Rice all the Year   44
4 Fêtes and Festivals   50
5 Korat and the North-east   60
6 The Chakri Dynasty and a Murdered King   73
7 Of Monks and Monasteries   98
8 Railway of Death   109
9 The Political See-saw   123
10 Police, Prisoners, Courts and Prisons   143
11 Schools and Universities   153
12 Chinese in Siam   164
13 The Lost City of Angkor   174
14 Mosques in Siam   183
15 Signposts to the Future   190

Index   205

Illustrations

———— ✦ ————

	facing page
The author's house up-country	32
A station buffet	32
Buses, their roofs piled high with goods. Punctures are common, accidents frequent	33
The Buddha at Ayudhya, old capital of Siam	33
The rice harvest	48
Threshing rice	48
Finger-nail dancing at Chiengmai	49
Army Day. A general kneels to receive the sword from King Phumipol Aduldej	49
A spirit house for the *Phra Phum* or *Chao Thi*	96
Monks return to the *wat* after their morning quest for food	96
The Temple of the Reclining Buddha in Bangkok	97
The Buddhist Library at Chiengmai	97
Murals in the Temple of the Emerald Buddha in Bangkok	112
The Kanchanaburi War Cemetery contains the graves of 5,061 Commonwealth soldiers	113
A Roman Catholic Mission secondary school up-country	113

Illustrations

Learning the alphabet in a school in the north-east   160

A school fair up-country   160

Thailand's newest university at Chiengmai; the science
  laboratory and the Council Buildings, used for
  ceremonies   161

Shipping the pottery in Bangkok   176

Visitors to Angkor Wat   176

Temple dancers in the Inner Courtyard of Angkor Wat   177

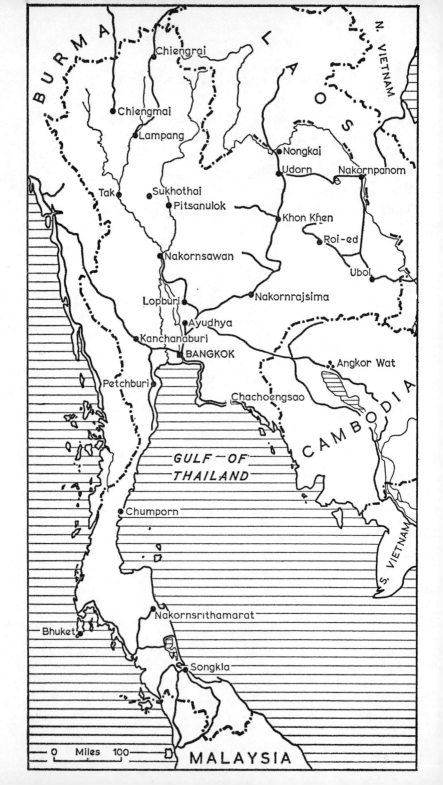

1 *Bangkok to Chiengmai and Misser Louis*

———————————⚬———————————

I had thoroughly enjoyed my two years in an up-country town. For ten months of that period, my wife Marian, and our two daughters Hilary and Jacqueline had lived with me in a wooden house on the fringe of the jungle. The very friendly community adopted this solitary English family. We had been invited to numerous weddings and cremations, and at all special events we were always privileged guests.

After they had gone home, I lived alone. My single state intrigued the townspeople, especially as my two servants could not be said to enhance Thailand's reputation for beautiful women. I think that there was a general feeling that I could have done better. However, they were pleasant girls, sunny-tempered and loyal. I am sure that if I had taken a mistress, few eyebrows would have been raised. It is possible that some assistance would have been forthcoming as to selection. Tolerance is an outstanding characteristic of the Thais.

My work was very interesting. A pilot project in education had been set up, and my duties were in the field of secondary education.

Just over a year later, my base was transferred to the capital, and I left my charming little house and garden, which had begun to look so attractive and colourful, with the shrubs and wild flowers. There was a magnificent flame-of-the-forest which I had watched grow until it nearly swept right across one side of the square garden; the bougainvillaea, frangipani, wild orchids and wild hyacinths. The latter grew in abundance in the pond and appeared to thrive on cutting. There were coconut palms and banana fronds, which appeared to be regarded as free for all. Roses which

I had planted bravely astonished me by flourishing. To this day I do not know if this was due to the efficacy of the manure from two water buffaloes, which a farmer friend had driven into the garden and left overnight, after listening with ill-concealed impatience and disagreement to a lecture on artificial fertilizers from a visiting official of the Ministry of Agriculture, or to beginner's luck. I was very sorry to move.

I had visited Bangkok many times, and so the capital was quite familiar. Life promised to be interesting, for I would have opportunities for travel. A cable to Marian, asking if she and the girls would enjoy a spell in Bangkok, brought back a prompt and delighted acceptance. They had no doubt that they would find plenty to do on the occasions when I would be away.

According to advertisements in the *Bangkok Post*, nearly all house-agents were women. I telephoned one at random, and in a matter of minutes a small Austin car appeared at the hotel, and a middle-aged woman fought against her ample girth, defeated the efforts of the car to keep her in and walked energetically towards me. She was unusually stout for a Thai but possessed remarkable energy. Her English was fluent but quaint, her explanations loud, picturesque and voluble.

She started off with a list of houses at a monthly rental of 4,000 bahts, or nearly £70. I demurred. What about something at 3,500? Her voice rang through the lounge. "Surely your wife would expect to see a nice erection?" Two American friends who were waiting to speak to me nearly choked and suddenly remembered an urgent appointment. She must have been proud of that word and unaware of any embarrassment it may have caused, for she used it freely when praising the houses we inspected. It is likely that no one has had the courage to correct her and that she still uses it today.

There have been several occasions when Thai business women have translated their names and displayed the English version without understanding its English equivalent. A large and most exclusive ladies' hairdressing saloon, patronized by Western women, exhibited the shop sign 'Nit Saloon' in massive gilt, until someone tipped off the proprietor.

She was tireless. She had us all moving at the double, including me, the landlords—and two of these were generals—and the servants. I felt that if this was an example of the newly emancipated Thai women I had heard so much about and who were the new business women of Thailand, then the economic future augured well for the kingdom, although I preferred those smiling, demure and often irresponsible girls I had known up-country.

I settled for a house in central Bangkok. It was built in the compound of a naval officer's house. Obviously used to the command of men, he had the unusual experience of being overruled, exhorted, cajoled and browbeaten. Her commission was two months of the annual rental, which I thought was generous. She departed as noisily as she had come. She was sure that my wife would be delighted by the erection.

It was a pleasant house, neat and compact, with an attractive garden, patio and servants' quarters. Running water, showers and flush lavatories were unaccustomed luxuries, for away from the capital there was no piped water supply.

One of our former girls was coming to work for us. We would find a chauffeur and another girl. I was about to leave the house the following morning when a young Thai came up to the door. He introduced himself as Vichit. He had heard that an English *farang* had moved in. I gathered that the house-agent had lost no time. His former professor at Chulalongkorn University was leaving for Spain and highly recommended his chauffeur. He beckoned him to come in, and a slightly built individual, whom I judged to be about 16, gave me the customary *wai* by placing his hands together and bowing over them. He turned out to be 35, married, with three children. The Thais have a remarkable facility for looking much younger than their years. It was arranged that he would start the following week when my family were due to arrive from England.

I persuaded Vichit to lunch with me, and we went to a restaurant in the Rajdammern Avenue. There he was greeted by three of his friends, who insisted that we join them. Vichit introduced the small party. There were two girls, Valluya and Savitri, both very attractive. Sanan, the other young man, was quite tall for a Thai and, as I was informed, a very good tennis player. All four were graduates from Chulalongkorn and Thamassat universities. Both Vichit and Sanan were lawyers. Valluya, the prettier of the two girls, worked in a Swiss import agency. Savitri was a secretary and translator.

They had also graduated from American universities, and were at pains to inform me that this was not as a result of U.S.O.M. fellowships. The United States Operations Mission to Thailand awards free courses of study with free travel to universities, colleges and hospitals, etc. in the U.S.A. Only Valluya had been to England. "Six months only when it should have been four years," she said with an air of mock severity, as if I were personally responsible. She had been unsuccessful in her attempts to enter Oxford. On completion of her studies in America, her parents had sent her to England for a consolation prize, as she put it.

It was a pleasant meal. Three more of their friends joined us. Then Valluya, Vichit and Sanan came in my car to see my house, while the others followed by taxi. I understood that it was quite usual for them to go out together in a group, but not in pairs. It would be very unusual for a girl from a good family to be seen out with a foreigner unless there had been arranged introductions, parental approval and the likelihood of marriage.

"The Americans are changing many of our customs, but not that one yet!" said Valluya. The others agreed.

I was told that the many night clubs and sleazy joints were well patronized by large numbers of American soldiers, and so they were well provided with distractions. Some had Thai girl friends, but numbers here were comparatively few and were mainly good-time girls. A spate of alarming stories had been circulated in Bangkok concerning their treatment of girls during the Korean and Vietnamese campaigns. I reminded Vichit and his friends that the threat of death in war was never far away, and this would explain the excesses by both soldiers and girls, and that in the case of Thailand there were so many Americans in comparison with other nationals. They were silenced if not convinced. Valluya was more outspoken than the others. She had not been particularly enamoured with life in America.

It was obvious that Vichit was very much in love with her. The descendant of a long line of army officers, he was dignified and correct. Her positive, democratic views and her open disagreement with some of his opinions embarrassed him. Savitri exuded good humour and good nature. Sunny-tempered and extroverted in outlook, she was outshone by Valluya's dominant personality. Sanan was brilliant. His career in law had already got off to a promising start. He possessed a quick and alert brain and was very well-read. I was glad of their company for the remainder of the week, for I was alone. We were to meet frequently during my stay in Thailand.

With the possible exception of Vichit, who was more difficult to know than the others, all of them were of independent thought and leftish views. Their education and experiences abroad had made them dissatisfied with conditions at home. Valluya was more leftish than the others. She was very bitter about the corruption, vice and favouritism which she also felt made Thailand appear a comic-opera kingdom to the countries of the West. She and Sanan had a deep admiration for Pridi Panomyong, who was regent during the Japanese occupation and was now in exile in Yunnan, Southern China.

The dawn in Thailand is always beautiful, and I was fascinated by the fantastic shapes and colours the clouds assume when the sun breaks through and rises higher and higher.

It was the same the morning my family arrived. The B.O.A.C. plane appeared through a magnificent sunrise like a flash of silver, right on time, and we were soon on our way to our new home.

Two days afterwards Savitri, Vichit, Valluya and Sanan made a charming gesture by calling and welcoming the family to Bangkok.

One evening when the quartet, as I now called them, were at the house, I mentioned that I would be visiting Chiengmai the following month. Valluya suggested that if I could postpone my trip for a fortnight they would be glad to have me with them. They knew the town intimately. I could stay with Vichit's relations or at the 'Railway Hotel'. I was delighted to accept. I was beginning to like this charming, lively quartet. Moreover, they would be of considerable assistance to me in Chiengmai and the teak country. I was anxious to find out something about Louis Thomas Leonowens, the son of the celebrated Anna. He founded the firm in Bangkok which bears his name, and had been one of the first to work the teak concessions in Chiengmai.

We went by train. The Thai Railways are justifiably proud of their service to Chiengmai. The sleeping compartments were very clean and comfortable. The shower cubicles were tiled. The enormous plate-glass windows afforded an excellent view. Chinese girls in smart and attractive green uniforms pushed trolleys up and down the platform. These were loaded with fruit, biscuits, cigarettes and cigars. I told Valluya that I was not used to this luxury. On many rail journeys I had bought my meal at a station halt. There a Chinese girl, who had been sitting behind charcoal braziers between the rails, called out the day's menu as soon as the train arrived. At one station there was one slim and pretty girl who looked upon me as a regular customer. As soon as I leaned out of the window she jumped up and brought me my lunch. She knew what it would be. Half a fried chicken on a skewer, a length of bamboo filled with sweet rice and sealed at both ends to keep it warm, bananas and a bottle of Singh beer. Her young brother waved tickets at me, his shrill voice exhorting me to lose my money, "Lotterlee! Lotterlee!" I always purchased at least one ticket, and I never won a prize.

The scenery was continually changing and at times was magnificent in its wild beauty. There were hills and valleys, massive boulders and roaring streams. We climbed through ranges of purple hills. More streams flowed between high ferns. Tall trees, the tallest I had as yet seen in Thailand, were covered with large white blossoms. Savitri called them snowball trees. A steep ascent took us through groves of magnificent teak trees and then on to the ghostly tunnel of Khun Tan. It was at this point that the coolies died in hundreds building the railway in 1925. We crossed the deep valley of the Me Ta on a bridge which had an amazing shape, like a cobweb. I was told that the design was not only original but brilliant and that the bridge was of great strength and durability.

At times there was dense jungle on both sides of the track; lush green valleys spotted with brilliant orchids, tobacco fields and fine teak houses. The train took us past the old walled cities of Lampang and Lampoon, and then on to journey's end and crowded platforms where a troupe of wandering classical dancers, complete with orchestra, were making a brave effort to entertain and perform the conventional movements of the dance, despite the large numbers of people who had come to greet their friends.

As I did not want to trespass on the hospitality of this friendly quartet, I decided to stay in the 'Railway Hotel'. They demurred at first, but eventually gave in, and it was agreed that they would call for me the following day. The 'Railway Hotel' is a collection of bungalows on stilts. It was not luxurious but comfortable.

Chiengmai is one of the most beautiful and romantic towns in South-east Asia. It has had a chequered history. Founded in A.D. 1296, it became the capital of the independent kingdom of Lannathai until 1558. Then it was occupied by the Burmese until 1774, when King Taksin drove them out. It became the capital of a Siamese vassal principality in 1794 and enjoyed a wide measure of independence. There was a Resident Commissioner from Bangkok in 1874.

Princess Dararasmai of Chiengmai was already a celebrated beauty at the age of 15 and lived in a kind of fairy palace on the River Ping. Princes and nobles from all over the kingdom, including Chiengrai, Lampoon, Nan and Payao, which towns still retained limited independence, were invited to a special function in her honour. At this time there was a clash between British and French interests in Siam. A rumour was officially leaked to Bangkok by the French that the British had planned to bring about a marriage between the lovely young princess and a leading Shan prince, the object of which would be to strengthen Britain's position in Siam. King Chulalongkorn, who had been invited to the ceremony, stepped in first. He sent his envoy with a proposal of marriage. Dararasmai's parents were delighted at the honour, and the young princess travelled with great pomp to Bangkok. At the age of 16 she presented the king with a daughter and was promoted to the rank of Fifth Queen. Chiengmai in this way lost much of its independence, for it was brought more closely into the kingdom.

Chiengmai women are renowned for their beauty. They are much lighter skinned than elsewhere in the country. The whole city offers a wealth of colour. There was a religious procession on the day we were there. The girls wore their traditional brightly coloured dresses, which made a pleasant change from the white blouses and blue skirts of the capital. They carried silver bowls full of blooms, bunches of flowers and the most beautiful roses I was ever to see in Thailand. Here the sturdy but plain bullock carts one sees all over the country looked very attractive on account of some excellent carvings. Some of the private houses which bordered the River Ping had attractive, well-kept gardens and were irrigated by a simple but ingenious system. Bamboo water wheels tilted bamboo containers and sent the water through a bamboo conduit on to the lawns and flower beds. I had the impression that I could have lived quite happily in Chiengmai.

The city is famed for its lacquerware and embossed silver bowls or boxes. One street is called Silver Street. Here the silversmiths carry on their work. A plain silver bowl is more expensive than one with designs, for it requires more time and a higher degree of craftsmanship to produce a surface free from flaws.

We climbed the 240 steps up Doi Suthep to the famous *wat* or temple. Some tiny children shyly offered us small bunches of marigolds and mountain roses. The object was to place them as offerings in the temple. A short way up we stopped at a small platform to look at the statue of a woman wringing water out of her hair. This is Nang Toronee, Goddess of the Earth. According to legend, evil spirits appeared before the Buddha when he was sitting under the bo tree and tried to divert him from his meditations with visions of more worldly forms of pleasure. Nang Toronee, seeing the danger, protected him by wringing out her hair so vigorously that a flood formed and drove the evil spirits away. I have heard more legends in Chiengmai than anywhere else in Thailand. A few were fascinating and delightful; others were quite ridiculous. To my amazement, Vichit accepted many of them, but Valluya was less credulous.

Seven-headed snakes guard the main flight of steps, their long undulating bodies, covered with glistening tiles, forming balustrades. Blessed water is reputed to gush from their mouths and spray the pilgrims as they climb, but on our day the water pressure was either too low or the snakes were not legend-conscious.

Wat Prabat Doi Suthep is one of the most famous pilgrimages in Thailand. Two ferocious-looking giants stand guard with drawn swords at the top of the stairway. The *wat* is a magnificent sight, with its yellow tiled roofs shining golden in the sunshine and its ornate red, gold and black doors and windows. There were about a score of Buddhist monks coming upwards. Vichit spoke to them. It was a pilgrimage, and they had come from all over the country.

The mountain ridge fell steeply away from the temple wall, and from that point we gazed into the misty space. Elsewhere a magnificent panoramic view of the city stretched before us. There was the silvery Ping, the purple mountains, a vivid splash of colour from the wild flowers and the green, white and red buildings of the *wats*.

We descended and made our way through the town. There are scores of *wats* in the city. They make a beautiful picture with their carved teak screens and tall Burmese interiors.

Valluya and Sanan had been hunting down possible sources of information concerning Anna's son, and we spent a most thrilling evening travelling to different parts of the city to listen to the exploits of this colourful figure.

In the teak country and in Chiengmai, which was the concessionaires' base and retreat, he is a legend even today. "Louis Leonowens? You mean *Misser* Louis!" I was laughingly corrected.

Anna arrived in Siam in 1862, accompanied by her young son Louis, aged 9, and her daughter Avis, aged 10. In 1867 she went to America with her children and never returned to Bangkok. Louis stayed there for a few years and then decided to seek his fortune elsewhere.

He told his friends that America was finished—"Played out!" His next call was Australia, where he joined the police force. This was to prove a toughening experience and an excellent preparation for a life of adventure and danger. Then, in 1882, at the age of 30, he turned up in Siam. His former classmate, Crown Prince Chulalongkorn, was now king. He made him an officer in the cavalry, but this lusty young extrovert was quick to see that there were fortunes to be made in other walks of life. He entered the service of the Borneo Company, which is one of the oldest and most distinguished foreign business houses in Thailand. It was also one of the earliest pioneers of the teak industry and was to be closely connected with it for over eighty years. Louis became its first forest manager.

The teak concessionaires had their own code. They were not allowed to bring their own wives, and it is likely that they thought this rule up themselves. They lived like Oriental potentates. They hunted, for there was game in abundance. They loved and they gambled.

Eighty years ago there were no trains. The journey of 500 miles took six weeks by pole boat. From Chiengmai to the teak forests the journey by elephant could take a fortnight. But Chiengmai was a paradise in those days. The teak concessionaires had laid out the city to provide them with all possible amenities for an enjoyable leave. In addition to the usual shooting, hunting and fishing, there was golf, tennis, squash and polo. Once a year they reported back to Bangkok. The Chiengmai maidens were famed for their beauty even in those days, and one concessionaire used to bring a few dozen willing lovelies with him as presents for his friends.

'Misser' Louis was first among the extroverts. The concessions were granted by the ruling prince of Chiengmai, the Chao Luang. In Louis he found a kindred spirit. Nearly every evening they gambled into the early hours. Their friendship even survived a crisis when one day they met in the forests and Louis was seen to have a larger escort of elephants than the Chao Luang! A man with a less engaging personality would have considered himself fortunate if he had merely been sent home, but the two continued to dine, wine and gamble.

If ever a foreigner was *sanuk* with the Siamese, it was 'Misser' Louis. He could do their work as well as they could. At celebrations and parties he was soon *sanuk* with everyone.

One incident highlights the anomalies in the legal system in those days. One day 'Misser' Louis was being carried through the streets of Chiengmai in a sedan chair. This was a serious case of *lèse-majesté*, for only the Chao Luang could be carried in this way. He was brought before the local court and informed that the punishment was death. Not surprisingly, he objected and was fined ten bahts! Almost any punishment could be waived on payment of a fine. The amount varied according to the status of the offender. In spite of his many privileges and the prestige he enjoyed, 'Misser' Louis was only a commoner in Siamese law.

He was reputed to possess unusual control over elephants and was well used to their sudden rages when they could be so deadly. He knew when a tusker was about to become *musth*. In this condition the huge beast will go berserk and trample to death its mahout and anyone in its path. Or it will seize the unfortunate individual with its trunk and then twist him on to its tusks so that they pass right through him. The elephant usually gives a tell-tale sign of being *musth*. An oily secretion, which has some connection with its sexual functions, exudes from a small hole near the eyes, but this is not always visible. Apparently 'Misser' Louis did not need the visual evidence. He knew his elephants. From what I heard, he led a charmed life.

In business he never missed an opportunity. He took out

concessions in the name of the Borneo Company, and, whilst he was about it, took out a few in his own! His boat, the *Captain Leonowens,* was a familiar sight in the teak rivers. Eventually his activities on his own account clashed with those of his employers, and he left the service. With the concessions he had secured, he joined the company's rival, Bombay-Burmah. Here, he continued merrily as before among his elephants and forests. He founded the business in Bangkok which bears his name and which is so familiar to residents.

The Siamese are quite lyrical about their teak and their elephants, and they associate 'Misser' Louis with the prosperity and prestige the industry provided for so long. Today there is grave anxiety as to the future of the teak reserves. The annual output has consistently declined. Recently the Ministry of Agriculture reported that the teak trees had been overcut three times their permitted yield, and that in twenty-five years there will be no teak left in Thailand unless the most vigorous steps are taken to ensure conservation and prevent theft. More severe penalties are urged. The existing ones have been in existence for over sixty years. Then the large lorries with their heavy loads are responsible for great damage to the roads.

The number of elephants has declined sharply. At the time of 'Misser' Louis there were 20,000. There are now less than 9,000. Although increased mechanization in the teak forests has reduced the need for elephants, large numbers have been slaughtered by organized mobile gangs, using high-velocity rifles and making their getaway with the tusks by fast cars. In many cases they have merely been shot for sport and left to die where they dropped. In some regions the elephant has completely disappeared. Fears have been expressed in well-informed circles that it is doomed to extinction. There have been urgent demands that the Government deal more drastically with the culprits and set up national parks.

White elephants are not actually white but are albinos. They are males, with pink eyes, and have twenty toes instead of the usual eighteen. In 1926 one was born in Chiengmai. It was worshipped wherever it was seen. The white elephant is considered to be sacred, regarded by many as the reincarnation of the Buddha. In accordance with custom, it was presented to the king who, with the queen, came to Chiengmai to see it. This was the first time that a Siamese king had travelled to the city. The royal couple were met at the station and escorted through the city by a procession, which included eighty-seven prize elephants. Later the elephant was taken to Bangkok, where enormous crowds, overcome with joy, lined the canal banks and roads. Unfortunately many people fell into the *klongs* (canals) and were drowned or crushed to death. The forest manager of the Borneo Company, in whose concessions the elephant was born, was awarded the Order of the White Elephant. Another was found in the south in March 1968.

Over thirty hill tribes inhabit the highlands north of Chiengmai and at times may be seen in the city. When we were there a group of Meos were walking about. They wore very bright clothes. The men were dressed in dark blue trousers and short jackets, with a bright crimson sash above their waists. Two of the men wore blue turbans. The women wore coloured aprons over their black trousers. Their hair was formed into a flat circular knob high on top of their heads. Both men and women wore several large silver collars, which indicated family wealth.

The women weave cloth from cotton and hemp. The Meos live in wooden shacks built of planks fixed upright; the roofs are thatched with palm leaves. Like some of the other hill tribes, they carry out a 'slash and burn' agriculture, slashing out clearings, cutting down trees to grow their crops, which include opium. The following year they hack out and burn another clearing. This denudes the soil, and the natural water storage which the trees provide is destroyed, causing droughts and floods. Every twelve years or so they move to a new region, taking their animals and chattels with them. The Bangkok government has tried for years to settle them but with little success. They are very independent and of unclean habits.

The Meos number about 45,000. They are animists and make sacrifices to the spirits of streams and forests. Their habitat is not confined to Thailand. They roam into Burma, Laos, Vietnam and South-west China, and if they run foul of the authorities in one country they turn up in another, in tribal territory. Sometimes their activities create difficulties between the neighbouring countries, although Thailand and Burma appear to have arrived at a clear appreciation of the situation and possible repercussions.

All the hill tribes cling fast to their old traditions and customs.

There are some 10,000 Yao from Southern China. They are usually skilled blacksmiths and silversmiths. The men wear blue baggy trousers with coloured embroidery. The women are very beautiful. Personal hygiene and cleanliness are two main characteristics of the race. They do not intermarry with the Thais.

There are 80,000 Karens. The numbers have increased following Burmese independence. A large number are animists, but there are many Christians among them. Unmarried girls wear a long white slip on a tunic of coarse homespun. One of the King's titles is 'King of the Karens'. There are Red Karens and White Karens. The former are dark-skinned, the latter are more fair and attractive. They are scattered over a region extending from Chiengmai in the north to Kanchanburi in the south. In the northern part a settlement of White Karens is ruled by hereditary chiefs. This tribe is strictly moral.

The Akha, of whom there are some 25,000, inhabit the mountain range north of Thailand. Some settlements are quite near Chiengmai. They are animists and dread evil spirits. Ceremonies are frequently held to drive them away. As they fear water spirits, they rarely wash. A man, known as the Ah Shaw, is appointed to deflower all virgins for marriage at certain specified ceremonies. The tribe lives by growing and selling opium.

The Lahu and the Lisu tribes are animists, although some of the former worship a man god. Lisu means 'Down from the roof of the world'. They left China because of oppression and migrated to Upper Burma, the Northern Shan States and Thailand. They live in houses built of wooden planks and raised on posts. The Lisu are ruled by hereditary chiefs. The men wear light blue coats, short trousers and turbans. The women's coats have wide striped sleeves and are covered with silver ornaments. Around their necks they wear double silver collars. The Lisu are excellent farmers and can cultivate almost vertical hill slopes. They grow opium but mainly for sale. The Lisu are one of the fittest of the hill tribes. Intermarriage is rare, even more so between Lisus and Thais. The women are considered to be very beautiful.

There are smaller tribes such as the Lawa and Khamu. The Phi Tong Luang are reputed to be the most primitive people in the world. The name means 'Spirit of the Yellow Leaves' because they are semi-nomadic and build temporary huts of leaves, which they abandon when the leaves turn yellow.

As Korat is the gateway to the north-east, so Chiengmai is the gateway to the tribes of the mountains north and north-west, as well as the opium-growing regions, which the quartet assured me the Government will never be able to stop. Even today many huge fortunes are made, and there is much bribery in high places.

Chiengmai has one of the finest hospitals in the country and also a very well-run leper colony. The doctors have a reputation for excellent and devoted work. Apparently there is little danger of their catching the disease unless they remain in the leper village too long without leave or become weakened by other illnesses. It has been estimated that there are 150,000 lepers in Thailand.

The magnificent new university, Thailand's latest and the first one to be erected outside the capital, occupies a splendid position in the city and will meet a need which has become urgent for a long time.

Vichit, Sanan and Savitri had decided to stay on in Chiengmai as one of Vichit's friends was due to take the saffron robe, and the ceremony was being performed in the famous *wat*.

I returned to Bangkok with Valluya and a small party of her friends and relations. They had graduated with her.

I was surprised to find that there was unemployment amongst those of similar background and qualifications in her age group. For this they blamed the Government.

When I told them that I had read that the women were in a stronger position than ever, in connection with emancipation and careers, they said that this was absurd. These stories were Government-inspired and also put out by foreign correspondents searching for a new slant. With the exception of a very efficient and capable few at the top, there were not many openings for women. They did not make much advance in the professions. Influence and nepotism often outweighed qualifications and experience. In families, boys were so spoilt that when they reached manhood, they expected the same treatment from their wives. Infidelity was quite common. Apparently, an ambitious woman who went into business could go far, and, for those who wanted to make money, this was the best avenue.

All thought that Thailand needed a civilian government and that all over the country people were tired of the old military clique. They told me that Thailand could have been a prosperous country years ago if some of the cabinet ministers had looked beyond Bangkok. But their vision was limited. The Government did not know what was going on outside the capital, for many ministers had not travelled far beyond it. The provinces could have been developed years ago. The communist threat was not even understood because few travelled up to the disaffected provinces to find out. They relied upon garbled reports from officials and advisers, mostly Americans. There had always been bandits in the north, and the occasional murders had been accepted as peculiar to that part of Thailand. Now they were asked to believe that they were the work of communists.

Valluya said that there were too many impractical women among the high-born of Bangkok who had never travelled beyond Ayudhya and Hua Hin. They organized schemes for the welfare of women. One she scoffed at was for the rehabilitation of prostitutes. They were offered domestic service, where they earned less in a month than they would receive from an American soldier for an odd evening.

There were not nearly enough jobs for those with good educational qualifications in Bangkok, and there was, at present, little future outside the capital. This was beginning to create a social problem which could have serious repercussions.

Valluya was critical of the effect of American influence. She said that the Government could not make any important decision in foreign affairs without consulting the American ambassador. Thailand was fully committed to the United States. Thai soldiers were fighting in Vietnam. Thailand had incurred the enmity of some of the countries of South-east Asia, when she could have aspired to the leadership of the region.

I asked if it were true that university students were politically apathetic. She said that quite a large percentage of students and lecturers had strong political views but were careful to avoid publicity. Criticism could so easily be labelled communism, and this was a very ugly and dangerous word in Bangkok.

I had the impression that if these views were a sample of those held generally by the young intellectuals, then they could well influence the trend of events in the future.

············

When the Siamese migrated from Yunnan in Southern China, large numbers settled in what is now Northern Thailand. They defeated the Khmers and Mons and established their first kingdom and capital city at Sukhothai in A.D. 1237. The immigration continued further southwards, where other principalities were set up.

Sukhothai prospered, particularly under the third king, Ram Kamhaeng. He had visited Peking and brought back Chinese artisans to build pottery factories and teach the craft to the Siamese. He sent annual tribute to China.

The kingdom was ruled by a simple patriarchal form of monarchy. A bell was hung outside the royal palace, and anyone who had a grievance could ring it and ask for the king's assistance.

He appears to have been a remarkable ruler, and is still held in reverence by students of Siamese history. He expanded the kingdom, was a devout Buddhist and a great lover. He excelled in war, wrote poetry and invented the modern Thai script and used it to write praise of himself and his kingdom on stone pillars. An extract from one of the inscriptions reads:

> When I grew up to be nineteen years of age, Khun Samchon, the ruler of Chot, came to attack Tak ... Khun Samchon approached. My father's elephant fled in disorder. I did not flee. I rode the elephant Nekbol. I drove in before my father. Khun Samchon fled. So my father gave me the name of Ram Kamhaeng. During my father's lifetime I served no other ... If I went to attack a village or town and brought back elephants, boys, girls, silver or

gold, I gave them to my father ... When my elder brother died, I inherited the entire kingdom.

After his death, more inscriptions were written on columns and walls by succeeding kings or nobles. One of them reads:

The people of this city of Sukhothai are charitably pious and devoted to almsgiving. King Ram Kamhaeng, the ruler of Sukhothai, as well as princes and princesses, gentlemen and ladies of the nobilities, and men and women, all have faith in the Buddhist religion.

Sukhothai was a wealthy and prosperous capital city. There was an abundance of elephants, oxen, horses, buffaloes; rivers and *klongs* were well stocked with fish; the yield from the rice fields was high, and the output of silver and gold was increasing. However, the rivalry between Sukhothai and Chiengmai, the new capital of Lannathai, became so destructive that another town was to profit by it, to grow in importance and eventually replace it as the new capital of Siam. This was Ayudhya.

The old capital of Sukhothai now lies in ruins. There is little to remind the visitor of the glories of her illustrious past. Everywhere I went I saw ruins which were in the process of further disintegration. Yet there was an air of wild, wistful beauty about the desolation. Flame-of-the-forest trailed across the ruins of former temples and palaces. In the centre of two lines of columns, a huge stone Buddha, almost completely framed with scaffolding, surveyed the crumbling remains of the former capital.

Along dry moats small boys drove water buffaloes. Goats bleated from paved and sunken walks. Three boys offered me small Buddha heads and pieces of pottery from the kilns which King Ram Kamhaeng's Chinese artisans built centuries ago. There was nothing grasping about these little salesmen, no mention of a price. A few ticals, and they were delighted.

In addition to the work on the huge Buddha, there had been some attempts to restore a few *chedis* (spires), but it looked as if most of the ruins had been neglected for so long that they were now beyond reconstitution and restoration.

I watched ten saffron-robed monks walking amid the ruins. They were moving purposefully. This was obviously not an excursion for them. I assumed that their *wat* must have been quite near. Birds of many colours were flying in and out of the mass of fallen walls, as if returning to their nests or setting forth in quest of food.

In 1419, Sukhothai was absorbed into the rapidly expanding kingdom of Ayudhya, and the former capital declined into insignificance. A new town was built only twenty miles away on the banks of a river. This provided it with an ample supply of water, which at times the old capital lacked. It is a typical provincial town and has a quiet, restrained atmosphere.

I gazed at the dense masses of water hyacinths which had spread across the river. With their pale mauve flowers and green leaves, they made a beautiful and peaceful picture. However, they had a pronounced nuisance value there, for I saw a boat pull up and men set to work cutting and slashing the thick clumps of blooms. The plant was brought from Java a hundred years ago, and it has spread so rapidly and with such density that it has choked many of the country's waterways. Much labour is required to keep the rivers navigable.

Ayudhya lies sixty miles north of Bangkok. It can be reached easily by road, rail or river. I found the visit most depressing. The former capital is one massive devastated area. Here and there one comes across scaffolding, but there is little of it, and one has the impression that it has been erected reluctantly and spasmodically.

Valluya and her friends were with us in 1959, and I made the comment that very little had been done in the way of reconstruction since its fall in 1767. I was surprised by the reaction of these young intellectuals. There was some resentment towards the Burmese, but the past as such had little interest for them. Their minds were on the future. Vichit made the laconic remark that the rubble, stonework and bricks of the nearly demolished city were needed to build the new capital of Bangkok. Valluya said that fear of further invasions from Burma persisted right up to the time of the British conquest of that country, and that Thailand was too busy with her defences. However, I have often met this lack of interest in former royal palaces and historic buildings away from the capital.

We came across hundreds of *chedis* and the ruins of palaces and temples in miles of streets. The whole area is a reminder of the crushing defeat inflicted by the Burmese and the savage and wanton destruction. The capital was sacked and completely destroyed. The king was killed. Princes and nobles and thousands of Siamese were taken to Burma as slaves. Of a population of over a million, only ten thousand remained.

As I gazed at the wilderness of ruins, I was reminded of a remark made by a brilliant student of mine, who had just secured a place in Thamassat University. I had remembered it because it had nothing to do with the lesson I was giving. "Our teacher says that we are not strong enough for Burma—yet!" That there were Thais who contemplated a war of revenge was something I had not considered. But I could understand that the appalling sight before me could well inspire anti-Burmese feelings. I told Valluya of the incident. She listened with interest. "All this", she waved her hands with an expressive gesture at the vast area of ruins, "is a reminder of what they did to us, as well as the shame of our defeat. One of the aims of Field Marshal Pibul Songkram, when Prime Minister, was to reach a better understanding with the Burmese. As a gesture of atonement, they gave large sums of money for the rebuilding of the city. The elephant stockade was restored, some Buddhist statues and sections of walls were renovated, but after Pibul's downfall work stopped, and has only just started up again—and as you can see—very little of it. However, many of us have not forgotten or forgiven."

We wandered past the slave market which must have witnessed some harrowing scenes in the old days. I had heard stories of archaeological treasures, of gold and silver work of great value, which the fleeing Siamese had hidden or flung into the canals and moats, intending to return later but failing to do so. It appeared quite likely, but I could not see how treasure hunts could be undertaken with any degree of success, for there were no records, and Nature had effectively concealed the secrets of the last days.

Perhaps a fortunate and intrepid few stumbled on some of them in the same way as small boys, like those at Sukhothai, came across the Buddha heads. These too were offered here in abundance, but the boys of Ayudhya were more commercially minded. There were fewer tourists in Sukhothai.

I walked on ahead to get a better view and disturbed some brickwork when climbing some broken steps. There was a sudden hiss, and three huge snakes shot out from a pile of masonry

and with lightning speed slithered into the encroaching jungle.
The ruins had some small measure of protection, even if Nature's
security corps were most unpleasant creatures.

In the 400 years of its existence, Ayudhya was ruled by thirty-
three kings, one-third of whom were murdered or had murdered
rival claimants to the throne. The assassins included a mother,
brothers and high officials of the state.

Few capitals could claim a more colourful or illustrious history.
It prospered from the date of its inception. It was situated on the
trade routes between China and India. The Chinese were the
earliest traders and settled in large numbers. The Portuguese were
the first European settlers, followed by the British and Dutch in
the sixteenth century. They reported back to their sovereigns
that Ayudhya had more splendour and majesty than London,
Lisbon or The Hague. Later the French were to be amazed at the
pageantry and pomp of the royal court, and the magnificent
palaces, temples, buildings and streets.

There were repeated attacks from the Burmese. One war
occurred when the Siamese, who possessed seven white elephants,
refused to give two of them to the Burmese king who had none.
A white elephant is considered sacred, and its possession a matter
of great prestige. The Burmese overran the country until they
reached Ayudhya, where they were stopped by its massive walls,
huge ramparts, forts, moats and canals.

One incident in the campaign, which the Thais recall with
reverence, concerns the former Queen Suriyothai of Siam. Her
husband, the King, and a Burmese general were fighting a duel
mounted on elephants. Seeing the King in danger, she drove her
elephant between them and received a mortal blow. Ayudhya
fell in 1569 after a siege of eight months. This time the city was
not sacked, but the walls were dismantled, and thousands of
families were taken as prisoners to Burma. Among them was the
legendary Black Prince, later King Naresuen of Siam. He took
advantage of his captivity to learn Burmese military secrets and
plans, and when he returned home he raised an army and declared
Siam's independence.

Burma invaded again through the Three Pagodas Pass, a name
also associated with the horrors of the Death Railway. He
decided on a scorched earth policy. Defences were destroyed so
that the Burmese could not use them. He fought a duel with the

Burmese Crown Prince and killed him. Later he honoured the bravery of his enemy by erecting a *chedi*. Unfortunately this was lost in the jungle, but was found again early this century, restored and unveiled by the present king of Thailand, Phumipol Aduldej, on 25th January 1959.

In the seventeenth century Ayudhya was once again a dazzling and prosperous capital. It was a walled city, six miles round, and folded in a bend of the Chao Phya River. Indians, Moors, Malays, Japanese, Chinese, Portuguese, Dutch, British, French and Scandinavians lived in compounds outside the city walls. The British, Dutch and French East India Companies had built their factories, which they fortified, not so much against the Siamese as against each other. There were at this time hundreds of beautiful *wats*.

There now appeared on the Ayudhya scene one of the most outstanding foreigners to feature in Siamese history. This was Constantine Phaulcon, known as the Falcon. At the age of 14 he went to sea in a British ship, and later joined the East India Company. Afterwards he decided to trade on his own. On one voyage his fearlessness, seamanship and courage attracted the attention of the king of Siam's envoy, who was a passenger returning from Persia. He persuaded Phaulcon to come to Siam. Here King Narai took an instant liking to the brilliant young Greek and in a very short time made him Prime Minister. This was an outstanding mark of favour, for it placed him second in authority to the King.

Phaulcon was a converted Catholic. The French were desirous of establishing relations with Siam, and he supported them. He persuaded King Narai to receive an official French mission, and in October 1685 the French Ambassador, Chevalier de Chaumont, was given a most lavish and spectacular welcome in Ayudhya. The letter he bore from Louis XIV was placed on a golden salver, then deposited in a golden casket, which was taken on board a gilded royal barge rowed by sixty oarsmen in crimson attire. After this it was laid on a golden palanquin and carried by ten men in crimson uniforms. There were magnificent river pageants and receptions in the capital.

Following the visit, French missionaries came over and built missions. French engineers built a magnificent summer palace for the King at Lopburi, and a palatial mansion in the same town for

Phaulcon, the ruins of which give the visitor today some idea of its former grandeur.

A mission was sent to France, and in it the first group of Siamese students to visit that country. Siam continued to send her students in ever-increasing numbers. The leaders of the *coup* which were to overthrow the absolute monarchy had studied in France.

Louis XIV wanted to convert King Narai to Roman Catholicism. Phaulcon had been rewarded by being made a Count of France and a Knight of the Order of St. Michael. Inspired by gratitude, or with the object of furthering his own interests, he made resolute efforts to assist in the King's conversion. He even considered launching a *coup*, with the support of French troops, to force the King to change his religion. This was indeed most ungenerous, even treacherous conduct towards the King who was his friend, and who had raised him up to the proud position he occupied and loaded him with high honours. Phaulcon had some premonition of the opposition his plan would arouse among the princes and court officials and decided to abandon it. He counselled the French to adopt a more cautious approach in this instance and to be content with an alliance, without the King's conversion as one of the conditions.

Phaulcon's influence over the King, and his importance in the country, had made him many powerful enemies. They realized that if the King were won over to Roman Catholicism France would constitute a serious threat to Siam's independence. Their opposition to Phaulcon became more bitter and more overt. King Narai, now a sick man, saw the danger which threatened his favourite, and, realizing that he could not now give him the protection he so desperately needed, implored Phaulcon to flee the country. Phaulcon was convinced that he could weather the storm, and declined the King's advice.

His enemies moved quickly. They sent him a letter purporting to come from the King, inviting him to come to the palace. The unsuspecting Phaulcon duly arrived and was thrown into a dungeon and put to fiendish torture to get him to confess that he had plotted with the French, not only in connection with the attempt at the King's conversion, but also in affairs of state. He was again tortured to make him reveal where he had hidden his wealth and to confess that he wanted the throne for himself. He

The author's house up-country

A station buffet

Buses, their roofs piled high with goods.
Punctures are common, accidents frequent

The Buddha at Ayudhya, old capital of Siam

declared that he had little wealth and reminded them of his services to the King and the country.

He had always expected that the French would help him if his life was in danger, but, although General Desfarges, the Commander-in-Chief of the French forces, and Abbé Lionne were at hand, they did nothing to help the one who had done so much for them. Phaulcon was dragged outside the royal palace and hacked to death. When King Narai heard the news, he was prostrate with grief and died four months afterwards. A great king and a brilliant statesman and politician were lost to Siam.

At the dawn of the eighteenth century Ayudhya was at the zenith of her power. Ocean-going ships sailed the seas. The arts and literature flourished. Among the foreigners, some forty-eight nationalities were represented. The King possessed a library of nearly 100,000 books. The literature of the period included books on medicine, architecture, archaeology, astrology, astronomy, sculpture, music, painting and fine arts, dramatics and boat building.

Towards the middle of the century, the proud capital began to decline under weak and ineffectual leadership. The Burmese, ever watchful, seized the opportunity and attacked. Ayudhya was besieged for nearly two years, and when it capitulated the Burmese took a fearful revenge upon the defenceless city. Elsewhere many towns, mainly in the north, were destroyed.

Yet although Ayudhya, the 'Light of the Kingdom', suffered such an appalling end, it is certain that eventually it would have met its doom as a capital city through another enemy. This was the sea. As it continued to recede, the importance of the city would have declined. Today it has a population of 25,000. It is an agricultural centre and the principal market for river-borne commerce, especially rice.

The new monarch, King Taksin, moved the capital to Dhonburi. He was so occupied with rebuilding Siam after the defeat by the Burmese that he did not concern himself much with any splendours for the new capital. However, General Chakri brought back the Emerald Buddha from Vientiane and installed it in Dhonburi.

After the execution of King Taksin, whose equestrian statue stands in Dhonburi, General Chakri ascended the throne. He moved the capital across the river to the opposite bank, so that the Chao Phya provided a moat and a natural defence against the Burmese.

For the site of his royal palace he chose the Chinatown area of old Bangkok, then owned by a rich Chinese merchant, who willingly moved the Chinese community to Sampeng. This is still the Chinese quarter of the capital. Chakri was crowned Rama I in an improvised wooden pavilion in June 1782. He gave the name Kroong Deb, which means 'City of gods', to the new capital. Bangkok means 'Village of the Olives'.

It rapidly took shape through corvée or conscripted labour. Everything built in his reign was in Ayudhyan style and mostly religious. These include the precincts of the Temple of the Emerald Buddha, Wat Po and Wat Sutat. The palace buildings which are still in existence are the Amarindra group and Dusit Maha Prasart. The royal barges were also built during his reign.

Rama II broke away from the traditional Ayudhyan style of architecture and added Chinese and European styles. He built Wat Arun. Rama III built the huge reclining Buddha at Wat Po, and had two large images of the Buddha crowned and dressed as Siamese kings and placed in a standing position before the Emerald Buddha. Rama IV built more royal barges, including one of outstanding grace and beauty, with a seven-headed Naga.

King Chulalongkorn built the Dusit Palace as a royal residence outside the city walls and connected it to the magnificent Rajdamnern Avenue, which was modelled on Pall Mall and the Champs-Elysées, with three attractive and stately bridges of Parisian style in marble to cross the canals. The Ananta Throne Hall, a vast, high-domed, marble edifice in Italian style, was completed in King Vajiravudh's reign.

All the Chakri kings built some great Buddhist edifice or palace to mark their reign. Hundreds of *wats* were built. In their zeal to beautify the new capital and perpetuate their own memory, they did not foresee that the upkeep of these buildings was to prove a heavy burden on future generations. However, between them they created a beautiful, colourful and picturesque city.

A hundred years ago *klongs* were the only highways of Bangkok, then a capital without roads or railways. French engineers laid out much of the city. They constructed two huge *klongs,* one running north, the other south, and connected most of the smaller ones to them. It was a simple but ingenious plan. The incoming

and outgoing tides sweeping up from the Chao Phya River along
the waterways would flush out the city, for *klongs* were the only
means of drainage.

The present New Road, which winds its way through Bangkok's West End and into the Chinese quarter, was the first road.

River traffic and transport must have moved in a very leisurely
way in those days. There were royal barges, some about 150 feet
long, made from the trunk of a single teak baulk. They were
magnificent and stately craft, with dragon or seven-headed Naga
prows and serpent sterns, and richly encrusted with gilt. There
were seventy-two oarsmen, dressed in crimson or crimson and
blue, to each barge, as well as two coxswains or steersmen.
Another, for timing the strokes, stood on a platform, and struck a
sounding board with a long rod.

There were the barges of the representatives of the accredited
powers to the royal court of Bangkok, the flat-bottomed river
craft of the merchants and lesser princes, the passenger boats,
punts carrying the saffron-robed monks to and from their
monasteries, teak rafts, sampans, deep sea ships from China and
ferry boats. Along the banks, the green, white, gold and red of
the *wats*, the ubiquitous flame of the forest tree, and the exotic
hues of the wild orchids completed the pageant of colour.

A few years ago the French Embassy brought the past back to
life on the occasion of a reception held at the riverside embassy.
All guests were asked to arrive at the landing stage by river craft
and to wear nineteenth-century dress. It was a brilliant success
and evoked nostalgic memories among those of the older
generation.

The Chao Phya remains as always a great river highway. One
afternoon I sat on the lawn of the 'Oriental Hotel', chatting to
Valluya, and watched a conglomeration of craft sweep by. There
were sleek warships of the Thai Navy; sampans heavily laden with
grain, water tanks, pottery or furniture, their decks almost awash.
I counted six flat-bottomed boats all loaded with pigs, each one in
a separate cane basket, *en route* for the slaughter house. There were
chains of barges; sometimes as many as seven towed by one tug.
There were boats piled high with fruit and motor launches
packed tight with passengers. Huge Chinese cargo ships, their
massive concepts (letters of the alphabet) proclaiming their
nationality above all others, moved slowly or were anchored.

Punts, crowded with saffron-robed monks, weaved their way in and out as they had done hundreds of years before.

We hailed a boatman to take us to Wat Arun, the beautiful Temple of the Dawn. The sun was setting and the temple was a magnificent spectacle. It is covered, layer upon layer, with a mosaic of tiny fragments of coloured porcelain. Valluya quoted a remark we had both heard before. "Thousands of cups and saucers smashed and fixed to the walls."

Wat Arun towers up from the river bank to a height of 250 feet. It is like a majestic pagoda, with four smaller ones of similar shape at the sides. Lights twinkled from the central tower. There were hundreds of these tiny bulbs in rows, stretching from the central tower to outline the smaller towers. Temple bells rang out their quiet and merry greeting.

One excursion I was never tired of was the boat trip to the Floating Market. The launch took me past the Temple of Dawn, with the mosaic glistening in the morning sunshine. I cruised some distance over the wide reach of the Chao Phya, then turned down a side *klong*. I could see saffron robes suddenly appear and vanish behind trees and buildings as the monks made their morning quest for breakfast. Houses, which were little more than rickety wooden dwellings on stilts, bordered the *klong*. There were barges which had semi-circular roofs of flattened corrugated iron and housed entire families. Children were swimming happily in the muddy water. Scores of boats passed, laden with fruit and flowers and nearly all poled by women. They were bringing the produce to sell in the Bangkok markets.

Banana fronds and palm trees dotted the banks; here and there a *wat* stood in colourful isolation. Then there were stretches with only a solitary hut. These usually marked an isolated farm. In some very humble dwellings the spirit house stood out very clearly in the gardens or yards.

The *klong* widened rapidly. There was a dense conglomeration of boats, but, as I came nearer, there was a clear passage between the avenues of craft. Where the *klong* narrowed the boats lined the banks. Most were full of fruit, but a few contained baskets, crockery and pottery, and that morning—like all others—the 'floating shops' did a roaring trade.

With my family I visited the Royal Palace. Here is the bequest of the Chakri kings in all its dazzling glory. It is almost a walled city. Enclosed within its area of one square mile are temples and buildings of exquisite design and colour. The golden roofs of the temples flashed in the eternal sunshine of Thailand. We passed from marvel to marvel, from surprise to surprise. We admired a beautiful mother-of-pearl door, then we turned to stare in amazement at a lion, a dragon or a *tepanom*, which is half girl and half cockerel. One wonders what they are doing there; why this hideous giant stood on guard outside this breathlessly lovely temple; why a Garuda, the mythical bird of the kingdom, appears in this particular spot. Most of these stone creatures came from China as ballast in the ships plying for trade. They had obviously been garishly coloured, and their ugliness made an effective contrast with the beauty of the temples they protected.

The eaves of the buildings are set in three overlapping tiers. They are decorated with red and green tiles lining the ridges. The gables are adorned with fantastic-looking dragons and mythical beasts. Graceful and well-kept bo trees and banyans provide welcome shade against the heat, but right in front of you, where you rest, on all sides are the castellated walls and flashing spires, and inlaid gables gleaming as if encrusted with jewels and precious stones.

The magnificent Chakri Palace was planned by a British architect, who copied the style of the Italian Renaissance. It has a magnificent roof in Thai style. The Dusit Maha Prasart is considered to be one of the finest edifices in the palace and a pearl of modern Thai architecture. It is built in the shape of a cross, the four arms enclosed with five-tiered roofs; and, where the roofs of the ridges meet, a superb spire or *chedi* of nine tiers rises. The base of the spire is supported by four huge Garudas. In this palace the king receives the ambassadors of foreign powers.

Behind the Chakri Palace is the Forbidden City within the City, where the wives of the former Chakri kings were housed.

Wat Phra Keo is the best known of the temples. It is the Temple of the Emerald Buddha. This *wat* is a cluster of pavilions. There are fragile, even ethereal friezes, porcelain-encrusted towers, mother-of-pearl inlay, golden spires, mythical creatures and fearsome-looking giant sentries. In the galleries around the cloister murals tell of the exploits of Prince Rama and the monkey General Hanuman in the Thai version of the Indian Ramayana.

Huge stone demons from the same epic guard gateways and doors. In front of the *wat* are eight circular towers lying north and south representing the Buddha, Law, Order, Disciples, Monks, the King, the preceding Buddha and the future Buddha.

On top of a richly decorated gilt altar, which rises tier upon tier from the marble floor, the Emerald Buddha sits under a seven-tiered umbrella. It is a jaspar image of the Buddha, about two feet high and attired in vestments and head-dress of pure gold, studded with precious stones. These vestments are changed three times a year, according to the hot, rainy and cold seasons. This ceremony is performed by the king, for the Emerald Buddha is the most sacred relic in the kingdom.

The scene inside the temples was the same everywhere. The worshippers left their shoes outside the door. They knelt down and shuffled across the floor in this position; they lit candles and joss sticks, burned incense; they fixed gold leaf on the face of the Buddha. The monks chanted, gongs boomed and shuddered across the courtyard. There was an atmosphere of deep piety, of adoration. Then, their devotions completed, they shuffled back from the altars and images, and my eyes popped as, still in the temple, they reached for their cigarettes and smoked!

The stately Borom Piman Palace, with its chapel and theatre, is comparatively modern. This was for a very short time the residence of the young King Ananda Mahidol on his return from Switzerland to take up the throne. He was murdered before he could be crowned. It is used today as a guest palace for visiting royalty and heads of state.

In the Royal Pantheon are life-sized statues of the former kings of the Chakri Dynasty, and close by is the Mondop or the Buddhist Library. It has a beautiful mother-of-pearl cabinet, of intricate design and containing the Buddhist scriptures. The floor is covered with a huge silver mat, and the four doors are guarded by human-faced serpents and demons. Close to the Mondop is a model of Angkor Wat. This was commenced during the reign of King Mongkut, when Cambodia was a vassal state of Siam.

Wat Po is the largest temple group. The special feature which distinguishes it from the others is the massive reclining Buddha, a figure 160 feet long, made of brick, with a casing of cement and heavily gilded. It represents the Buddha entering Nirvana.

Wat Benchamabopitr, or the Marble Temple, is constructed of

white marble from Carrara in Italy, with glazed yellow tiles all edged with gilt so that it appears to have a roof of gold. Its walls are of solid white marble with a row of latticed windows, set in gilt frames on either side, surmounted by a series of images of the Buddha in different positions.

Wat Sutat is considered to be one of the largest and most magnificent temples in Thailand. It is composed of two large chapels. The Viharn is built on a high terrace in the centre of a courtyard enclosed in a roofed gallery which contains many sitting Buddhas. The doors of the Viharn are exquisitely carved. The Bote is seventy-five yards long. At the base of the altar is a group of statues. There is also a huge Buddha, represented as presiding over a meeting of his eighty disciples.

Wat Traimitr houses the Golden Buddha. In 1956, on the occasion of the celebrations to commemorate the twenty-fifth centenary of the Buddhist era, this statue, which is larger than life, was chipped while being moved. A dull yellow substance was revealed, which on examination was found to be pure gold. It is believed that it was camouflaged in this way centuries ago to conceal its real value from the invading Burmese.

Wat Sraket is known as the Temple of the Golden Mount. It is one of the most picturesque landmarks in Bangkok. A number of small caves and spires have been carved or let into the mount, and are planted with trees which give an alpine aspect to the lovely monastery. Two winding staircases lead to the summit of the Golden Mount, which is crowned with a *chedi* or spire. A piece of one of the bones of the Buddha is said to be enshrined in the *chedi*.

Thai classical dancing is a very colourful spectacle, as well as one of great beauty. The Khon depicts scenes from the Ramayana. The performers, all males, wear masks and the singing is done by a choir under the direction of a leader. There is a small orchestra called a *piphat*, consisting of oboes, drums and gongs. The characters are identified by the colours of their costumes. Lakshaman is dressed in gold, Rama in green, Hanuman in white and Sugriva in red.

In the Lakorn both men and women take part. With the exception of the giants and other mythological creatures, the characters do not wear masks. The motif consists of romantic stories composed in verse. The movements are complicated, but the dancers, particularly in the Lakorn, execute them with great skill and exquisite grace. They make great play with their hands, turning the fingers, which have artificial nails projecting more than an inch, right back until they almost touch the wrist.

They wear tapering crowns on their heads and long jackets or coats of heavy brocade covered with precious stones and chains. Glittering ornaments cover the chest. The breeches or skirts, of rich and heavy brocade, sparkle with stones, while gold bangles shine on their arms and feet.

I had the impression that classical dancing is losing its appeal among the younger Thais. On one occasion, when I purchased some tickets from a Thai doctor friend who had been persuaded to take more than he needed, Valluya and her friends did not appear to be particularly thrilled by my invitation. When I was persuaded to buy some more tickets at a later stage, Valluya conjured up a more pressing engagement. Eventually she admitted that she and her friends did not like Thai classical dancing. However, when I told them that it would be difficult for me not to go, they rallied with commendable good nature to the support of the *farang* (Westerner).

Thai boxing is a robust affair, and, like the classical dancing, is not confined to Bangkok. The contests commence with the contestants praying and making obeisances. Then follows a dance which is intended to frighten the opponent. The actual boxing allows full use of elbows, fists, knees and feet. I wish they would dispense with the orchestra of pipes and drums which play non-stop, a shrill wailing monotony. I never missed an opportunity of watching a contest, but I never became accustomed to the music.

Bangkok is an outstanding example of a great city literally changing before one's eyes. In the late Fifties there were about eight really good hotels. Then they began to spring up like proverbial mushrooms. Skeletons of scaffolding appeared all over the capital, and huge and lofty blocks of luxury apartments began to take shape.

The population has not so much increased as exploded. In the past twelve years it has doubled. It is now nearly 2½ millions.

I watched *klongs* being filled in to make more roads and accommodation. Sometimes the roads were laid too quickly, with the result that the waters seeped through, and whole stretches were flooded, creating chaos with the traffic. The older generation were despondent. "Bangkok is becoming a concrete jungle," some told me.

Thai and foreign business men invested in more restaurants, cinemas, hotels and apartments; *samlors* (tricycle taxis) were taken off the roads. The numbers of Austin and Morris taxis dwindled, and their places were taken by Japanese taxis. Large and flashy new cars crawled through the densely crowded streets of the capital. Busy thoroughfares became even more congested. New districts developed.

The opening of the 'Erawan Hotel', near the British Embassy, was a social event in 1958. An hotel in Bangkok with bathrooms! I remember how I enjoyed the luxury of a full-length hot bath after years of river water from a Shanghai jar in our house in the jungle. Today the Erawan has many rivals.

The thousands of American 'military tourists' had much money to spend. They were based in the capital or they came in to enjoy their leave from the huge American bases in Udorn, Nakorn-panom, Korat, Takli, Don Muang, Ubol, or Sattahip.

To Don Muang, Bangkok's modern airport, come the huge air liners of twenty-five international airlines. The new highways have opened up the capital to thousands of Thais, who come to seek their fortune, to find employment or to admire the sights and enjoy the night life.

And what an exotic night life Bangkok provides! The few massage establishments where, as I found by experience, the luscious young masseuses knew nothing at all about massage, but went through the motions and did not press their delectable charms upon you unless you made the first move, were closed down by Field-Marshal Sarit in his campaign to clean up the capital. They soon reopened as before, with the difference that Bangkok then was like a Sussex market town compared with what it is today.

Sathorn Road, in embarrassing proximity to the Soviet, Burmese, Australian, Laotian and Italian embassies, offers every conceivable form of sexual indulgence. Petchburi Road proclaims its vice by flashing lights and signs. There are restaurants without tables but furnished with long couches and discreet curtains; private 'nursing establishments', where the smiling, attentive nurses have never seen the inside of a hospital; luxurious night

clubs; elegant restaurants and clubs where one can take the
family without embarrassment—Bangkok caters for all tastes.
Brothels, strip tease, sleazy joints, the capital has them in abundance.

However, all this could be stopped if the authorities ever wished
to adopt strong and resolute action, but the old Bangkok has
gone for ever. Its physical appearance has changed with furious
urgency. Boom-town Bangkok has not yet achieved the peak
of its prosperity. There are 36,000 American 'military tourists',
as some Thais cynically describe them. All are lavish spenders.
Then the United States last year stepped up its foreign aid to
100 million dollars, which included further construction and
development work in the capital, and more fortunes were made.

No city in the world has changed as rapidly as this jewel of
South-east Asia. Many Thais are very sensitive over American
influence and their pride in their independence is as strong as ever.
Yet, as Sanan and his friends had told me more than once, "We
shall never be completely independent while the Americans are
here, but without them it is doubtful whether we would keep
our independence for long."

One afternoon, when walking through Bangkok with Valluya,
I stopped to watch some workmen putting the finishing touches
to the roof of a new hotel. We turned into Suriwongse Road,
which is a bustling centre of the motor-car industry, and strolled
in the grounds of the Nelson Hays library. Valluya clutched my
arm tightly and pointed. Outside the library, and only a few
yards from the busy street, a small girl was standing motionless
and petrified. About ten feet from her there was a huge snake, its
head reared. As I considered my next move, I realized that the
snake was unaware of the girl. Its eyes were fixed upon a huge
frog which squatted helpless, hypnotized. Everything happened
at once. The snake struck and in a split second had disappeared
with the frog.

Valluya turned to me with one of her spontaneous observations:
"Do you know," she said, "we've got the jungle at our back
door. We've got the snakes in the streets. None of that has
changed. Perhaps everything else is explained by the march of
progress. If only it did not have to happen so quickly. If only we
had been allowed to get used to it by easy stages."

However, Buddhism remains constant, as constant as the

Northern Star—as an abbot of a monastery in Bangkok told me with pride. Chapters of its saffron-robed monks continue to officiate at the openings of new buildings in modern Bangkok, to chant their prayers, extol the Buddha, thread the sacred string through their fingers and wind it up again in a ceremony which absorbs all into a religion which is as old as the national life.

Rice all the Year

Thailand is often described as the 'Rice-bowl of Asia'. Rice is certainly the basis of life. It is grown on 90 per cent of the cultivated land. Nearly the same percentage of the population lives in rural areas, and these people are mainly occupied in growing rice.

The Trade Treaty signed between Britain and Siam in 1855 was to have far reaching effects, for, in the years following World War I, Siam became one of the leading exporters of rice. Production of rice paddy in 1966 was nearly 12 million tons.

When I lived up-country, I was able to watch closely the all-the-year-round cultivation of rice. In the month of April the rice season gets under way. The monks walk in procession to the land and bless it. Rice maidens join in the ceremony and are always an attractive sight. All that month the farm workers, a large number of whom are women, swarm on the land. They are always dressed in black and wear wide-brimmed straw hats as a protection against the blazing sun. They fire the straw stubble to soften the ground for ploughing. Then, after the first rains have fallen and before the water rises too high, the soil has to be ploughed and cultivated to a muddy tilth. This is the work of the water buffalo, the tractor of the rice-fields.

The farm workers are up before the sun, and they work until dusk, with a long break when the sun is hottest. In the majority of cases the farm is a family holding, for 80 per cent of the farmers own their land.

Water is always a vital problem, and its efficient use is important if the crop is to flourish. The rate of ploughing must match the filling of the fields with water. During the growing season it requires about twenty inches a month. In order that it can be made to flow on to the growing plots, bunds are built between the fields. A series of water-raising contraptions, such as windmills and chain buckets, are erected at intervals, and these enable the fields to be flooded or drained.

When the fields are soaked, the seedlings are planted by hand. The process of transplanting from the seed-beds to the paddy-fields commences about a month to six weeks after the seed-beds are first planted. The seedlings must be at that state of growth when they can be safely transplanted into the paddy-fields, which should be wet enough to take them. They are pressed into the slushy mud by the more experienced workers, and it is done in the coolest part of the day to protect the young seedlings. The narrow, flat-bottomed boats, loaded to the maximum capacity, move off to the various fields. At times I have had the impression that the whole village has mobilized itself, with some of the workers gathering the seedlings into bundles, placing them in the shade, stacking them in the boats, paddling the boats and un-loading.

At the end of the calendar year harvesting of the early varieties begins. The water-machines are stopped about two weeks before harvesting, so that the land dries out for the workers, who cut the crop close to the earth with a short sickle. The crop is placed on the stubble and left there for four or five days to dry, then the stalks are gathered into bundles or sheaves and carried on long poles to the threshing plot. This is a floor of hardened mud and buffalo dung.

Before the threshing actually begins, it is usual to offer prayers and give thanks to the Earth Goddess. A pole or post is fixed in the middle of the floor and hung with offerings to the goddess. The threshing process varies according to the size of the crop. The small family farmers strike the sheaves on the ground. The grain is tossed in the air to blow away the chaff. In the larger farms water buffaloes are harnessed in teams of four, muzzled and set to work trampling the rice. Power machinery is used only to a very limited extent. The Government Rice Department has invented a machine called the Iron Buffalo. This is intended to take the place of the water buffalo, but it will be a very long time before this sturdy animal is superseded. Then manual labour is very plentiful and cheap. However, more power machinery is in use on the big

farms. One-fifth of the cultivated land is composed of farms
exceeding twenty-five acres.

The drying process continues for about a week, the grain being
continually raked over. Then it is ready to go to the mill. I have
often watched it loaded on a sampan, and, as the craft has settled
lower and lower in the water, I have wondered if both farmer
and sampan owner were taking a risk with crop and craft. Yet
sooner or later a flash of the hand has signalled a full load. I have
assumed that this was the result of years of experience and a
practised eye, yet knowing and liking the Siamese as I do, the
feeling is never far away that they are always taking a chance.

At the mill the rice is weighed and tested for quality, which is
usually according to five grades, then loaded into sacks. From the
mill it is sent to various centres, or stacked on to sampans and
transferred to sea-going lighters or to cargo ships lying off shore.

It is a very pleasant sight when the baked and cracked ground
gradually changes to a pale green mist, then to a gently moving
floating rice-field, which thickens to a lush green density and then
to a golden-brown. Sometimes I have stopped the car and got out
to admire the scene. Here, indeed, is the earth giving forth its
riches in abundance, and Thailand is most fortunate.

On some of my visits I have been recognized and greeted with
a friendly 'Sawadi'. It was not always possible to recognize the
workers, for in some parts the rice-fields stretch to the horizon,
and only their hats could be seen above the green walls of rice.
They appear to enjoy their work and are happy together. Yet
danger threatens them all the time. Three incidents I shall always
remember illustrate this point.

On one occasion I had stopped to change a wheel, when a young
girl came running out of the paddy-field. In her hands she gripped
a large snake. I could not identify it. She looked at me and
smiled. Suddenly her expression changed, a knife flashed, and she
flung the snake from her. It writhed for a few seconds and then
was still. The girl made a delightful picture standing there and
then walked over to look at the snake, which she had obviously
brought over to show me, but at the last moment had lost her
nerve or realized that she could not hold it any longer.

On at least four occasions I was halted at the roadside by a small
group, one of whom carried a dead snake. Another had obviously
been bitten. The request to drive them to one of the 700 centres

for an injection was never made with any degree of urgency. Snakes are an everyday occurrence, for they infest the paddy-fields. The farm workers learn to live with them and do not easily panic.

The other incident was when I was held up by a toothless, elderly farm worker. He had a large wooden box in his arms. He opened it a little to reveal a writhing mass of snakes. I agreed to his request to take him to the next village, a distance of about eight miles, on the strict understanding that he sat in the back of the car and kept his rear portion firmly on the lid. He shouted with laughter and climbed in.

I drove with one eye over my shoulder and a prickly sensation up and down my spine. Each time our eyes met he smiled happily, and pressed his bottom more firmly on the lid to show that he was co-operating. When we stopped, three of his friends were waiting, all with sacks. They greeted him like a long-lost brother. I gathered that he had missed the bus, and they were all wondering what to do. Into an ancient lorry went box and sacks. Then I understood the object of their journey and my part in it. The sacks also contained snakes, and they were taking them to the snake farm in Bangkok where they would sell them.

Thailand is plagued with snakes, and this, I thought, is one way of helping to rid the country of them, as well as providing serum for snake bites.

Often, when I have been driving up-country, a snake has shot across the road, and I have been unable to avoid it. It has spun itself into a coiled spring, but the wheels have caught it, torn and flattened it, while above in the sky black specks have become larger and, while I watched, have taken shape and swooped.

The ordinary cobras and banded kraits are found almost any-where. I have seen them in Bangkok in the gardens and *klongs*, where they hunt rats and frogs. The ordinary cobra strikes when its hood is up and front part of its body erect. Its hiss is a warning and often its undoing, if the reactions of the one threatened are quick enough. The king cobra, which fetches a very good price at the snake farm, is very aggressive, particularly during the mating season. It will attack instantly if disturbed. It can be as much as twenty feet in length.

There is rice everywhere one travels in Thailand, although the central region is the most fertile. In the valleys of the north, a region of subsistence agriculture, it is the principal crop, and, when irrigation is adequate, there are two crops per year. In the vast plateau of the east it is cultivated in irrigated fields in the valleys and again is the main crop. It is also grown in the flat coastal areas of the south-east, which is the wettest region of Thailand.

In addition to the needs for sufficient labour and water buffaloes, Thailand's rice yield naturally depends upon an adequate supply of water. The Government, determined to maintain its export trade and feed its large population, has tackled the problem of irrigation with energy. In 1952 work was begun on the Greater Chao Phya project. Its central feature, the barrage across the river at Chainat, was built four years afterwards. The entire project was completed in 1961 and has provided flood control and irrigation for an area of $2\frac{1}{2}$ million acres of arable land.

The Phumipol Dam of the Yan-Hee, named after the king, will irrigate 2 million acres and control further floods in the Central Plain. In 1958 the Ministry of Agriculture started to build 500 irrigation tanks in the fifteen north-eastern provinces. The same year a scheme for exploiting the underground water resources of the vast Korat plateau was launched. It was proposed to drill 300 wells. These irrigation works will not only increase the amount of land available for cultivation, but will permit of double-cropping in some areas.

When one compares the paddy yield per acre with other countries, then at first sight it is disappointing. It is the second lowest of all rice-producing countries. Japan's yield is thirty times as high. However, that country uses a hundred times as much fertilizer per acre as Thailand. Then, as fertilizer costs five times the price of the paddy, intensive cultivation under existing conditions is not always profitable.

With the improvement in communications, completion of more irrigation projects and production of fertilizers on an economical scale, an increase in crop yield and profit is inevitable. Farmers in the north-east have quoted the old Chinese saying to me: "Water makes the harvest and manure makes it big." In recent years fertilizer production has become a booming industry. At Mae Moh in the north there is a large plant built by a West German concern. Four more are planned, including Thai

The rice harvest

Threshing rice

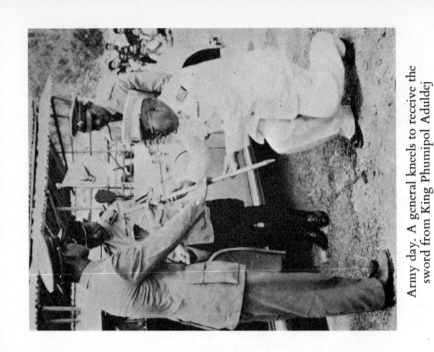

Army day. A general kneels to receive the sword from King Phumipol Aduldej

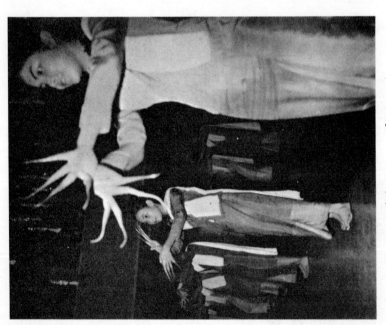

Finger-nail dancing at Chiengmai

Chemical Industries. This bulk production within the country will slash the costs.

For the past 1,000 years, Thailand, assisted by simple, man-made but efficient small-scale irrigation works, has had to contend with the vagaries of Nature. Now modern techniques with power-driven machinery are coming to supplement the work of Nature and offset its deficiencies. The outlook is bright.

The Government is anxious to diversify the agricultural crops, which include sugar-cane, cotton, tobacco, soya beans, maize, ground-nuts and coconuts. Eighty per cent of her exports, worth 250 million pounds, are agricultural. Rice and rubber export earnings for 1960 were equal.

However, the vast majority of Thai farmers, large and small, are at present disinclined to take up the challenge. They have "rice in their veins", as a frustrated official of the Ministry of Agriculture described it to me. "A rice obsession!" said a worried, hard-working, American agricultural expert whom I met in the north-east, after his interesting and factual talk to a group of Thai farmers had been laboriously translated by a counterpart, whose sympathies, I suspected, were with the farmers.

Although some success has been achieved with the policy of diversification, rice is the crop around which the lives of so many millions revolve. Moreover, it provides a market and a simple cash economy, which brings a measure of security.

Some idea of the importance of the crop, when viewed nationally, is shown by the 1965 export figures, when rice accounted for half the export earnings and double those of rubber.

In 1857, it was 54,000 tons; in 1905, 868,250 tons. In spite of her soaring population, Thailand exported nearly 2 million tons in 1964, which brought her 100 million pounds. The principal customers, then as now, are Indonesia, Japan, the Philippines, Malaysia, India and Ceylon. She is indeed the 'Rice-bowl of Asia'.

One of the most pleasant characteristics of community life in Thailand is its sociability. All who participate appear to be enjoying the occasion, as if they had looked forward to it for some time and were determined to do their part in making it a success.

I think that this quality is due to the importance the individual Thais attach to being *sanuk* or acceptable. For one not to be *sanuk* means that you would not enjoy an evening with him, that he is odd man out. There have been occasions when I have been discussing a list of guests to be invited to a party at my house in Bangkok, Chachoengsao or elsewhere, when someone has interrupted with the remark, "Oh, no, not him. You wouldn't find him *sanuk!*"

However, the Thais love celebrations, ceremonies, fêtes and special holidays, so much so that they cash in on those which are associated with other religions and national fêtes of other countries. If the *farang* wanted a holiday on Good Friday or Christmas Day, that was fine. What puzzled many of them was the lack of any visible evidence that he was enjoying himself. But if the French colony liked to liven up Bangkok on July 14th, well the Thais would go along and give them support.

Everything which goes on in the community is the concern of all, whether it be Wan Phra or Buddhist holy days, temple worship, events to herald the commencement of the Buddhist Lent, marriages, the consecration of land or the consecration of new houses and buildings by a chapter of Buddhist monks. The Ramwong, which is a communal dance to celebrate an unusual

event, and the Moh Ram, or rhyming duets, which are a feature
of the north-east, will attract large crowds.

My gardener, who, as a young man, had entered the priesthood for a few months, never missed an opportunity to take food
to the monks. It happened that there were an unusual number of
Wan Phras all within what seemed to be a very short time, and he
was continually asking for time off to go to the monastery. To me
he was the personification of happiness and contentment, and any
joke would send him into fits of laughter. I had pulled his leg over
his repeated visits to the monastery, observing that he gave plenty
of rice but the monks did not appear to put on weight. After this
he would frame his request for leave with, "Can I go make
monks fat?" and disappear, laughing loudly.

Even funerals are a gay affair, for the Buddhists have an altogether
different conception of death, and an entertainment is in progress
in the precincts of the *wat*, while the monks are observing the
various formalities and rites. This can go on until the early hours.
With my wife and two daughters, I was invited to all of them,
both in the provinces and in the capital. These included those in
honour of the King's birthday, Chulalongkorn Day, Police Day
and Teachers' Day.

In Bangkok these festivals were very spectacular and often
quite moving, but, although they were organized on a less
elaborate scale in the provinces, they were also always impressive
there. Moreover, they possessed an air of intimacy which was
lost in the impersonal life of the capital.

From March until May it is the kite-fighting season. The vast
Pramane Ground in Bangkok is crowded with people. Some
have come from outlying provinces to enter their kites, support
their friends or merely to watch the spectacle, which at times can
be very exciting. As the Thais love to bet, the festival provides
opportunities in abundance to make or lose money. Kite-fighting
is a sport for adults and is not to be confused with kite-flying, for
children. Some of the kites are very ingenious in design and
construction and are the result of many months of patient work
and trials to prepare them for the annual event.

Although the kites fly to considerable heights and are an attractive and graceful sight, the actual flying is not the purpose of the
kite flyers. The kites are of two kinds. One is the *chula,* or male
kite, the other is the *pakpao,* or female, and the object is for one to

bring the other to earth in its own territory. Usually it is the female or *pakpao* which is vanquished. The *chula* is a more robust and star-shaped kite, while the *pakpao* is smaller, diamond-shaped and more feminine-looking, with a white cloth tail. It has a loop with which it endeavours to capture the *chula* in flight. Sometimes I have seen the female turn the tables on the male, and this happens to the accompaniment of roars of approval, for it is the result of outstanding skill as well as much patience and strength on the part of the kite flyer. The manœuvring for position and strike, the sudden jerking away, the upward flight to safety, the evasive tactics used by the flyer, then the capture and kill, all make it a thrilling spectacle.

The festival which follows on this one takes place about the middle of April. It is the Songkran or Water Festival, and it was one that I always looked forward to. Its origin was associated with ancient fertility rites. Water was thrown to ensure a bountiful season with plenty of rain. During the festival boys and girls are able to meet without being chaperoned, but it is not always easy to pair off. In former days men were married at about the age of 20 and girls at 14. The girls wore belts below their blouses. These were of gold, silver, brass, or were jewelled, and were an indication of the wearer's worth on the marriage market. The young admirer who could pay the price approached a third party, who entered into negotiations with the parents, and, if all went well, the astrologers were called in to fix the most propitious day for the wedding. Although the marriage could be said to be arranged, the young couple did profit from the festival to the extent that they had actually seen each other and, therefore, knew who their parents were talking about when the subjects of marriage and dowry were raised.

Today it has its religious and merry aspects as before. The water-throwing is a free for all, and everyone takes it in good part. The *farang* is not exempt. He may even be the favourite target. I have been drenched to the skin and changed into dry clothes, only to be soaked again. After that I walked about in my dripping clothes. Water was thrown over me from silver bowls, jars and vases. It was squirted down my neck by water pistols accurately aimed by attractive girls, who were convulsed with merriment every time an unfortunate victim was caught.

One year three young women smiled at me so demurely and

wai-ed with such assumed innocence and courtesy that my hands fumbled as I clasped them to return the salute. (The Thais do not shake hands. Their greeting is to clasp the hands together, as if in prayer, and to bow over them.) This is what they had been waiting for. Water cascaded over me. It streamed over my head and down my body. It was an incitement to the others. I was penned against the wall, and when I finally escaped I was breathless.

I staggered into a shop and watched the events from an upstairs window. Marian and the girls had already been soaked once and had decided that this was enough. They watched the activities from the balcony of a government building.

The procession was led by about sixty girls. They wore bright flowers in their hair and were dressed in coloured *pasins* and blouses. Fifteen lorries followed them. These were decorated with saffron flags, and in each lorry there was an enormous statue of the Buddha with several monks in attendance. One of them was standing up and swishing lustral water over the crowd, which at times was so dense that a way had to be made for the lorries. Men and women pushed their way towards the monks, holding out bowls to be filled with water. I noticed that they did not look for suitable targets but took it away. I learned that this was for use in celebrations in their own homes.

Outside two *wats* entire families were building the traditional sand piles, which they decorated with flowers and tiny, coloured-paper flags. Then they sprinkled them with perfumed water. The water-throwing continued in this place, but the crowds were not so dense, and one had a better chance of escaping. Men and women went into the *wats*, where they washed the statues of Buddha and the feet of the monks, their parents and grandparents. This was all part of merit making.

In May it is the Festival of the Ploughing. This is considered to be of special importance on account of its close ties with agriculture. It is an old custom and was used by the kings of Thailand as a signal for the people to commence ploughing. The king performed the ceremony. Today he appoints a *Phya Rackna*, or Lord of the Festival, who officiates at the Pramane Ground.

Three cloths are presented to him. He selects one, and the amount of rainfall is forecast. A richly decorated red and gold plough, believed to be sacred, is drawn by bulls decorated with garlands of flowers. This is followed by royal guards dressed in scarlet costumes. Brahmins chant and blow conch shells. Four celestial queens carry baskets filled with paddy. The animals are solemnly presented with seven varieties of food and the one they choose foretells the crop. It is now time for the *Phya Rackna* to scatter the rice. As this is considered to bring good fortune, the spectators hurriedly pick it up and take it away with them.

The whole festival provides a pageant of colour, with the central figures standing out solemn and clear. There are large numbers of uniformed officials and guests. There is the royal guard and the king with his entourage and thousands of spectators, among whom are a large number of farmers who have made the journey to the capital from all over Thailand.

During the same month the Buddhist Festival of Visakha Puja is celebrated in the *wats*. This is in commemoration of the three episodes of the Birth, Enlightenment and the Attainment of Nirvana by the Buddha. It is an occasion for making merit, and in the grounds of the *wats* processions form up with candles and move in a clock-wise direction around the Convocation Hall. Artistically decorative lanterns, which have taken months to prepare, are carried. Each procession must make a triple circuit of the Convocation Hall. It is a very dignified occasion, but the atmosphere is not unduly restrained, for Buddhism is such a friendly religion. Visakha Puja draws the ties between the *wat* and the individual even closer.

Loy Krathong, a very popular festival and one which appeals to all age groups, both for the entertainment and spiritual comfort it provides, is celebrated at the end of October or beginning of November. *Loy* is 'to float' and *krathong* means a 'leaf cup'. The festival consists of putting lighted candles, with food, incense and money, in tiny boats made of banana leaves and flowers and floating them on rivers and *klongs*.

For some weeks before the event the *krathongs* are on sale. Stalls are set up in the streets and on the river banks. The *krathongs* can be purchased for a tical, which is fourpence, or for several times that amount, according to the size and design. There is always a wide variety of shapes. Some take the form of an aeroplane covered with tiny flowers, others are miniature battleships, dragons, houseboats. Exquisitely beautiful flowers, with a backing and base of banana leaves and candles set up in the middle, delight the eye. Most of them are made by the Chinese shopkeepers and are a tribute to their artistic ability. They all sell like proverbial hot cakes.

On the actual night of the last Loy Krathong I attended the crowds which lined the banks of the Chao Phya River—the Mother of Waters Most Noble—were so very dense that I think that it was chiefly on account of the customary courtesy shown to the *farang* that they automatically made way for us. The broad and fast-flowing river was packed with river craft. Motor boats were speeding in both directions, their wash sweeping over the legs of those on the water's edge. Fireworks exploded and sprinkled the sky with rich colours or sent up patterns of great beauty, which hung suspended for a few seconds before commencing slowly to disintegrate. Above the noise the shrill tones of the xylophone orchestras blared.

Large numbers of *krathongs* floated past us, their candles burning brightly and bravely. We watched them until our vision was obstructed by a passing boat, or water lapped into the *krathong*, extinguished the light, and the tiny craft sank. We placed our four *krathongs* gently in the water and sent them on their way. One rode out bravely, and within a few seconds had moved into the current; the second followed it in a more leisurely way, while the other two turned back towards the bank. Here they were turned outwards by someone in the crowd.

Suddenly the high-pitched voice of an elderly woman hailed us from a punt. We stepped in, and she poled us downstream. As we continued on our way, more punts passed us. Hilary and Jacqueline were a little shocked to see those in the punts reaching out and seizing the *krathongs*, but they were lost in admiration and envy at the antics of large numbers of small boys who swam out, dived under the boats, and clutching the tiny floral craft searched them for money of which there appeared to be a generous supply. I think our two girls regarded the incident as another delusion.

It was obvious that Loy Krathong was intended to provide a good time for all. On our way back to the house, we passed small groups of people floating their *krathongs* in the smaller *klongs*, well away from the crowds. There was no evidence here of the high spirits we had seen on the river banks. The event was taken much more seriously.

There are various explanations as to the origin and purpose of Loy Krathong. Several Thais I met that night said that floating away the *krathong* was symbolic of floating away one's sins, that it is an atonement for boating over the footprints of the Buddha or images of the Buddha embedded in the sands of the river. I thought that there was little that was religious about the festival.

According to one legend, a lady fed the Buddha and after the meal floated the bowl down river, hoping that the merit this deed had given her would make her a Buddha in the next incarnation. A daughter of a Brahmin living at Ayudhya is the central figure in another legend. She is said to have made a raft of such elegance and beauty that the king desired to launch it. As a Buddhist, however, he could not bring himself to take such an important part in a Hindu custom, until he thought of dedicating the *krathong* to the footprints of the Lord Buddha where they had pressed into the sands of the river. He prayed that any merit accruing to his act should pass to the daughter of the Brahmin. His nobles emulated his act, and Loy Krathong thereafter became an annual custom.

What is more likely is that it is looked upon as a yearly offering to the water spirits, as well as the floating away of all sins and warding off future calamities. In Chiengmai and the north-east provinces huge *krathongs* are built and lighted with torches. Clothing and food are placed in them, and they are then sent on their way. It is hoped that poor people will take the contents and also accept responsibility for the sins incurred by those who launched them. Again, they are intended as a thanksgiving to the Goddess of Water.

Some well-educated Thais admitted that it is now only a very pleasant way of spending an evening. "You float away your cares. Loy Krathong has long lost any religious or ritual meaning it may have had."

Buat Nak concerns the admission to the priesthood. During the months of June or July, before the commencement of the Buddhist Lent, the candidate, accompanied by his family and friends, presents himself at the *wat*. His head is shaven, and he is dressed in white. He takes his vows and receives the saffron robes.

Another ceremony which has a national appeal, and although essentially Buddhist and monastic, is Kathin. This takes place towards the end of October, when new saffron robes and accessories are presented to the monks all over the country. There is a procession of brightly decorated boats along the *klongs* and rivers.

The occasion is enlivened by songs and folk dancing. The royal barges move in stately procession, and the king is rowed in the state barge to the Temple of Dawn, where he presents the saffron robes. In the closely knit community the ceremony has a simple dignity and a special intimacy, for the centre of the village life is the local *wat*, and on the occasion of Kathin it assumes a special importance and dignity.

The same month and during early November pilgrimages are made to Pra Chedi Klang Nam or the 'Pagoda amidst the water'. This pagoda is situated on the west bank of the Chao Phya River, about fifteen miles south of Bangkok. There are processions of decorated boats and organized races and games. In some years a special feature of the pilgrimage, which is also a fair, has been a demonstration of spinning raw cotton into cloth—the various processes of spinning, weaving, dyeing and stitching it into robes for presentation to the monks.

One custom which is an institution all over the kingdom is the Phra Phum Chao Thi. *Phra Phum* means the Lord of the Land or Place. *Chao Thi* has the same meaning and is used more in the north of Thailand.

In the compound of Thai houses a miniature house resembling a monastic temple is fixed on a post so that the house is about eye level. Its walls are about eighteen inches square or more. It houses the guardian spirit of the house, the *Phra Phum* or the *Chao Thi*. When the land is cleared and the house built, an expert is called in to select a suitable place for the shrine. He will decide which day is most propitious for erecting it, and, if he is not an astrologer, which he usually is, he will call one in for consultation. It can face north or south, but is generally sited north. The actual house or building must not throw its shade or shadow over the shrine, for it is believed that man and spirits are of different worlds and cannot inhabit the same place.

The shrine is raised on an earth platform. Most shrines consist of a single room with an outer platform which is a little lower. The inner room is intended to be the living-room for the *Phra Phum* and the outer platform for the offerings. A picture of the *Phra Phum* is painted on wood and then cut out. It is placed in the shrine, with its back to the rear wall. It represents a god or *devada*, with a halo of light around the head in the shape of a leaf, corresponding to the outline of the god's head and its spire-shaped crown. The right hand of the god holds a double-edged sword. With the left hand he holds a book.

An invocation is made to the *Phra Phum*. He is invited to take up his abode in the shrine, and to give protection to the house and those that dwell in it. Offerings of food, consisting of rice, sweetmeats and water, as well as sticks of incense and flowers are placed on a small table in front of the shrine.

My landlord in Bangkok owned a house with a large amount of land, so spacious that he built two houses on it which he let to Westerners. I occupied one of them. He was an admiral in the Thai navy and had spent some years in England. His prolonged education and experiences abroad had done nothing to shake his implicit faith in the *Phra Phum*. On special occasions he would place fresh food and flowers in the shrine. As he was always glad to explain the customs of Thailand to me, I ventured to point out that the food never grew less. "They only require the smell," he assured me. It would have been embarrassing to question the logic of this statement.

The ceremony, as I have seen it in Bangkok, is a mixture of Buddhism, Hinduism and Animism and is often conducted in Pali. In the rural areas, and particularly in the north-east, the ceremonies are simpler, and the site of the *Phra Phum* is usually selected in accordance with local traditions. However, it loses none of its significance. Wherever sited, it is venerated.

I have come across *Phra Phums* at lonely crossroads, at bends in the road, by the side of *klongs*. An immediate explanation has always been forthcoming as to the reason for its presence. Perhaps there had been a succession of serious accidents; a bus had overturned, or a boat had capsized. All this had occurred because the spirits had been dispossessed or were angry. And had there been any more fatalities since the erection of the *Phra Phum*? None! The *Phra Phum* is now pleased and gives his protection!

Some of the *Phra Phums* are very beautiful, others are quite simple structures. They are made of stone or concrete, clay or wood. I have come across small factories in jungle towns, where there have been several dozens of them of different colours and designs, all stacked in the courtyard awaiting customers. Apparently the demand for them does not diminish.

It is usual for the residents to worship the *Phra Phum* every evening, and for the traveller from another part or village to ask its permission and protection before settling down for the night. In the morning, he will give thanks before continuing his journey. This is more common in remote areas. In very many ways it is a very personal shrine, and the supplicant will, entirely on his own, light incense sticks and give thanks, as well as ask for favours.

My gardener sought its intercession every time he purchased a lottery ticket. He never won, but he never lost faith, and when I left Thailand he continued to buy and to pray. He was never tired of telling me of the night when he discovered a deadly snake in the garden. He tried to escape but his retreat was cut off. So he fell on his knees before the *Phra Phum*, and when he dared to look behind him, the snake had gone!

———————————••••••———————————

"You must go to the north-east. There you will see an altogether different Thailand, an impoverished region which has contributed nothing to the country's economy. It isn't a friendly place. It is a breeding ground for communists."

My informant, whom I had met on several occasions at various functions, worked in the Ministry of the Interior. I remarked that I was due to visit Korat the following month, and then to tour some of the provinces. At once he showed lively interest. "Then drive down. Use the Friendship Highway. It's a wonderful road, and halves the time from Bangkok. When you get there, call on Nai Panan. He owns a garage, and may be of help."

He scribbled some words on a visiting card and handed it to me. I thanked him, and we continued to chat about the north-east. I was disappointed to find that he had never been there and that what knowledge he possessed was entirely political.

I had seen the construction of the Friendship Highway right from the early stages. It was a magnificent feat of engineering. The Americans used such ingenious and massive equipment that the road literally progressed while you watched. Unfortunately, my car, which had been damaged in one of the inevitable collisions in Bangkok's traffic, was not ready, and I travelled up by train.

The train arrived right on time at Korat. Outside the station a *samlor* boy smiled at me and pointed to his vehicle. I climbed in and told him to take me to the 'Celestial Heaven' hotel. I had stayed there overnight a year ago, but had seen little of the town. He shook his head. The owner had disappeared. "Over the

Mekong, pretty damn quick!" he whispered, looking mysterious. There was 'Vale of Enchantment' or 'Paradise' or 'Delicious Slumbers' but 'Vale of Enchantment' very good, and he get there "pretty damn quick". I nodded, and got in.

In the streets, bicycles, bullock carts, *samlors* and jeeps mixed themselves up, sorted themselves out and were about to move on until the next obstacle stopped them. A water buffalo, its massive head and horn span swaying slowly from left to right, surveyed the scene and tried to help. A small boy ran out and, with shrill cries, hit it with a switch. Then he climbed on its back and, with more cries, steered or was steered by it to the side of the road. A policeman halted a coach for a particularly glaring example of dangerous driving, but his anger suddenly changed to loud laughter when a large durian fruit rolled off the roof and bounced off the driver's head.

Korat, or Nakornrajsima, to call it by its Thai name—which nobody does—is a very old town, with a proud history. The ruins of the ancient walls and gates are well preserved, but they do not mark the boundary. The city has been extended far beyond those old walls and is taking over more territory.

'Vale of Enchantment' appeared to be very much the same as the general run of Chinese hotels. A pot of China tea appeared in a matter of seconds, and, after a shower and a meal, I went into the street. I was walking slowly, looking at some fine new buildings, when I heard the ringing of a bicycle bell. "Pretty damn quick" shot across the road. I climbed in and told him to take me around the town. There appeared to be an extensive building programme in progress. Bamboo supports, tied at junctions as in comic pictures, were springing up in several places. There were cinemas and Chinese theatres. The streets were full of people. Radios blared from shops and restaurants. Korat is a very noisy town.

The town is aptly described as the gateway of the north-east. Fast traffic speeds along the Friendship Highway. Trains from the capital disgorge their passengers and freight at Korat, or they come in from the frontier town of Nongkai in the north or from Ubol in the east. Thai Airways run an efficient service. Communications to some of the north-east provinces are good, but internal services between them, as well as within separate provinces, are totally inadequate. There are agricultural experimental stations, irrigation projects and good roads.

The Korat region is famed as a cattle-breeding area. It has 5 million water buffaloes, or over 80 per cent of the entire nation's stock. I have seen them loaded in large numbers on cargo ships in Bangkok docks for export. Pigs are bred and find a ready market in Thailand, as well as in other countries of South-east Asia.

In the square stands a life-size bronze statue of Than Poo Ying Mo, saviour of Korat. This remarkable woman is a national heroine. In 1827, she rallied the women of Korat and, with feminine guile, captivated the Laotian soldiers who had captured the town of Korat when the Siamese armies were away on another campaign. Then, when they were drunk, she released the Siamese prisoners they were taking home. She led a combined onslaught which resulted in the deaths of many Laotians, while others fled.

Monks picked their way, leisurely and unruffled, through the traffic. A huge circular Shell sign towered above and behind a very old *wat*. Strangely enough, the new blended with the old. The colours and design of the station harmonized with those of the monastery, but this may not have been intentional. The green, snow-white, red, green and gold of the *wat,* the saffron robes of the monks, the brilliant colours of the shrubs and trees, the soft blooms of the orchids enhanced the natural beauty of the surroundings and faded out harshness.

I wandered down a very narrow street to escape from the noise of the traffic and the strident loud speakers and found myself in the grounds of a *wat*. Four monks were seated on a bench. Facing them, a few yards away, was a young nun dressed in white, her head shaven. She held her right arm outstretched. Her eyes burned into their faces. For some minutes she stayed motionless. I walked on and found the main street. The explosion of noise greeted me more vibrantly for my having strayed from it.

The Korat plateau consists mainly of villages and hamlets. The largest towns, in addition to Korat, are Khon Khen, Nongkai and Ubol. The plateau is drained entirely by the Nam Mun system, which empties itself into the Mekong.

I called on Panan and gave him greetings from his friend in Bangkok. He gave me a warm welcome, and, when I explained the object of my journey, he showed a most lively interest. He said that three of his friends were travelling north on the following

day. They expected to go as far as Nongkai on the Laotian border.
If this interested me, he would ask them to take me. He warned
me that the roads were unpleasant at this time of the year, and I
might prefer to go by plane and bus, in which case he would work
out a route.

The prospect of company appealed to me. Then I would see
something of the countryside if I travelled by car. I said that I
would be delighted to go, if they would have me. He asked me to
wait while he called them. He was soon back with the good news
that on the following day we would make an early start.

Early the next morning we set off. My companions were
Boriboon, a rice farmer; Chet, a teacher, who was the only Thai
I had ever met who had won a prize in the National Lottery. He
was on holiday in Korat. The third was Chitra, a local government officer from Sakol Nakorn, one of the north-east provinces.
We were soon on easy terms, and the journey was pleasant and
uneventful for the first sixty miles. After this I found the countryside unchanging mile after mile. We were well into the north-
east.

I soon found it a depressing region, desolate and dry. A layer of
dust rose up from the baked road. It was a painful contrast to the
lush green of the fertile central plain. Everything appeared to be
crying out for water. There were clumps of dwarf shrubs and
stunted flowers, large numbers of withered and dying trees. The
dust sometimes flew up in a cloud. I asked Boriboon what it was
like for the rest of the year. "Damp, muddy and steamy. A moist
heat everywhere. It's like breathing steam. Everywhere the same.
A wretched region," he said, morosely.

I had heard that there was never enough water, even in the
rainy season. It is only a quarter of that in the central region, while
the coastal stretch, between Bhuket and Ranong, has about
twenty-five times as much.

The following day was just as depressing. More dust from the
baked roads; lonely villages and hamlets with little sign of life;
and what livestock we saw was of poor quality. In the early
afternoon we came to Nongkai and the Mekong. I decided to
cross the Mekong the next day and have a look at Vientiane.

That evening, when, as Chitra said, we had got the dust out of
our hair, we walked round the town. There were large numbers
of Vietnamese. They were taller than the average Thai, and they

walked with a proud independence. They did not smile as easily as the Thais. They made no attempt to hide their nationality. The women wore black trousers, white surcoats and the conical Chinese straw hats one sees all over Thailand.

Coloured pictures of King Phumipol adorned the walls of some of the shops, and I remarked on this to Chitra, who grinned and replied, "And one of Ho Chi Minh, or Uncle Ho, all ready to put up in its place!"

Back at the hotel, Boriboon called for iced beer, and we settled down to a long chat. He had studied farming in the United States. In his view there had been gross neglect of the fifteen provinces for the past fifty years. The people there had no time for the Bangkok government. In the early Fifties, they had attempted a separatist movement. Police-General Phao, following his usual repressive methods, had the leader, a deputy named Tiang Sirrikhan, executed, and many were imprisoned. Field-Marshal Pibul Songkram, Prime Minister, had visited the north-east following the Vietminh invasion of Laos in 1953, to see if it would be practical to resettle the Vietnamese minority away from the north-east. There were demonstrations and wild scenes. Women lay down in front of his car. Some committed suicide by cutting their throats. A defeated and dejected Pibul returned to the capital.

Arising out of the Geneva agreement of 1954, the Bangkok government expected to receive the freight on American aid goods for Laos and extended the railhead to the south bank of the Mekong, opposite Vientiane. The Friendship Highway linked Saraburi to the Korat delta. The United States had replaced the timber bridges with concrete structures and had built airstrips. But, as Boriboon pointed out, those small towns and villages away from the main roads or the railways remained as isolated as before. Sometimes the villagers had to trudge two miles for water.

Disease was rife. There was a high rate of malaria, cholera, jaundice and dysentery, and intestinal diseases. Doctors were scarce, and there were very few hospitals. Most of the schools were of the old sala (with open-sided classrooms) type, and it was very difficult to get teachers, for there was nowhere for them to live. It was not unusual to find over a hundred children with only one teacher.

It had been estimated that wells were needed for as many as

15,000 villages. An attempt had been made to drill some. In many cases they had been successful, but in others they had struck sea-water or obstructions. One-third of the population, or 10 million people, lived in these provinces.

Reverting to the problem of the Vietnamese immigrants, this was not new. It had been going on for the past 300 years. The Vietnamese had moved continuously from the densely populated areas in the Red River delta of Tonkin into Laos. Towards the end of the last century they migrated in increasing numbers into eastern and central Laos. Some crossed the Mekong to settle in the fifteen north-eastern provinces, where they intermarried. Large numbers penetrated the passes from the coastal plain by the South China Sea and crossed the Mekong to what is now the Thai town of Nakornpanom.

One result of the Indo-China war was that there was a rush of Vietnamese into Siam. They settled in Thakhek in Laos. After the defeat of the Japanese in 1945, the Viet Minh occupied Thakhek. The French recaptured Thakhek and other Laotian towns from the Lao Issarak rebels and their Viet Minh allies. This sent large numbers of anti-French Vietnamese and Laotians over the Mekong and into the north-east. It was not until 1958 that the Thai and North Vietnamese governments made an agreement to repatriate all refugees in Thailand who were sympathetic to the communist régime. They were put on trains, which were then sealed, sent to Bangkok and shipped to Haiphong. Repatriation has now been stopped by the Hanoi government, but it has left Thailand with an acute problem on her hands.

In Bangkok it was estimated that there are now between 35,000 and 50,000 refugees, but I have been told that the figure is nearer 100,000, for children under 18 had not been included in the repatriation lists. It is doubtful whether they will be assimilated by the time they are adults!

I asked Boriboon whether he and his friends had ever been *bhikkus* (monks) and what they thought of the religious side of the dispute in the Vietnamese war. He said that all of them had taken the saffron robe within a year or so of each other. I gathered that the friendship between them was of several years' standing and very close.

Chet said that President Ngo Dinh Diem and his family had close connections with the Roman Catholic Church. They persecuted the Buddhist monks and followers and kept Buddhists out of the high offices of State. The object was to strengthen the position of the Roman Catholic minority. The persecutions had already aroused much indignation in Thailand. However, the situation in Thailand, where the Sangha, or Buddhist monastic system, is centralized under the authority of the king, was vastly different from that which obtained in Vietnam. There they followed the Mahayana, or Greater Vehicle, of the northern school, which he said was a breakaway movement. Thailand belonged to the Theravada, or southern school. This was the purest form, less complicated and adhered more closely to the teachings of the Buddha.

I felt that this was over-simplifying the problem. A charming and intelligent monk, whom I had met in Nakon Sawan, discussed the religious difficulties in Vietnam, where he had spent some years after the withdrawal of the French. He told me that the monks were much more militant than those in Thailand, possibly because of the influence of former colonial rule. There was a growing tendency on the part of the younger ones to resent the authority of their seniors. In general, the abbots wielded less authority than was the case in Thailand. Moreover, Buddhism, as understood in the West, was not the principal religion or philosophy of Vietnam, although it was widespread. Taoism in all its manifestations, and this included the worship of spirits, ancestors and of Vietnamese national heroes, was the real religion and in some respects resembled that of the Chinese.

There was also Cao-Daism, which was a religious combination based on Buddhism, Confucianism and Christianity, and, since its foundation in 1926, now had about 2 million followers. There was the Hoa Hao sect, which was a form of Buddhism, and had over a million followers. The political and military powers exercised by the Cao-Daist and Hoa Hao sects were broken by the Government in 1955 and 1956. Then the Roman Catholics had seized their opportunity and had asserted an authority out of all proportion to their numbers, for they made up only 20 per cent of the population. That they had been repressive could be explained, although not justified, by the conviction that, if the country fell to a communist take-over, the Church was doomed, but Buddhism would live on, adapting itself to changing conditions, as it had done in China.

The persecution in Vietnam had been interpreted as an attack on Buddhism. Buddhists took the view that differences between the sects were of less importance than the threat from an alien religion and the ill-treatment of those who were, in some ways, their brethren. The monks believed that the Church had not reconciled itself to the position where the colonial powers which had supported it for so long had departed. Nor had it realized the extent of the unpopularity of the pro-Catholic régime.

The four of us talked into the early hours. Then we went to our rooms. I showered, and was about to climb under the mosquito net, when I heard a faint tapping at the door. I opened it to find the waiter alternately beaming and yawning at me. "*Poo-ying? Poo-ying?*" he inquired. He waved his hand down the short corridor. An attractive girl appeared and gave me a respect-ful *wai*. "*Hah sip* baht!" murmured the waiter. I thought that fifty bahts was indeed a bargain for such a young lovely, but sleep was threatening to snatch me in a matter of seconds. I declined her favours with an apologetic, "Another time," and they went away.

The next morning at breakfast I told my friends about the charming intruder. Boriboon nearly choked himself on his papaya when schoolmaster Chet unblushingly admitted to having spent an excellent night for eighty bahts. Chet said that she must have been an Anglophile, but Boriboon pleased Chet by saying that she knew that she would have to work harder and so raised the price!

Chet drove me to the ferry-boat jetty, and I crossed the river to Vientiane. There was a distinct French atmosphere about this tiny capital of Laos, which was not entirely due to its French lay-out. French was spoken freely, and, although Vientiane was the administrative capital of the kingdom which had recently won its independence, I formed the impression that there were some who were still proud of their French culture. I had the same feeling two years earlier in Beirut. The French depart, but they freely send back their school-teachers and advisers, as in North Africa, and they are generally accepted.

There are a large number of pagodas in Vientiane which I found very attractive. The porches were worked in teak and over the years had acquired a delightful silky finish. There were some

Americans in the restaurants, all looking bored, although, with that clannishness which they seemed to possess so much more than the British, they had crowded around one table. I would have liked to have stayed longer, but that would have involved visa formalities. I bought a bottle of brandy to take back to Boriboon and his friends. A Frenchman half rose from his table and invited me to join him. He was going back on the ferry, and pressed me to help him to finish off some of his cognac in the opened bottle.

He said that it was ridiculous for either side to be too fussy over the ordinary day traveller's contraband. "Just think," he said, "a thousand miles of river, and the smuggling which goes on at night, for you've got some of the finest sailors in South-east Asia living in these parts. The Thai police have got an impossible job. Who can supervise a boundary that size? The Laotians send their agents over by boat or helicopter. Both sides trade with one another. Most of the Thais in the north-east speak the Lao language, and they've been pals for years. When the Laotians turned on us in 1946, Prince Soupanouvong and his big boys, communist or otherwise, made a dash for the north-east and holed up there comfortably. Look at the Pathet Lao! The Vietminh troops do the fighting, and then the Pathet Lao take over, but the north-east like them because they help out. Their agents live with them, even bring helicopters over with medical supplies, food and money. Pathet Lao's attitude is, 'Feed a hungry man and then he'll listen to you.' Phao said, 'Beat them over the head.' Just look at the mess that's landed the government in."

It transpired that he had lived for years in Saigon and Hanoi. I asked him whether he thought the communist threat was exaggerated. He was very cynical. He said that there was little basic difference between the North and South Vietnamese. Both sides hated China. Ho Chi Minh was a clever old fox and would never let the war get out of control and so let China take over the North and have a ready throughway for her troops. Even if both sides went communist, they would still oppose China. He could not understand why America did not realize this and come to terms with Marxism out there. He believed that De Gaulle was about the only one on the target. French agents were subsidizing the rubber planters and factory owners, and through them the Vietcong. De Gaulle was banking on a neutral state as the

ultimate conclusion, and this would give France access to Hanoi
and the north.

We left the café and boarded the ferry. On the passage across I
asked him if many people, Frenchmen or otherwise, thought as
he did. "Frenchmen, yes, and what aren't my views are plain
facts, common knowledge. You won't get an American to argue.
Before long he is in a state of near hysteria over the talk of
communism. That's why the U.S. government gets milked all
over South-east Asia. They feed them with talk of communist
plots, and America pays up." We parted at the jetty, where I
found Boriboon waiting with the car.

The next day we struck the Mekong again, stopping at Nakornpanom. The drive was as depressing as before. The grass was
bleached white by the sun, and the trees stood like gaunt skeletons. I visited some schools. Most were closed because of the water
shortage. However, I found one that was open. Like the others it
was dilapidated, with little equipment, old and broken benches
and seats. The children were charming and most polite. Their
smiles made my spirits rise. A crew-cut American shot out of one
of the classrooms, and a gale of laughter followed him. The
headmaster introduced him. "This is Doctor . . ." The American
interrupted him. "A turd tester," he grinned. He held up some
small circular tins, like those which contain film strips. He had
come to test for intestinal parasites.

Back in the car, Boriboon told me that this American was
sanuk, *sanuk* everywhere. I believed him.

At Nakornpanom, on the Mekong, I left the trio and stayed
for a couple of nights in the town. It had an animated, colourful
appearance, and the shops were full of articles. There appeared
to be more police about. There were no obvious signs of communist propaganda, but I was told that there was much activity
in this province, and there had actually been cases where local
officials of importance had been murdered by communists when
they could not be won over or were in active opposition to the
party. This may have been true, but I could not escape the feeling
that communism was often a convenient scapegoat.

I returned to the capital, deep in thought. In fairness to the
Bangkok government, it must be stated that a start has been made
to improve conditions in the north-east provinces, however
belated. The United States has been generous with her technical

and economic aid programmes. More irrigation systems are being built. New roads are being constructed. Schools and hospitals are going up. Much of this could have been done many years ago. The resources of the mighty Mekong, which flows through China, Thailand, Laos, Cambodia and Vietnam, could perhaps have been harnessed. However, there are, no doubt, political complications which the ordinary person knows little about.

At the same time, Nature can be a pitiless opponent. A vast stretch of land, poor soil and inadequate rainfall, a people who have established over the years a closer bond with the Laotians and the Vietnamese than they have with those from the rest of Thailand—these are problems which are indeed of great magnitude. For too many years the people of the north-east provinces have been cut off from the rest of Thailand. This is largely the fault of the Bangkok government. It would assist in bringing about a better understanding if some factual knowledge of the appalling conditions were disseminated throughout the kingdom. Young Thais might be persuaded to work there. The United States and, to a lesser extent, other countries, annually award large numbers of fellowships for free travel and study abroad. The administrators of these awards should insist that, on their return, the students should work for a time in the up-country districts or even in these provinces, instead of cluttering up the capital.

I have discussed this matter with some of the staff of the American-aid missions and have been told that they try to do this, but too many have influence in the capital. My reaction is that surely the remedy is in their hands.

Then too many of these fellowships are awarded to students and teachers, who wish to study at a university in the United States, obtain an easy degree and, on their return, receive graduate allowance as teachers of English. The United States makes generous provision for the study of English in Thailand, and their classes are well supported. It would appear unnecessary to spend so much money on fellowships abroad when reasonable facilities exist in their own country. Moreover, Thailand is desperately short of technicians, and fellowships in this field are a matter of urgent priority.

Religious persecution in Vietnam reached its height in May 1963, when the Government tried to prevent Buddhist celebrations in Hué on the occasion of the Buddha's birthday. There was so much brutality by the police and the military against the Buddhist monks that foreign governments protested. In August special forces, on orders from President Ngo Dinh Diem's brother, Ngo Dinh Nhu, stormed pagodas and arrested hundreds of monks and students. Seven Buddhist monks committed suicide by burning. Rumours that Ngo Dinh Nhu was seeking the good offices of the French in order to reach accord with the communists on North Vietnam swept the country. There was more unrest in the north-east.

The United States suspended economic aid to South Vietnam and financial support for Nhu's special forces. On 1st November there was a *coup d'état*, led by General Duong Van Minh, who was Diem's military adviser; General Tran Van Duong and General Le Van Kim. President Diem's régime, which had ruled since 1954, was overthrown. The President and his brother were shot. Much to the astonishment of many foreign observers, the communists did not follow up the advantage given by the upheaval. This, and a calmer religious atmosphere, improved the situation.

The United States has built massive military bases at Udorn, Nakornpanom, Ubol, Korat and Takli in the north-east. These bases help her to prosecute the war in Vietnam; they also protect Thailand from attack. The administration of the north-east provinces is a domestic affair, as the Bangkok government has been at pains to point out to the United States forces in Thailand.

If the situation is examined critically, it would appear that at the present time the communist threat has not assumed serious proportions. It was reported that in the summer of 1968 there were some 1,400 known communists in the north-east, which would suggest that the agitators have made little progress over many years! Communist subversion is under alien control and alien leadership, which probably explains what amounts to apathy towards the movement in Thailand.

With her frontiers protected, Thailand can concentrate on an all-out drive to bring prosperity to the north-east. This would include irrigation, buildings and agricultural projects and improvements in communications and the social services. There are welcome signs that some plans in these fields are under way. It was reported that in 1966, 85 per cent of the 43 million dollars was spent on counter-insurgency projects, mainly in the north-east. These include rural development schemes.

6 *The Chakri Dynasty and a Murdered King*

·⟨❀⟩·

During the siege of Ayudhya, a brilliant Siamese general, Taksin, realized that the city was doomed. He rallied about 600 soldiers, escaped with them through the Burmese lines and fled to Rayong, on the eastern coast of the Gulf of Siam, which he turned into a fortress town. Thousands of Siamese joined him. With a fleet of a hundred boats and an army of 5,000, he sailed up the Chao Phya River and captured Dhonburi. He beheaded the Siamese puppet governor who had been installed by the Burmese, sailed on to Ayudhya and defeated the Burmese soldiers. He united the provinces under his rule, and proclaimed himself king. Then, in 1771, he invaded Cambodia, and, after a short struggle, forced the Cambodian king to accept Siamese overlordship, a position which continued for nearly a hundred years.

The Burmese made several further invasions, but Taksin drove them out. One of his generals, Chakri, successfully defended Chiengmai. He defeated the Burmese armies and marched into the Laotian states of Vientiane and Luang Prabang. Here all resistance crumbled, and both states were forced to accept Siamese hegemony. In only twelve years, Siam had regained her unity and was extending her frontiers. From 1778 to 1893 much of the territory of present-day Laos was under the jurisdiction of Siamese kings.

While General Chakri was becoming more popular, Taksin's influence was declining. He had crowned himself king and had married several princesses of the old royal line, hoping to consolidate his position. The old dynasty had disappeared, and he considered himself the founder of a new one and, as such, the rightful king of Siam. However, his tyrannical rule alienated the loyalty of many of his former supporters. They spread a rumour that he was mad and that the kingdom was in danger. As a result of a successful conspiracy, he was executed.

The obvious choice of a successor was the brilliant general, Chakri. He commanded the army and, in any case, was acceptable to the nobles who had plotted against Taksin. A year after the death of Taksin he ascended the throne and founded the Chakri dynasty, which is the ruling house of Siam today. Chakri took the title Rama I. The present king, Phumipol Aduldej, is Rama IX.

Although unity had been restored to Siam, some principalities retained a measure of independence in certain internal matters, but subject to the authority of the throne. Then the immorality and corruption which were largely responsible for the country's defeat were still rife. Chakri was determined to curb the power of the princes, and also to clean up the country.

In his attitude to the princes, he played the old Siamese game of intrigue, conferring favours on some and making rivals of others. A large number of monks led lewd lives. Taksin had taken a strong line here, following the fall of Ayudhya, when a number of monks led by Ruan, who had proclaimed himself King of Fang in north central Siam, had turned to banditry, murder and vice. Ruan declared himself to be the priest-king, and, with his followers, he wore the saffron robe.

He besieged the city of Pitsanulok which capitulated after two months. The governor was murdered, and his corpse hung over the central gate. Flushed with an easy victory, he set out to subdue central Siam. Taksin had led an army against him, recaptured Pitsanulok, killed many of his followers and hunted the priest-king through central Siam. His followers deserted him, and Ruan took refuge among the hill tribes of the north.

The lesson was not lost on Rama I. He ordered the arrest of all profligate monks, who were then disrobed and put to forced labour. Abbots were required to keep registers of all monks under their authority and were held responsible for their conduct. All monks and novices were ordered to prove their identity, and the abbots were required to issue each one with an identity card, which was usually a statement inscribed on a palm leaf. He decided that the Buddhist canon should be revised and brought up to date, in accordance with the reforms he had introduced in the priesthood. He called a council of 250 high dignitaries, who sat for nearly six months in Wat Mahathat. It produced a set of regulations and a code of morals and worship which are still used today.

In 1785, or just three years after Chakri had been crowned, the Burmese invaded, but the Siamese fought back savagely, and the Burmese were hurled back beyond the frontier. In 1810 they made yet another attack. Burmese armies invaded from the south. They seized the island of Bhuket and besieged the town of Chumporn, but the Siamese drove them out.

In 1806 Rama I died at the age of 72. He was succeeded by his son, Prince Isarasunthon, who took the title of Rama II. The heir to the throne was usually nominated by the ruling king before he died, sometimes on his death-bed. The choice had to be approved by the Accession Council. If there were rival claimants, then the disappointed prince was well advised to accept the choice gracefully, otherwise he stood a good chance of losing his life by being sewn up in a velvet cloak and clubbed to death with ebony clubs, the method employed for executing those of the royal blood.

Only three days after he had been crowned, Prince Isarasunthon had Prince Kasatra and his followers executed for treason, although, according to Siamese law, they had merited clemency by confessing. However, Rama II was determined to protect the dynasty and give a salutary lesson to others.

He attempted to bring about a more equitable system of taxation. His officials were sent into the ricefields, orchards and plantations to assess the yield. Those fields which were irrigated from rivers or canals were taxed according to their acreage, irrespective of the value of the crop, but ricefields on high ground, which depended upon seasonal rainfall, paid tax only on the yield. If it were proved that the farmer's record for the past three years was unsatisfactory, he was dispossessed, and the property given to the king.

Those guilty of the sale or smoking of opium were exhibited publicly for three days on land and three on a boat. For failing to inform the King's officials of cases of opium smoking, the penalty was sixty lashes. In actual fact, the opium smoker had to be a person of strong nerves. All kinds of lurid stories as to the appalling fate which would overtake them gained credence. Insanity, blindness, impotence—the latter has always been dreaded by the Siamese—and convulsions, were among the list of ultimate afflictions. Even the supernatural was invoked.

It was said that the dead smoker turned into a huge and hideous form of spirit, a *prade*, which was always very hungry and stank abominably. It gave warning of its approach by a high-pitched, terrifying scream. The *prade* carried on its head a sharp-edged circular knife, which gradually cut its neck, so that blood gushed out. However, the wound would heal, and the sawing would recommence, which kept the *prade* in perpetual agony. The only way in which peace could be restored to its tormented soul was by the relatives acquiring merit. The vision of the *prade* in action may have sent shudders down the spines of the nervous, but the opium habit grew. It would, therefore, appear that, in time, the supernatural lost its terrors, and the smoker decided that the pleasure was worth the risk!

Rama II was a devout Buddhist. He restored the old Ayudhyan custom by which the people were exhorted to join in a three-day period of merit making. The consumption of alcoholic drinks was forbidden. The city was decorated with flowers and lights, and there were processions to the temples.

He changed the old law by which Buddhist monks guilty of immorality were expelled from the order and executed, and substituted life imprisonment with hard labour. He allowed other religions complete tolerance. The Christian missionaries were making fewer converts, and Rama II believed that this was due to the reforms his father had made in the practice of Buddhism and the improved conduct of the monks and the monasteries. Most of the Christian converts were descendants of the Portuguese immigrants who had married Siamese girls.

Throughout his reign there was always the threat of invasion from Burma, and Rama II built up a large army. He turned some of the towns into fortified cities. He had formed an army of 30,000 trained soldiers, armed with muskets supplied by Britain, Portugal and America, and with spears and swords. In 1810, the Burmese attacked Talang Island, Ranong and Chumporn but were driven out.

He continued to maintain good relations with China. That country looked upon Siam as a vassal state, but did not assert itself. His relations with the Malay provinces became more difficult with the increase of British influence in the peninsula, especially following the cession of Penang by the Sultan of Kedah. Later the Sultan demanded its return and started a minor insurrection against the British, but he soon abandoned it.

Rama II's foreign policy became more aggressive. In 1821, annoyed by the defiance of the new sultan—the old one had died leaving ten sons, mostly by different mothers—he ordered him to report to Bangkok. The Sultan refused. Possibly he was afraid of a usurper from among his brothers. Rama II sent an army. The Sultan appealed in vain to the British for help. The Siamese army was victorious, and the Sultan fled to Penang. Rama II promptly abolished the sultanate and sent a son of the Governor of Nakorn to govern the state as a Siamese province.

In 1822, the Marquess of Hastings, who was Viceroy of India, sent John Crawford to Bangkok, with a letter of introduction. It informed the king of the growing might of the British Empire and of his earnest desire for friendship between the two countries. He also sent 300 muskets.

During his reign Rama II built some magnificent buildings and temples. Rama I had concentrated on rebuilding Ayudhya in Bangkok, which meant that everything took on the Ayudhyan style. Rama II varied the architecture, including Chinese and European styles. He built the beautiful Wat Arun, or the Temple of Dawn, and had gardens, lakes and pagodas laid out in the grounds of the royal palace. He was a talented artist and poet.

At the age of 56 he died. He left seventy-three children by thirty-eight wives. He had been too ill to nominate the heir to the throne, otherwise he would have chosen his favourite, Prince Mongkut, who was the eldest celestial son. Mongkut was 5 years old when his father ascended the throne in 1809, and in 1812 he was given a magnificent ceremonial bath on a brilliantly decorated raft moored on the Chao Phya River, close to the Grand Palace.

At the time of his father's death, he had already entered a monastery, and he stayed there when the Accession Council gave the throne to Prince Chesda, who took the title of Rama III. Rama III was 37 at the time of his accession, and already had thirty-eight children. He was a leading patron of the arts and was popular with the Court.

Rama II had acted without his usual wisdom and foresight by appointing princes to high offices of state, and some of these offices were handed down to their children. This was to lead eventually to an abuse of power by a privileged class, which continued to increase in numbers and to be one of the causes of the 1932 *coup*.

The opium trade had become very profitable, and the loss to the royal coffers was considerable. It was now largely in Chinese hands. Feuds between the secret societies had become so deadly that Rama III decided that they had to be wiped out. He acted with energy and ruthlessness. In one operation in the provinces over 3,000 Chinese were killed.

He built more ships, for trade was increasing and the output from the silver mines was soaring. More canals were dug. The rivers were dredged and widened. He increased the taxes on gambling and the sale of alcohol. The Chinese traders who held these monopolies had to bid for them. The Chinese minority at this time did not create difficulties. About 16,000 a year entered the country. Intermarriages were on the increase, for there were few women among the immigrants. This meant that the Chinese were being assimilated, perhaps to a greater degree than at any other time.

He accepted foreign missionaries but was more appreciative and grateful for their medical work than their preaching. However, he recognized in their tireless efforts, despite discouraging results, a challenge to the saffron robe. He sent visiting commissions to monasteries far afield and ordered the expulsion of 500 monks for unsatisfactory conduct. He had nine new temples built and eighty others extended. The enormous ninety-foot statue of the reclining Buddha in Wat Po was built during his reign.

Captain Burney, an English officer in Penang, was sent to Bangkok, under the pretence of asking the king for help in the struggle with Burma, but the real object of the visit was to secure ships and supplies for the campaign. He also wanted to negotiate over Malaya. Burney suggested that Siam could attack Burma in the north but not interfere in the south. Rama III realized that it would be disastrous not to negotiate with the British and agreed, and so the first commercial treaty between a Chakri king and a Western power was signed in June 1826.

This led to conflict with Laos, where a rumour was circulated to the effect that Burney had presented an ultimatum to the Siamese king, and that the British were preparing to invade Bangkok. Prince Anuwongse of Vientiane saw his opportunity. The Laotian states had been under Siamese hegemony for many years, and they surrounded Siam from north-west to the south-east. He decided to capture Bangkok first and then make himself master of all Siam. He made a lightning thrust at Korat and occupied the town. An advance force pushed down to Saraburi, which was only three days' march from the capital.

Rama III fought back. The Vientiane troops were driven from Saraburi. Before the advancing Siamese forces, Anuwongse retreated from Korat to Vientiane, and then to Vietnam. The Siamese armies followed him and occupied Vientiane. Rama III ordered that all elephants and horses be rounded up and sent to Bangkok and the walls and forts demolished. He was urged to destroy the city as a warning to other states, but he saw that a weakened Vientiane was an easy prey to Vietnam.

Anuwongse was finally captured and sent to Bangkok, where Rama III had him placed in a large iron cage and put on public exhibition. After a week of this punishment he died.

The King believed in the old adage that no one is as strong as he who has successfully crushed a revolt and now took a stronger line. When, in 1833, the Vietnamese of Cochin China rebelled against the central government of Hué and attempted to form an autonomous state, Rama acceded to their request for help and sent a large army and naval force. Unfortunately, the Cambodian king changed sides to the fury of the Siamese, who were forced to withdraw but not before demolishing the walls of Pnom Pehn. This destruction of cities was an old Siamese custom.

However, the King continued to have difficulties over opium. An Englishman, Robert Hunter, began to import the drug and was soon in trouble with the authorities. He appealed to the British government for help, but they would not interfere. This refusal encouraged the King to restrict trade and impose more regulations.

The President of the United States sent Joseph Ballestier to Bangkok in 1849 to obtain more concessions, but the envoy and the King fell out over matters of etiquette. The Siamese chamberlain informed the captain of the American ship that he would not risk arranging another audience with the King, as Ballestier was so bad-tempered and ill-mannered. The same year Sir James Brooke visited Bangkok on a mission of friendship and trade.

In 1849 Rama quarrelled with the Roman Catholic missionaries. There had been a serious plague the previous year, and he ordered a period of deep devotion and piety. The missionaries refused to observe some of the religious rites and called on their converts to ignore them. He was furious and threatened to expel the priests and demolish their churches. Fortunately, the Roman Catholic bishop intervened, and said that the missionaries had displayed an excess of zeal.

Rama III was now very ill, and he asked the Accession Council to appoint a successor. They chose Prince Mongkut. If the court astrologers had told Rama III that Mongkut was to take two of the King's granddaughters as wives, and that the hero, King Chulalongkorn, and all future kings would trace their descent from him, he would have been incredulous. But that is what transpired.

Mongkut, or Rama IV, is the best known of all Siamese kings among the Western powers, on account of the novels by Anna Leonowens and Margaret Landon and the films and musical based on them. These accounts of the king were highly coloured and inaccurate and bitterly resented by the Thais. Today he is revered as one of Siam's greatest monarchs.

He had spent twenty-seven years in a monastery before his accession, was a devout Buddhist and had acquired a high reputation for his knowledge of Buddhism. He had studied English and the history and politics of the countries of the West. He realized that he would have to arrive at some working relationship, particularly with the European powers, if he was to preserve Siam's independence. His diplomacy here was brilliant. Britain was in control of the Malay States right up to the Siamese border and could well be a threat to Siam. While in the monastery, Mongkut had heard of Britain's victory over China in 1842, and the news had made a profound impression on him. China had looked upon Siam as a vassal state for centuries, and, if Britain could subdue this great country, then her power must be tremendous.

He decided to seek Britain's friendship, and, in 1855, or four years after his accession, he concluded a Treaty of Friendship and Commerce. The British envoy, Sir John Bowring, was given a brilliant reception. The capital was *en fête* for several days. Mongkut was determined that the imperial envoy of Queen Victoria should be treated with the highest honours. Bangkok was to be the show window of South-east Asia, a country worthy of the friendship of the mighty British Empire, and, in the name of a prosperous and independent country, the King of Siam greeted Sir John.

The treaty concluded between the two powers gave important trading concessions to Britain. Her nationals were allowed to rent or own land near Bangkok. All British subjects were granted extra-territorial rights. However, the shrewd Mongkut took care to see that Britain's power did not threaten the independence of Siam. When the American envoy, Mr. Townsend Harris, was negotiating with Mongkut, the King inquired whether the United States could be counted upon, at least for arbitration, in the event of a dispute with Britain. Townsend Harris refused to commit his country. The French envoy was also approached with the same object and gave the same reply. It is not known whether all envoys heard of Mongkut's diplomatic move with amusement or respect, possibly the latter. The treaty with France gave French missionaries a wide measure of freedom.

In an attempt to control the opium menace, Mongkut established the first opium *farm*. This meant that the monopoly was sold to the highest bidder. The royal coffers received a fixed sum from the monopolists. Until the end of the century, opium, lotteries, gambling and alcohol monopolies accounted for nearly half of the state revenues.

He was the most learned student of Buddhism. He decided that, for most people, there was too much mystery and elaborate ritual. Merit could be bought. The simplicity and nobility of the Buddha's message was being lost. He founded a reform movement, the Dhamma Yutta or 'Adhere to the Doctrine'. This was most successful.

He was well aware of the intentions of the French Roman Catholic and American Presbyterian missionaries to convert him. He had studied their religions but was well content with Buddhism. He told them that man cannot even attempt to emulate the omnipotence of the God they described, but every-

6

one could follow the path trodden by one whom all knew was once a man like them.

He brought advisers to Bangkok from several countries, for he was determined that there would be no clear imprint of one nation's influence upon the country. His son, Chulalongkorn, who was to succeed him, was careful to follow this policy. Finance was entrusted to experts from England. Experts from France advised him on law reform, the Dutch advised him on agriculture, the Danish trained his navy, the Germans his army and the Americans trained his Foreign Office in external affairs. French engineers laid out the waterways of the capital.

Much has been written about Mongkut's harem. In actual fact, it was quite modest by Siamese standards, especially when it is remembered that, before his accession, he had spent twenty-seven years in a monastery and had kept his vows.

He was to leave eighty-two children by thirty-five wives. Mr. H. G. Quaritch Wales refers to *The Bangkok Calendar* of 1863, from which he tells us that there were twenty-seven royal mothers in the King's family. One had seven children, two of them each had five, another had four, two of them each had three, four had two each, and all the others had one each. At that time there were thirty-four concubines. Each received a government salary designed for the support of her own person, not including her children. Besides these thirty-four concubines, there were seventy-four daughters of noblemen, who had been presented to the King by their fathers, with a view to serving as maids of honour. Concubines were known as Nan Ham or 'Women forbidden to leave the palace'.

The staff of the harem consisted of elderly women who acted as judges in cases of breaches of discipline, tutors entrusted with the education of younger concubines, and a small army of slaves. No eunuchs, and no one save the King ever entered the palace, which was a small town inside the Grand Palace.

H. G. Quaritch Wales says that recruitment to the royal harem was effected through different sources:

Sometimes one took the king's fancy, or he receives a report that so and so is a beautiful girl whose parents have a connection with royalty. If the king wants her, he sends a royal messenger to conduct her to the royal palace to be educated and trained, and then admitted as a Nan Ham. Sometimes parents send their loveliest daughters as presents, hopeful of favours.

Another source was provided when the Prince ascends the throne. All the other princes, nobles and lords present their most beautiful daughters. Thus royal concubines have been very numerous, even a thousand or more.

"King Chulalongkorn had thirty-four sons and forty-three daughters," boomed the stentorian voice of the guide who had conducted us on a tour of the capital during my first month in Thailand.

A lovely, irrepressible American girl from Auburn, Alabama, whose spontaneous quips had kept the party in fits of laughter, rose to the occasion. "I don't think these Siamese kings were all that good. They must have had some help!"

Actually it was recognized state policy for the Siamese kings to have large harems. It guaranteed the succession, as well as the loyalty of those families, for the daughters were hostages. However, the 'princely' class was growing more and more numerous.

Chulalongkorn was only 11 years of age when he ascended the throne in 1868. Prince Bunnag was appointed Regent and tutor until he came of age. The new king was to reign for forty-two years. He is the most revered of all the Thai kings and is known as the 'Hero King'. He visited Europe on two occasions and was to send all his sons there for their education. They were allotted special courses of study, so that, on their return, the ideas and knowledge they had acquired could be adapted and put into practice. Perhaps this modernization process might have been better served had he sent men more mature and experienced in their particular fields, but Chulalongkorn wanted to keep it, as far as possible, a family affair.

He continued his father's policy of bringing technicians over from Europe and attaching to each small groups to study their methods, a forerunner of the counterparts as we understand them today. (The Thai government provides the United Nations or foreign government experts with a 'counterpart', a Thai, who works with the expert and takes over when he leaves the country.) In his reign, Siam was to have a fine network of railways, as well as electricity, post and telegraph.

He was interested in democracy and in democratic institutions which he had seen on his travels abroad, but he was convinced that the time was not ripe in Siam for any move away from autocracy. One of his sons, Prince Chira, had studied in Denmark and was Commander-in-Chief of the Siamese army. Against much opposition from the palace circle, he brought in conscription which, later, was to exert a controlling influence over the privileged classes.

Chulalongkorn realized that Siam could not be a truly united country as long as there were some states or principalities such as Chiengmai, which had a measure of independence. Accordingly, he took the daughters of the ruling princes of these regions as wives.

Throughout his reign, his major policy was to preserve Siam's independence.

In 1890, France made new demands on Laos. She insisted that these were reasonable because the Laotian kings had once rendered tribute to the King of Annam. Siam opposed these claims, and sent more soldiers to Laos. Three years later France demanded all Siamese territory east of the Mekong River, moved forces from Vietnam into Siamese territory and followed up this move by sending warships to the mouth of the Chao Phya River. The Siamese opened fire. The French retaliated. There were casualties on both sides. France then presented an ultimatum. Siam was to evacuate all territory east of the Mekong, to pay an indemnity of 3 million francs and to punish the officers for firing on French ships. Siam agreed to pay the indemnity and punish the officers, but asked for negotiations over the proposed cession of territory, for much of it had belonged to Siam for years.

Britain, in response to an urgent appeal from Chulalongkorn, sent warships to the Gulf of Siam and asked France for an explanation. France promised that the independence of Siam would not be threatened. Britain then advised acceptance of the French demands, which had now been raised to include the evacuation of all armed forces from Siemrap and Pratabong. These towns had once been part of Cambodia. In 1896 both France and Britain guaranteed Siam's independence.

Chulalongkorn was disappointed that Britain did not give him more support. But both France and Britain were preoccupied with their own affairs. France was looking uneasily towards the Rhine; the war party were still clamouring for the return of the lost provinces of Alsace-Lorraine. Britain had recently fought the Boer War and found that she had fewer allies than she had thought. Then she was alive to the danger from a powerful Germany.

One of his greatest political triumphs was the Siamese king's switch to a pro-Japanese policy, following Russia's defeat by Japan in 1904. Chulalongkorn had cultivated friendly relations with Russia in order to have support in resisting the claims of the French. He had sent several of his sons to the military academy at St. Petersburg and had persuaded princes and noblemen to do the same.

He saw that Japan, by her victory, had proved herself to be a great military and naval power and could be a very useful ally. The Japanese people had the same conception of monarchy as the Siamese. Moreover, the two countries were now the only independent states in the Far East. His advisers had told him that revolution in Russia could not be long delayed. Clearly, Siam's interests were best served by establishing good relations with this young, vigorous and rising power in the Far East.

The last decade of Chulalongkorn's long reign was a golden era of culture, in which Bangkok shone as a great capital in Southeast Asia. Music, art and literature flourished. More schools were built. Some magnificent new temples adorned the capital and the provinces. The saffron robe exerted a mystic hold all over the kingdom, but it was never at any time oppressive. It brought the people even closer to a wise and great king. In 1907 he made an official visit to the European capitals and was delighted with the warmth of his welcome.

He had married three sisters who were daughters of King Mongkut and, therefore, his half-sisters. They were given the titles of first, second and third queen. The eldest, Sunanda, and her son were drowned when the royal barge capsized. The horrified courtiers looked on helplessly, for no one could even touch the sacred person of the king or queen under penalty of death.

H. G. Quaritch Wales quotes this law in his book *Siamese State Ceremonies*.

If the boat (royal barge) founders, the boatmen must swim away; if they remain near the boat, they are to be executed. If the boat founders and the royal person falls into the water, and is about to drown, let the boatmen stretch out the signal spear and throw the cocoa nuts so that he may grasp them if he can. If he cannot, they may let him seize the signal spear. If they lay hold on him to rescue him, they are to be executed.

He who throws the cocoa nuts is to be rewarded with forty tikals of silver and one gold basin. If the barge sinks and someone else sees the cocoa nuts thrown and goes to save the royal person, the punishment is double and all his family is to be exterminated. If the barge founders and someone throws the cocoa nuts so that they float towards the shore (i.e. away from the royal person) his throat is to be cut and his home confiscated.

At Bang Pa In, where the Queen and her son were drowned, the King had beautiful gardens planted in her memory. A very moving message, in Thai and in English records the tragic event.

To the memory of Queen Sunanda Sukhumalai, Queen Consort who was wont to spend her most pleasant and happiest hours in the garden amidst those loving ones and dearest to her, this memorial is erected by Chulalongkorn Rex, whose suffering from so cruel an endurance through those trying hours made death so near, and yet preferable. 1881.

The new king, Vajiravudh or Rama VI, was the son of the second queen. He had studied at Oxford, had served with the British army and had conceived a deep affection and admiration for Britain. He introduced several British institutions and customs to Siam. The famous Vajiravudh school in Bangkok is known as the 'Eton' of Siam.

Vajiravudh was not interested in politics. It is doubtful as to whether he really wanted to be king. He was an intellectual. He wrote and produced plays and operas and surrounded himself with the company of young men whom he brought into his productions. They came from all classes, their main assets being good looks and acting ability.

He formed a King's Army Corps. It became known as the 'Wild Tigers' and was commanded by his favourite courtiers. It consisted of court officials, young actors and their admirers. The object of the corps was to offset the power of the army, which his favourites said was opposed to him. He needed large sums of money to finance his vast army. Vice and corruption were so prevalent among the Wild Tigers, that there were angry protests from some influential nobles at court, and high ranking army officers complained that the money spent on the Wild Tigers was sorely needed to pay for the equipment and wages of the regular army.

His brother, Prince Chakrabongse, for whom the king had a high personal regard, had told him of a conspiracy against the throne and later had warned him of the growing resentment of the masses at his extravagance and favouritism and of the abuses of privilege among the Bangkok princes, of whom there were a large number because of the royal polygamy of the Chakri kings. He took some heed of his brother's advice, for there were rumours that the Bangkok garrisons were in a state of mutiny and preparing to march on the palace. The Wild Tiger Corps lost much of its influence, although whether this was on account of a lessening of the King's interest or because jealousy and corruption caused so many splits that it practically dissolved itself, it is difficult to know. Unfortunately, it left in its trail a number of feuds which divided the capital.

Vajiravudh loved to retire into his world of fantasy, his operas and his pomp and pageantry, but he did more than any Siamese monarch to emancipate women, and he endeavoured to make monogamy the only legal form of marriage.

Throughout his reign, he persecuted the Chinese minority. He had not forgiven the Chinese secret societies for the general strike they had organized only a few months before he became king. After the Chinese Revolution of 1911 he introduced more severe measures. In 1913 the Nationality Act was passed, and the persecution increased. The following year he published under a pseudonym a pamphlet entitled *The Jews of the East*, which was a scathing attack on the Chinese. There was more corruption during his reign than that of any other of the kings of the Chakri dynasty.

His policy was consistent with that of former Chakri kings in one respect, and that was to watch the developments of the struggle for power and make such moves as would benefit the country or preserve its independence. Accordingly, he declared war on Germany in July 1917.

About 1,200 Siamese troops arrived in France. The larger number served in a motor transport corps while the rest were pilots and aircraft mechanics. The Armistice was signed shortly afterwards. As a result of her action, Siam was granted the right to be represented as an equal at the Peace Conference in Paris and to serve as a charter member of the League of Nations.

When he died in 1925, he left only one child, a baby daughter born just before his death. The ghosts of the former Chakri kings, famed for their virility, must have stared at each other, received silent but unanimous agreement and promptly black-balled him from the Chakri Valhalla.

He was succeeded by his brother, Prince Prajadhipok or Rama VII, who ascended the throne in 1925.

Prajadhipok had been educated at Eton and had formed a deep admiration for the British way of life. The British public schools and universities have done much towards establishing good relations with those countries whose nationals have been educated there. I have met, in the capital and up-country Thais, who are quite lyrical in their praise of these institutions, and I have satisfied myself that this has not just been a case of courtesy to a foreigner. Prajadhipok never forgot his old school. He presented it with a famous garden and brought Old Etonians over to serve as advisers in different ministries.

However, the star of the Chakri kings was now setting. The new king was quite unfitted to govern. His brother's death at the early age of 50 had been a great shock, and Prajadhipok had not expected to succeed him.

There was an old superstition that the Chakri dynasty would last just 150 years. King Vajiravudh is reported as having replied to those royal princes who reminded him of this superstition, "They said that about the British in India. Their role was supposed to end one hundred years after Plassey, and they've already lasted another sixty!"

The royal astrologers at the Siamese court had also been making similar forecasts from time to time. However, it was apparent that an extremely difficult time loomed ahead. The world-wide economic depression had involved Siam, where it became more serious because of the extravagance of the previous king. The officer class was still smarting over the humiliations experienced at the hands of the Wild Tigers and King Vajiravudh. The young intellectuals were well aware that Siam was almost the only absolute monarchy among the kingdoms of the world.

Given time, it is possible that he might have solved some of the problems and even have granted a constitution before he was forced to. He was a conscientious king, and was determined not to make the same mistakes as the previous kings. He was convinced that trouble was brewing, but when he confided his views to his advisers, they dismissed them out of hand. "Where are the leaders?" they asked. They insisted upon the retention of absolute monarchy. Prajadhipok reminded them that there had been leaders in 1912 and that the conspiracy had been well organized.

Following his usual custom of leaving the capital during the hot season, the King had gone to the seaside resort of Hua Hin with his court. In June 1932 the conspirators struck. The revolt was well organized. A document with the forged signature of the prince in charge of the royal military arsenal was sent to all up-country garrisons, ordering all arms to be sent to the capital before 15th June.

However, the Chief of the Siamese Police had not been idle. He had compiled a list of the conspirators and, as more names were whispered, some quite illustrious, he was horrified. Believing the revolution to be imminent, he dashed to Hua Hin to confront his superior, Prince Nakorn Sawan. He begged him to order the arrest of all the conspirators, but the incredulous prince refused. The matter could await further investigation when he returned to the capital.

Before dawn the next morning, 24th June, almost the entire Bangkok garrison had been marched, without arms, to the huge square in front of the Dusit Palace to watch an alleged anti-aircraft demonstration. There the guns of the tank corps were trained on them. There was no resistance.

Working to a preconceived plan, the conspirators dashed into the houses of the princes. They were arrested, some in their pyjamas, and imprisoned in the throne hall of the Dusit Palace. All the ministries were taken over. The leaders sent a warship to bring the King back from Hua Hin. He told them that he would return by train. The revolution was over. To the amazement of the entire world, it had been bloodless. King Prajadhipok was the last of the absolute monarchs of Siam.

Four names appeared prominently on the list of the leaders. These were Pridi Panomyong, Colonel Pahol, Colonel Song Suradet and Major Pibul Songkram. The king signed the constitution, which was written on palm leaf, on 10th December

1932. By his act, he prevented foreign powers from intervening in Siam's internal policy.

Ten months afterwards, Prince Boworadet gathered an army together and marched on the capital. The revolt became known as the Royalists' Insurrection. It was completely crushed in four days. Boworadet fled the country. Six of the leaders were sentenced to death, and over 300 to terms of imprisonment. King Prajadhipok came under suspicion of having connived in the plot, for, instead of standing by Pahol's government, he fled to Songkla and did not return until the issue had been decided.

Shortly after this, with Queen Rampai, he sailed for England, on the pretext of seeking medical treatment. He could not bring himself to sign the death warrants of the political prisoners, and the events of the past year had been too shattering. He never returned to Siam. On the 5th March 1935 he abdicated and asked that there be no uprising on his behalf. He lived a quiet life at Virginia Water, Surrey, where he died six years later.

He left no issue. The crown passed to Ananda Mahidol, grandson of King Chulalongkorn, a 10-year-old boy at school in Switzerland. A three-man Regency Council was appointed to govern the country until he came of age. In 1938 the young prince was given a vociferous welcome when he visited the capital for two months. He was only 13 at the time. He returned to Switzerland and lived there during the war years with his mother who was now known as the Princess Mother, his brother Phumipol and his sister Galyani.

On 6th September 1945 Pridi, in his capacity as Regent, wrote to him, pointing out that, as on 20th September he would have attained the age of 20, the regency would be terminated. He asked the young king to return to the capital and direct the government of the kingdom.

Ananda replied to the effect that, while anxious to serve his country, he felt that he would be more equipped to do so if he were permitted to complete his studies. This would necessitate a further two and a half years' study for his doctorate, but he would return to the capital at once for a short stay before resuming his studies.

On 5th December King Ananda arrived to a tremendous welcome. He was fêted wherever he went. He planned to return to Switzerland on 13th June. On 9th June he was found dead, shot through the forehead.

At first the court officials and doctors believed that he had committed suicide. The revolver was cocked for firing, and only one round was missing. However, they thought that an announcement that he had taken his life would bring the throne into disrepute. Eventually they agreed upon a communiqué, and this was broadcast to the deeply shocked nation in the evening. It stated that:

> The King was found lying dead. An examination was made by the Directors-General of the Police Department, and the Department of Medical Sciences, as the result of which it was concluded that the King must have played with the pistol as he was fond of doing, resulting in an accident.

In the Dusit Palace the monks commenced the official ceremony of One Hundred Days. At the same time the National Assembly, on Pridi's advice, offered the crown to Phumipol, the dead king's brother, who accepted.

The period of official mourning had not long commenced, when Bangkok was seething with the wildest rumours. Doctors from Chulalongkorn hospital, who had prepared the body after his death, reported that they had found a wound in the back of his head which was smaller than that in the forehead. They deduced from this that he had not committed suicide, nor had death been accidental. He had been shot from behind.

Other doctors disputed this deduction, and rather grotesque experiments were carried out on human corpses and live pigs. As a result, the Chulalongkorn doctors' hypothesis was disproved, but much harm had been done. Rumours named several people as the murderer. One of the first to be so accused was Pridi. As Prime Minister, he was responsible for the King's safety. He became the centre of the storm. It is likely that the monarchists and former privileged classes had a hand in spreading these rumours, which at first Pridi impatiently shrugged aside. The princes had not forgiven him for the indignity of their arrest, and of the later restrictions on the privileges they had so long enjoyed.

Some of the more fanciful allegations included a charge that the conspirators intended to murder the entire Royal Family. Then there were whispers that King Phumipol had murdered his brother. Pibul was also named as having engineered the murder. It was also said that the murderer or murderers had been smuggled into the palace to kill the king. This meant that the royal pages were implicated. Even the Princess Mother did not escape malicious slander, for it was said that Phumipol was her favourite son and that she would have preferred him to be king.

Rumour followed rumour. A major in a Thai parachute regiment told me that Thailand will never learn the real truth until there is a successful communist uprising. I have also been told that only the Royal Family know the identity of the murderer.

Ananda had been unwell the previous day, and early on the day of the murder he was first visited by the Princess Mother, who slept in a wing of the same building, the Borom Piman Hall. About eight o'clock a royal page named Butr took the King his customary glass of orange juice and the morning papers. Some minutes later another royal page arrived. This was Chit. He had reported a couple of hours earlier than his normal duty time because of a royal errand. Butr explained that the King had been to the bathroom but refused his orange juice and gone back to bed. A quarter of an hour later, Prince Phumipol passed by. He inquired of the two pages as to his brother's health. They told him that it was nothing serious but that he was still in bed.

Ten minutes later a shot was heard. Chit rushed to the room of the Princess Mother and gasped out the news. She tore into the King's room, followed by the royal nanny. Prince Phumipol had heard a cry, and, on going to investigate, he met the lady-in-waiting, who told him that his brother had shot himself. He went at once to his brother's bedroom, arriving just a few seconds after the nanny. He took in the situation, went out and told Butr to fetch a doctor. Then he went back to help his mother. The Chief of the Palace Guards telephoned the tragic news to the Chief Major Domo. Pridi was also notified and at once called the Minister of the Interior and the Director-General of the Police.

Pridi set up a Commission of Inquiry into the King's death and busied himself with the elections, and his victory by a large majority gave him the impression that most people believed him innocent of the allegations of regicide. He saw King Phumipol and the Princess Mother off on their return by R.A.F. aircraft to Switzerland, where the King was to continue his education, and then resigned from the office of Prime Minister, which he had never really wanted. Admiral Dhamrong, a personal friend, took over, and Pridi returned to his former position of Senior Statesman.

This was the position at the end of October when the Commission of Inquiry completed its report. It rejected the original verdict of accidental death. The Government called for increased police investigation. The police allowed seven months to pass before they set up a special committee, and its members had made little progress sixteen months later. It appeared as if over the whole country there was a strong desire among the masses to let the unexplained tragedy slip gradually into oblivion. No one had been arrested. The two royal pages, had they so desired, could have disappeared, even left the country. A former royal secretary, Chaleo, whose name was also linked with the death of the king, had actually been given a seat in the Senate.

Then, on the evening of 7th November 1947, tanks roared through the streets of the capital. Thailand, the land of *coups*, had just added another *coup* to its list. Pridi at once saw the danger. He made his way to the house of the British Naval Attaché, who took him in and called on the ambassador, Sir Geoffrey Thompson, to whom he reported the danger which threatened their war-time collaborator. With the help of the American ambassador, he got Pridi out of the country. From Singapore, he sent a letter to Lord Killearn, Special Commissioner in South-east Asia, denying on oath that either he or any member of his entourage had anything to do with the death of the king. This was because the leaders of the *coup* had declared that its main object was to solve the mystery surrounding the death of King Ananda. Its real purpose, as revealed later, was to get rid of Pridi.

The trial opened in September 1948. Chaleo and the two royal pages, Chit and Butr, were charged with having plotted with others to kill King Ananda. The actual charges varied slightly. Chaleo was excluded from the second charge, which named the two royal pages and accomplices "who are still abroad". A third charge concerned Chit alone. It stated that he knew that the ·45 was not the revolver which fired the fatal shot and that he had endeavoured to protect his accomplices from lawful punishment by pretending that King Ananda had committed suicide.

The judges were making leisurely progress, when, on 26th

February 1949, there occurred yet another *coup d'état*, which forced the court to adjourn. Pridi had made an attempt to return, but the *coup* was crushed in a matter of hours.

While the trial was proceeding, King Phumipol had visited London from Switzerland and had fallen in love with a beautiful Thai girl. She was Sirikit, the daughter of the Thai ambassador. A few months after his return to Switzerland he had a car crash. One eye was permanently injured, which explains the dark glasses he wears today. He informed the Bangkok government that he was returning with Sirikit for the wedding.

On 30th March 1950 the remains of King Ananda were cremated. A month afterwards King Phumipol married. Later, he was called to give evidence at the trial. Then the court adjourned to Switzerland to hear the evidence of the Princess Mother. The royal pages maintained their innocence. Their families had been in the service of royalty for generations. During their imprisonment they had been chained, beaten and injected with truth drugs. Chaleo made a spirited defence.

The following September the court delivered judgment. It ruled that King Ananda had been assassinated. Chit was found guilty and sentenced to death. Chaleo and Butr were found not guilty and released. Both prosecution and defence appealed against the verdicts. Again there were lengthy proceedings, and the results of the appeals were not delivered until fifteen months afterwards, that is in December 1953. This time Butr was found guilty. Chaleo was again found not guilty and released.

An appeal was made to the Dikka, Thailand's supreme court. The final judgment was announced on 13th October 1954. Chaleo had been taken into custody only two days earlier and must have had a premonition of his fate. All three were found guilty and sentenced to death.

In the early hours of 16th February 1955, they were shot. Police-General Phao had visited the prison earlier and had a long conversation with the men. Later he said that what they had told him he would keep to himself. It is most unlikely that it was a confession of guilt, for their long imprisonment would have induced an earlier confession if they had been guilty, or they might have pleaded guilty to avoid further interrogation and ill-treatment. The police witnesses testified that under the truth drug they had not confessed.

The mystery is still unsolved.

Rayne Kruger has made an exhaustive study of the case, and in his book *The Devil's Discus* finally comes up with the verdict that King Ananda killed himself. I would disagree here and say that the verdict should have been murder by a person or persons unknown. A brief examination of all explanations is of interest. The suicide theory has its supporters. It is said that in Switzerland he had fallen in love with a beautiful girl, Marylene, but that there could be no future, as a mixed marriage would not be permitted. At the trial Butr stated that he saw the King burning letters the night before he died. He certainly was in no hurry to take up the kingship and it could well be that he did not relish such an onerous task at a most crucial period in Thailand's history. Both brothers were fond of playing with guns at the Villa Watana in Switzerland, and they continued with this hobby in Bangkok. The revolver was always kept in a cabinet in the King's bedroom. Yet they were both very experienced with firearms.

In September 1957, when there was discontent and disorders in the capital over the rigged elections, I wandered one day on to the Pramane Ground, the Speaker's Corner of Bangkok. Huge crowds were listening to the speakers. I was astonished to hear one of them shout at his audience. "You want to know who killed the King? I'll tell you!" He pulled a pair of dark glasses out of his pocket, put them on and ruffled his hair. It was a good impersonation of King Ananda's brother, Phumipol, the present ruler of Thailand.

My two friends gave a horrified gasp and slipped away with a frantic signal to me to follow them. I noticed that several people gaped at the speaker, and turned to each other in amazement as if unable to believe their ears. Others stared at him with admiration for his recklessness. I inquired what would have happened to the speaker if he had made that accusation when Phao was in office. "He would not have dared," growled one of them. "Even now . . ." He left the sentence unfinished.

The other repeated what I had heard before, which was that death was accidental. The revolver had either gone off while the two brothers were playing with it, or else Prince Phumipol fired under the impression that it was not loaded. If this were indeed the true version, then the royal pages must have known, but would their testimony against one so high have been believed?

Another theory is that it was the work of one or more of the supporters of Pibul or Pridi, hopeful of high reward, or of an extremist determined to remove all obstacles to Pridi's reforms. This does not follow that either man ordered it. Pridi was at the · zenith of his power. Pibul, on the other hand, was discredited, only recently released from prison, but there were many who had not forgotten the enormous power he had wielded during the war and believed that he was Thailand's man of destiny. To a large number of Thais an aura of glory has always surrounded his name.

The fantastic rush of rumours which swept through the capital following the news of the King's death and the pointing of the finger at Pridi, whose open contempt for the allegations antagonized so many, had gladdened the hearts of his enemies. He gave them the opportunity they had awaited so long. Put the suspicion on Pridi. Topple him from the pedestal to which the fickle masses had raised him. Down Pridi! Up Pibul!

The blunt statement in December 1956 by General Praphass, Deputy Prime Minister, that "The November, 1947 *coup* group staged its *coup* in order to rid Thailand of former Premier Pridi Panomyong", was received with mixed feelings of anger, amazement, cynicism and disgust in Thailand and abroad. Clearly, with Pridi out of the way, it would be an easy matter for his enemies to discredit him further, and he would not be in a position to refute the charges. That he had taken refuge in China was regarded as evidence of communist sympathies, which was untrue.

There were many who collaborated with Japan during the war. Pibul had many friends in high places. He could not have held Pridi responsible for his imprisonment as a war criminal, for he must have known that had he been handed over to the Allies he would not have escaped so lightly.

Another story concerns the royal pages and Chaleo, the former secretary. It is said that they had powerful friends and benefactors in whom they placed their implicit trust right up to the time when the executioner led them out, when they realized too late that they had been betrayed. One cannot but comment that a faith which will withstand the rigours of seven years' imprisonment and repeated death sentences must be exceptional.

Many people maintain that it would have been impossible for an outsider to have eluded the sentries and got into the palace, but

A spirit house for the *Phra Phum* or *Chao Thi*

Monks return to the *wat* after their morning quest for food

The Temple of the Re-
clining Buddha in
Bangkok

The Buddhist Library
at Chiengmai

others are equally positive that a determined man could have done it.

With the execution of two pages and a former secretary, it can be said that the cause of Justice had been served, but the verdict and the carrying-out of the sentence have left large numbers dissatisfied. Grave doubts assail the minds of too many people and there are those of all parties who wish desperately that the case against the three men could have been dismissed early in the trial on the grounds of insufficient evidence.

The present ruler, King Phumipol Aduldej, Rama IX, was therefore the first of the Chakri kings to be crowned as constitutional monarch since the 1932 *coup* ended absolute monarchy. He has already ruled eighteen years and is well liked throughout the kingdom, while there are large numbers who look upon him with the traditional reverence the Thais have for their kings, which may explain the prompt declaration of loyalty to the throne made by the leaders of successful *coups*. His official titles include His Majesty the Supreme Divine Lord, Great Strength of the Land, Incomparable Might, Greatest in the Realm, Lord Rama, Holder of the Kingdom, Sovereign of Siam, Chief of the Sovereign People, Supreme Protector and Monarch. However, all over the kingdom he is Nai Luang. When a policeman has asked me to make a diversion, it is because Nai Luang was driving through. When my driver has been late, it was on account of the crowds waiting to see Nai Luang. It is a simple and affectionate term. Nai, of course, means Mister. Nai Luang, the Greatest of Them All, or The One Who Dwells in the Palace.

His wife, Queen Sirikit, is a woman of great beauty and charm and is very popular. They have four children—Princess Ubol Ratana, born in 1951; the Crown Prince Vajiralongkorn, born 1952; Princess Sirindhorn, born 1955, and Princess Chulabhorn, born 1957. And so the continuation of the House of Chakri, which has given Thailand its kings for nearly 200 years, is assured.

7

Of Monks and Monasteries

Sometimes when driving through different parts of Thailand I have had to reduce speed and follow a small procession. When the road has been clear for me to pass, I have been greeted with smiles and cheerful sallies from all in the party. In the middle was always the most important figure, sitting in a *samlor* or in an open car, sometimes dressed in white, with a flower between his clasped hands. A man, of any age, but in most cases having recently reached manhood, on his way to the monastery to join the kingdom of the saffron robe.

I have watched several ordinations in *wats* or monasteries in the capital and in up-country towns. A magnificent and moving spectacle was the mass induction of 2,500 monks to mark the twenty-fifth centenary of the Buddhist Era.

They sat in rows in a beautiful golden pavilion. It was like the movement of long parallel waves. A blaze of saffron which moved forward and backward, as if its timing was synchronized by a master of ceremonies, which, of course, it was not. The waves murmured, grew louder and louder, then the volume subsided. Heads were bowed and bowed again, even lower; the waves merged into one smooth sea, as 2,500 monks prostrated themselves, praised the Buddha, then made their way out of the huge edifice into the world.

The previous year the young king Phumipol had given the celebrations a good start by taking the saffron robe and entering Wat Bovornines, where King Mongkut had served as an abbot over a hundred years ago. The king of Thailand is 'Defender of the Buddhist Faith'. He appoints all high dignitaries in consultation with the Grand Patriarch and generally presides over the religious ceremonies of the state.

Buddhism exerts a strong influence over the Thais. How powerful this is can only be understood if one gets to know them intimately and in different walks of life.

For some years I had been very friendly with a doctor in an up-country town. We played chess until the early hours, and, with his wife, we made some enjoyable excursions to places of interest. One day I was walking across a dry paddy-field and came upon a deserted, rickety bamboo hut. Inside I saw three young puppies. Only one was alive, and it was in a shocking condition. It was emaciated and covered with sores. It snapped feebly at me when I picked it up. I took it to the car and drove home with it. With care and good food, it made phenomenal progress. It learned a number of tricks more quickly than any dog I had owned in England. The two girls could do anything with it, but to strangers he was a bundle of ferocity. We never succeeded in teaching Bimbo, as we called him, good table manners. He literally fell on his food as soon as he saw it and devoured it with a speed which prompted a friend to observe that his ancestors were cheering him on or else he expected the plate to be taken away before he had finished. Bimbo had acquired some embarrassing habits. I am sure that he took on paternity at an age which would have been judged a miracle in England. However, when my family returned to England, and I moved my base, we did not know what to do with him. All our friends had dogs. In the end I asked my doctor friend if he would put him to sleep. He was clearly put out and made several alternative suggestions. One was that I should drive several miles and then turn him loose, another that I leave him at one of the *wats* some distance from home, where it would be fed. I did not like any of them. We had grown very fond of Bimbo. Although he was very strong, he was unprepared to join the legion of wild dogs, many of which hunt in packs.

I asked the doctor if his refusal was concerned with Buddhism. He agreed without hesitation that it was. If he did what I wanted, he would interfere with the dog's cycle of existence.

I approached four more Thais whom I knew quite well. I called on a dentist to whom I was giving English lessons. He had been educated at a Presbyterian Mission school and had become a Christian. However, his earlier Buddhist upbringing and background was still strong. I heard later that he also attended the *wat* quite regularly. He was very sorry but quite unable to help me. Fortunately an American family took over my house, and were glad to have him, despite his growls and barks with which he introduced himself, and which they ignored, much to his surprise.

It was said that Field Marshal Sarit offered the infamous Police General Phao the choice of the saffron robe or exile.

I have visited schools and found as many as six teachers away at the same time, all having taken the saffron robe for a month or more. I have found familiar faces absent from offices of public administration, from all spheres of employment, and all for the same reason.

Thailand has over 21,000 *wats* and a fluctuating priest population of nearly 400,000 monks and novices, and half this number of boys serving as temple attendants or students. There is no doubt that such a large force is a brake on the economic progress of the kingdom, but, if the Thais realize it, they accept it. They know that throughout their life the *wat* is always ready to offer them sanctuary and peace. Most enter on attaining the age of majority, but at any age a man who feels the need for spiritual comfort, or for the assurance of eternity, can seek admission. He must swear to follow the rules of the new life, and when he wishes to leave all that he has to do is to hand in his robes. Even one who has entered with the intention of spending the rest of his life there can leave without question at any time. He may have lost the sense of vocation with which he entered, or he may be assailed with doubts. However, if he seeks re-admission later in life, he must start again at the bottom, not where he left off. The majority do not remain long, but the priest in charge, the *Chao Khun,* has spent a lifetime dedicated to prayer and study.

Buddhism in Thailand is founded on the existence of a brotherhood of monks who have forsaken the world, if only temporarily, to take the saffron robe. Ordination does not require everlasting vows, except when a monk is remaining in the brotherhood for life. The saffron robe has been worn for the past 700 years.

To all priests, and to those to whom they preach, not only in the *wats* but in the small congregations who come to those making a pilgrimage across the country, Nirvana is their conception of heaven. The principles do not differ so much from Christian principles. Six are similar to the ten commandments.

A good friend of mine, Dr. Luang Suriyabongs, was a brilliant German scholar, as well as a physician of some repute. He was an acknowledged authority on Buddhism and the author of several books on the subject. Our long conversations usually centred on Buddhism, which he has described as the elimination of all desire, a way of life; "an ethical method for escaping the misery of actual life by the practice of meditation upon one's self which leads to Insight and Wisdom, to lasting peace—to Nirvana." Nirvana is the Buddhist goal. It is the consummation of the spiritual struggle to free one's self of delusion, ill-will, greed and of human passion in order to escape from all suffering and from the Circle of Re-birth.

He goes on to say that

Buddhism foregoes the idea of a God Entity and the theories of a permanent individual soul. The whole universe is in a state of flux . . . all is subject to the universal law of Karma. The whole universe and all life in it is bound to the Wheel of Life, to the Circle of Re-birth. Thus, man is born according to his past Karma which, to-gether with his present Karma, will determine his future existence. His past Karma cannot be undone, and whatever Karma has been committed must inevitably run its own natural course until the effects of his will-actions have exhausted themselves, which may occur either in his life or in some future existence . . . Buddhism thus places the fate of man squarely in his own hands . . . He can, by avoiding evil, and by doing good, and by purifying his heart from greed, ill-will and delusion, create a better Karma for himself which will lead to his salvation, or he can use his power to do evil, which will inevitably create bad Karma, and bring still further suffering and will retard his salvation from 'The Circle of Re-birth'.

I do not think that it is possible to live alone in a jungle district where the life of the community revolves around the *wat,* with-out becoming deeply interested in the practice of Buddhism. I have found that the ordinary Thai one meets is more interested in reincarnation, and that to him Buddha is the Christian God, to whom he prays. When I have made this observation to some abbots, they have replied that. what the worshipper does is to express the wish that the merit acquired by him in the accomplish-ment of some deed, may have, by virtue of the law of Karma, the result according to his desire, and that he does not pray to Buddha. I have had the impression that the prayers were of intercession.

Prince Chula Chakrabongse, speaking of the eight precepts, said of the third, not to commit wrongful sexual acts: "it is far wider than the forbidding of adultery, it covers rape and seduction, both by lies and promises, or by the lure of gold. In fact, a wrongful sexual act is one which harms someone, and not the mere act itself."

The philosophy is easily understood by the most uncomplicated individual. Do good, receive good; do evil, receive evil. And in these four simple words lies much of its strength.

The Buddhist monk, and the teachers in the schools, whether appointed by the State or by the Buddhist Church of Thailand, do not have a complex message for those who seek their guidance. The five commandments of Buddhism, exhorting believers not to kill, steal, lie, commit adultery and drink intoxicants, are a simple creed. Much of the comfort which Buddhism gives its followers comes from the exhortation to make merit, and here the priest or instructor suggests ways in which this can be done. Among all those who teach the precepts of Buddhism—the monks, the instructors, the more qualified preceptors appointed by the Buddhist Church of Thailand to lecture on the faith— there is sympathy, compassion, and tolerance, an acceptance of one's weaknesses and failures, but no condemnation, rather an exhortation to do one's best.

Prince Chula Chakrabongse maintains that the fourth precept, not to tell an untruth, is not to be carried to absurd lengths, and that the fifth, not to partake of intoxicants, is controversial even among Buddhists. "Are we then not to touch one drop of alcohol, or can we drink moderately on suitable occasions?" He reminds us of the advice of the Buddha, which was to take the Middle Path.

The Thais have adapted this friendly and helpful religion to suit their way of life, but it is a guiding force. In the homes and in the schools, children are taught to say: "I worship the Buddha, the law and order." To a very large number this simple creed becomes a way of life and a creed throughout life. One of the explanations as to why so many of their *coups* have been bloodless is that they abhor the shedding of blood.

Buddhism has never produced religious fanatics and has never been the cause of a religious war. Other religions have been allowed full freedom, with only one exception, which occurred during the reign of King Phetraja (1688–1703). This did not assume serious proportions and, as an anti-French movement, was directed only against French Christians. Christians of other countries, including Siamese converts, were not involved.

The actual ceremony of ordination varies in certain details in different *wats* and in different regions. I watched three candidates being ordained the same day. One was a school caretaker approaching middle age, another a young barrister, while the third was an artist.

The floor of the main hall of the *wat* was bare except for a *pai-si*. This consists of flowers and leaves, built up into seven tiers and veiled by white cloth. The *pai-si* is symbolic of the Kao Phra Sumen, the Hindu holy mountain in the centre of the world.

The heads of the candidates had been completely shaved the day before. Abbots have told me that the origin of this particular part of the ceremony was to make them less attractive to women and therefore less likely to be tempted. In the case of two of them, the abbots were possibly right, for, as the shaving continued, they had begun to look quite forbidding, but the appearance of the caretaker became almost angelic.

Friends and relatives stood by, watching intently, and were dressed in their best attire for the occasion. Parents of the two young initiates poured lustral water over them. In the case of the caretaker, this was done by the school head. This was in token of ritual cleansing. Then their bodies were smeared lightly with saffron-coloured paste. After this they put on spotless white shirts, a wide waist band and belt. They wore loose fitting jackets of flimsy material, adorned with gold stars made of paper, over their shirts.

Friends gave them bunches of flowers wrapped in banana leaves. They passed the bouquets to their parents as a gesture of peace and atonement for past wrongs. Again, the school head stepped forward and received them from his caretaker. Then, with more flowers held tightly in their clasped hands, they knelt on cushions, their heads bowed low.

The *pram* then took over. This is a Brahmin term, but the *pram* in the ordination ceremonies in Thailand is usually a local figure. He commenced to chant in Pali, invoking the blessings on the initiates. There was a monotonous pitch about the chanting, and just when I was getting used to it it was punctuated by a shrill sound like a wail. To the accompaniment of music from the ubiquitous xylophone, string instruments and drums, the *pai-si* was unveiled.

Candles were assembled in threes, secured to a leaf, lighted and passed from hand to hand around the large room. As they were handed on to the next guest in the line, the hand was swept well forward. This is to brush away evil spirits. In some ceremonies in Bangkok, when honours are being conferred, candles are passed around in the same way, usually three times. There is always a huge portrait of the King, and the hand in this case is swept towards the picture, to convey good wishes to the King.

After the passage of the candles had been completed, the *pram* rose to his feet, holding lighted candles. He threw his arms upwards to extinguish the flames, and then, with a speed remarkable for his age, he moved quickly towards the *pai-si*. This is symbolic of the flight of the gods. Each candidate's forehead was anointed with a white paste. Then they were given food and orange juice. The *pram* resumed his chanting. He called upon the spirits to re-enter the bodies of the initiates, and, after a short pause, he tied strings around their wrists to prevent the spirits from escaping.

The candidates moved across the floor on their knees and asked the abbot for ordination. He received them kindly and with dignity and then made a speech, in which he reminded them of the impermanence of the body, of birth, death and decay, which comes to everything, from a thought to an empire, and lastly the three great sanctuaries of Buddha, which are the Lord Buddha, the teaching and the priesthood.

Then the candidates took their vows, which included the basic ones of charity and chastity. They swore that they would not eat at forbidden times, not to possess jewels or perfume, not to dance, or to accept money. They swore to observe the 227 silas. The ceremony concluded with the presentation of the saffron robes.

In some *wats*, especially those which are famous, the ceremony is more elaborate, and it is more difficult to be admitted to the priesthood. At some ordinations I have attended, where there have been some high officials of the state present to watch the ordination of the sons of their friends, the *wat* has looked most decorative, a pageant of colour provided by the dresses and uniforms of the onlookers and the masses of flowers.

It is more usual for candidates to proceed to full ordination as *bhikku* (monk), but in the north-east a large number are satisfied with entrance as *samaneras* (novices). Here the ceremony is shorter, and the candidate takes fewer vows.

The life of a monk is not one of ease. I lived for over a year less than a hundred yards from a *wat*. Sometimes I would be awakened before 5 a.m. by the noise of the *wat* coming to life. About half a dozen measured strokes on a bell, followed by some dozen in rapid succession or the beating of a drum, was the signal. As soon as it is light enough to read the lines on the hand, they take their alms bowls and leave the *wat*.

There are only two meals daily, and the second one must be taken before noon. Then follows study and free time. Those who have not mastered the *Tripitaka* (the Buddhist writings, comprising the three divisions of sutras, or discourses of the Buddha for the laity) must continue to study it. The *silas* (rules of discipline and Buddhist morality) are read once a day. On the eighth and fifteenth day of the waxing and waning moon, the Wan Phra or Buddhist Sunday is observed. On these days the people visit the *wat* for the reading of the scriptures.

Study is well organized. There are nine ecclesiastical grades, but very few reach the ninth. The honorary title of *Maha Barien* is awarded to those who do reach this stage. Pali and Sanskrit are studied, and in some cases English. Those above the third grade have reached a recognized standard of learning and are exempt from military service. They receive a small salary from the Government for their personal use. This exemption is also granted to those who have progressed to the second. Those who fail to reach the first grade, which I thought comparatively easy, must fulfil their normal period of two years' conscription, but they can always rejoin when it is completed.

For novices the day begins at the same early hour, with praises to the Buddha. Breakfast is at 6 a.m. followed by two and a half hours' instruction. Lunch is at noon. Then there are three hours' instruction, a break of one hour, and another hour's instruction. Although neither *bhikku* nor *samaneras* may eat after midday they may drink orange juice, but not milk, for this is considered to be a meal. They may smoke as much as they like.

A monk cannot be arrested without permission of the abbot, but he may ask him to surrender himself. The abbot can expel monks for offences against the order or for a breach of the regulations of the *wat*. One such expulsion took place at a *wat* I knew quite well. The conduct of one of the monks near the *wat* aroused the suspicions of a policeman who asked him to remove his hat, which he did, to reveal his shaven head. The saffron robes were found hidden under a tree. In shirt and trousers he accompanied the policeman to the abbot, to whom he confessed that he had been to a brothel. He was at once expelled. The following day several people were discussing the incident in a café, and I was interested to note that there were no lewd comments. Rather was there some compassion for his lapse, especially when someone said that he had earlier intended to leave the *wat*.

Some monks have made a special study of astrology, and are in great demand all over the country. Many are quite outstanding scholars. There is an excellent Buddhist University in Bangkok, a Buddhist library and a hospital for Buddhist monks. As would be expected with such large numbers, there is an enormous difference in the mental ability of monks, except in the more celebrated *wats*. I have visited schools in the provinces, and seen monks sitting in classrooms with boys of about 12 years of age. In these cases, the abbot has insisted upon an improvement in the educational standard.

I have found that monks in the north and north-east are closer to the people than those in Bangkok and the big towns. This may be due to the more closely-knit communities among which the former work.

The attitude of tolerance displayed by the kings and governments of Thailand towards missionaries is indicative of the supreme confidence they have felt and continue to feel in the people's satisfaction with Buddhism. If Buddhism had ever been threatened or allowed itself to be threatened by Christian or other doctrines, the same delightful tolerance which has for centuries been an endearing characteristic of the Siamese would never have endured.

The *wat* has been the hub of community life for centuries, and this accounts to a great extent for the close bonds which exist between the monks and the people, as well as the affection and devotion of all to Buddhism. To build a new *wat*, improve or extend another, has always been the proud achievement of kings of Siam, as well as a collective community effort. A humbler, but no less dedicated, work would be the building of a *stupa* or *chedi*. In some *wats*, there are dozens of these spires.

The traditions are very old and far-reaching. In the former capital of Ayudhya there were over 300 *wats*, many of indescribable beauty. All glory to the Buddha! After the city was sacked by the Burmese in 1767, the Siamese built their new capital at Dhonburi, later Bangkok. This city today has more than 500 *wats*.

In recent years the Buddhist Society of Thailand has begun to send out missionaries, although so far the project is on a very limited scale. I have often wondered why this has not been done earlier, for the Thais have freely accepted those of other religions for centuries. During their visit to England in July 1966, King Phumipol and Queen Sirikit anointed the name plate of the First Buddhist Temple in Europe, or the new Temple of the Light of the Buddha. This was at East Sheen. Five of the ten monks who officiated had flown over from Bangkok.

There are comparatively few nuns in Thailand, and their status is low. I have seen them in the compounds of the *wats*, but they do no work of any importance there. Their heads are shaven, and they wear white robes, but the monks do not accept them, neither do the people. They do not go out with their alms bowls for their food. Valluya, who was well disposed towards them, said that it was very doubtful as to whether they would be given any. I was rather surprised, but when I asked several people of different age groups and background, I found that it was the general view. They live in separate quarters, in small houses in the compound of the *wat*. They look lonely and lost. It is difficult not to feel sorry for them, for they are pious women and are content to serve the Buddha in the humblest capacity.

Of all the countries of South-east Asia and the Far East, none has a priest population which can compare in size with that of Thailand. Although it could well be a political force, and it is possible that propaganda could be disseminated in the *wats* and by the monks themselves in the course of their pilgrimages, there is little evidence of any participation in political activities. I have seen statements in the Bangkok press to the effect that there are agitators from outside the order who argue that there is much in common between the doctrines of Karl Marx and the Buddha, but this is nothing new. It has been a favourite argument in communist propaganda for about half a century, with little success.

Those who take the saffron robe do so to escape from the world for a short time, to be spiritually cleansed and spiritually recharged, to find the answers to many questions, to seek peace and enlightenment. And they can only enter when their affairs are in order. Then they can join this vast brotherhood of monks.

Railway of Death

••◦⟨∘⟩◦••

The cinemas in Bangkok are very comfortable. They are air-conditioned, which affords a welcome escape from the heat, and the films are recent releases. One which stands out in my memory is *The Bridge on the River Kwai*. Bangkok audiences are usually quiet, but on this occasion there was an atmosphere of concentrated interest and suspense. The railway had been built through their country, which had known Japanese occupation. The scenery was familiar to many of them. There were a large number of *farangs* present, and perhaps that made for a bond of sympathy and understanding. In two cemeteries, one at Kanchanaburi, the other at Chungkai, nearly 7,000 allied soldiers are buried. Kanchanaburi, the larger, contains 5,061, of whom 3,459 came from the United Kingdom. The American authorities removed their dead for re-burial in America.

In Thailand one comes across perhaps a dozen former Allied prisoners who had worked on the railway. I have generally found that they fall into two groups. There are those who, after the passage of years, are inclined to be magnanimous towards the Japanese, on the grounds that they were sometimes even more brutal towards their own men and that by Japanese standards a prisoner of war is the lowest of the low. Moreover, some of the Korean guards were even more brutal. The other group has not forgotten the indignities and the atrocities, and their hatred of the Japanese has increased over the years.

I experienced an example of the latter one evening in the Bamboo Bar of the 'Oriental' hotel. My wife and two daughters had just returned from a holiday in Tokyo, and Hilary, the elder one, was telling me of the little courtesies and kindnesses they had received.

A tall, emaciated Dutchman was listening with growing impatience to the conversation. Suddenly he jumped to his feet, and came across to our table. "I saw another side of them, perhaps the real side. I was a prisoner of war on the Death Railway. They are the cruellest race on earth." For a few seconds he glowered at us, his eyes blazing with fury. Then with a tremendous effort, he muttered an apology and strode from the lounge.

An Australian, whom I had met several times in this bar and who worked for one of the car firms in Suriwongse Road, grinned at us in an attempt to help us out of our obvious embarrassment, and as my wife and daughters went out to do some shopping, he joined me. I learned for the first time that he, too, had worked on the railway. Every year he attended the annual ceremony of laying wreaths by the ambassadors of Britain, New Zealand and Australia. He invited me to accompany him on the next one, but, as I moved to Chiengmai a few weeks after this, it was some three years before I managed to join Bill, as he was called, on a visit to both cemeteries.

The brutal truth is that the railway was necessary to ensure Japan's communications with Burma. It is the manner of its construction which was to horrify and sicken the civilized world, and bring shame and ignominy on Japan.

A start had actually been made before the war on the construction of a line from Moulmein, in Burma, to Bangkok, but both countries had abandoned the project. It was found to be impracticable as well as too costly.

When the Japanese offensive began, their communications in this region lay through a long and exposed sea route to Rangoon, via Singapore and the Malacca Straits and along a road unsuitable for continuous heavy traffic which stretched from Raheng, via Kowhareik, to Moulmein.

The Japanese High Command had realized that this was altogether unsatisfactory. They decided that the railway commenced before the war should be completed. This would provide them with excellent communications and enable them to maintain a large Japanese force in Burma. They had an almost unlimited supply of labour which would be forced to work very long hours. Then the maintenance of this enormous labour force could be achieved at very little cost. It meant that about 250 miles of railway from Thanbyuzayat in Burma to Bahn Pong in Thailand had to be built. Much of the line had to be laid through mountainous country, dense jungle and in adverse climatic conditions.

During the construction of the railway, over 16,000 prisoners of war died and were buried alongside the line. The Burmese and Malay workers, pressed into service by their Japanese masters, died in their thousands. The actual number is unknown. The Japanese did not keep any records, but it is estimated that the total lies between 80,000 and 100,000.

One evening, I returned from up-country and found Bill in his usual place in the Bamboo Bar. As soon as he saw me, he said that he was going to Kanchanaburi in three days' time. This time I was glad to be able to accompany him.

We left the capital and drove off in Bill's jeep. Kanchanaburi lay some seventy miles to the west. It was a pleasant drive, and the road was quite good until we drove out of Nakon Pathom, from which point onwards the jeep found all the potholes and ridges. At Bahn Pong we turned right at one of those clock towers, which are becoming so common in Thailand and which give a modern touch to old and rural places.

This took us on the road to Kanchanaburi. It was a peaceful and pretty stretch. We drove through some attractive countryside, while here and there flame-of-the-forest stretched out in bright profusion as if pointing the way. Small towns and villages appeared to come to life, and at irregular intervals we came across the ubiquitous Coca Cola sign suspended above a hut made from the wood of the district. As we pulled up outside one of these bamboo, *atap* and wooden structures, I found myself wondering if the demand for this drink was sufficient to yield a profit and where the ice came from. Like so many others, the owner of the shack was Chinese and possibly was content with a small margin. Then he also sold rice and noodles.

We drove slowly past a large Chinese cemetery and then came into the mountain range. A signpost in English and Thai directed us to the Kanchanaburi War Cemetery. At the entrance there were plaques commemorating the fallen and one read 'Kanchanaburi War Cemetery 1939–1945'.

I followed Bill on his tour of the cemetery. He said very

little. Now and again he stopped at one of the plaques and I imagined that the memory of a former comrade was drifting back to him over the years. There are 1,362 Australians buried in this cemetery, and 1,896 of the Royal Netherlands Forces.

It has been laid out with imagination and an accurate realization as to what it would look like when Nature joined her gifts to the skill of Man. The graves were set out between plants and flowering shrubs. Each grave was marked by a simple concrete block surmounted by a brass plaque with the name, rank, regiment and age of the one buried there. The gravestone also bore the crest of the particular regiment and either a brief text or a message from his family. The rows were surrounded by grass verges and banks. At the far end there was a large white cross with a sword surmounted on it. Beyond rose the mountain range which made a majestic and fitting background.

I thought that it was a beautiful cemetery and well-maintained. Much credit was due to the War Graves Commission and the gardeners who worked in it. The hedge which surrounded the cemetery had been neatly trimmed and gave an air of dignity and privacy.

We were walking out of the grounds when a flash of yellow in the distance caused Bill to turn. Three Buddhist monks walked slowly towards us. Their gaze was turned on Bill, full and intent. It was serene and interested. Whether Bill realized its significance I don't know, but involuntarily, or so it seemed, his hands swept together as he bowed his head. They accepted his *wai* but did not return it. Buddhist monks never do. Bill watched them disappear, and, turning to me, he said in a far away voice. "A lot of Thais were mighty good to us. They gave us food when they hadn't got much themselves, and helped us where they could. I like this country."

We left the cemetery, went slowly down a winding road for just over a mile and arrived at the River Kwai and the bridge. The river was little known, even in Thailand, until Pierre Boulle startled the world with his book *The Bridge on the River Kwai*. It became a best seller. The Kwai at this time of the year was shallow and easily forded, flowing between valleys, jungle hills and mountains, broken by rapids. During the rainy season it can rise as much as fifty feet, and the current can be very swift and dangerous. The bridge loomed up, dark and forbidding. Perhaps

Murals in the Temple of the Emerald Buddha in Bangkok

Photo: Commonwealth War Graves Commission

The Kanchanaburi War Cemetery contains the
graves of 5,061 Commonwealth soldiers

A Roman Catholic Mission secondary school up-country

it was its iron structure which afforded such a sharp, brutal contrast with the lush countryside and the permanently blue sky of Thailand.

During the construction of the railway several bridges were built by the prisoners. Two of them were of wood. All were bombed and destroyed by the Royal Air Force. Several spans of the existing bridge were smashed during bombing raids in 1945 and after the war were replaced by two larger spans.

The Japanese War Memorial stood at the foot of the bridge. It was built during the war by the Japanese army. It is of simple design and has an octagonal base with a flight of steps facing the cardinal points of the compass. The ashes of those Japanese soldiers who lost their lives in the building of the railway are buried here. Far below flowed the river.

The single track railway line is still used by the Thai State Railways and runs to Saiyoke Waterfall. While we were there a train came in sight. It crossed the bridge at very slow speed. People were wandering across and others were cycling over, with a complete disregard for their own safety and that of others, for only three planks are fixed between the narrow lines.

An elderly peasant who was standing next to us grinned at Bill, told us that he lived close by and said that there had been occasions when some people had not been quick enough even for the slow speed of the train and had been sent hurtling down into the river. The bridge was built to carry the railway across the Kwai Yai into the valley of the Kwai Noi. At strategic points Japanese engineers had supervised the construction of railway trestles over the river, which was a very dangerous job and responsible for many fatalities.

There was a restaurant close by, where one could purchase postcards and souvenir models in wood, but there was very little sign of commercialization.

Kanchanaburi was the largest of the three main camps. Most of the prisoners of war passed through this town on their way to other camps.

Bill hired a small motor launch to take us across the river to the other cemetery at Chungkai. This town was quite unknown until the construction of the railway. The journey was quite short, for the cemetery is only about three miles from the main one at Kanchanaburi. We drifted slowly to a rickety wooden

8

landing-stage and climbed out. A short walk between the trees brought us to the cemetery.

The entrance pavilion is built of local materials and roofed with coloured Thai tiles. Trees have been planted to add to those already growing, and these provide much welcome shade.

The cemetery is the original burial ground started by the prisoners. Most of those buried there died in the hospital which the prisoners built. The number of graves is 1,740, and of this number, 1,329 are British and 313 are Dutch.

Chungkai cemetery is even more peaceful than the main one, perhaps because it is more secluded. It can only be reached by boat.

The lay-out of the graves is similar to that at Kanchanaburi. It has an attractive garden effect, which is enhanced by two beautiful trees which are close to the central cross. They tower above the shrubs and the large mango trees. When in flower they are a beautiful sight. Just inside the entrance gates a large marble slab catches the eye. In letters of gold is the simple but impressive message 'Their name liveth for evermore'. This cemetery, like the one at Kanchanaburi, was built by the Army Graves Service, who transferred all the graves. At the end of the war the Thai State Railways bought the railway from the Allies for 50 million bahts.

We returned to Kanchanaburi and then drove back to Bangkok. Late into the night, and indeed well into the early hours, Bill told me of his experiences. I think that the visit had made a profound impression upon him, and he wanted to talk about it. He had worked right through to the end. Apparently the Japanese plan required the line to be completed in fourteen months, or at the latest by the end of 1943. Work was commenced in June 1942. One force was to work from the Burmese end, the other from the Thailand terminus. Both parties met at Nieke in November 1943, and the completed line of 273 miles was completed in December 1943, which was a Herculean achievement.

Bill was one of a large number of prisoners who were marched from Singapore station and packed in railway trucks. They went by ship up the Malay peninsula, through the Kra Isthmus, and thence into Thailand. There has been some talk in recent years over a project to build a canal here and so save the long journey around Malaya. Pridi actually wrote from exile in China to the Bangkok press, urging that the work be carried out without further delay.

The first job the prisoners were given was to build camps at Kanchanaburi and Bahn Pong in Thailand, and at Thanbyuzayat in Burma. The accommodation for the guards had to be built first, and this was laid down as the procedure to be enforced at all the staging camps along the railway. Next came cook-houses and huts for the working parties. Last in order of priority was provision for the sick. The accommodation throughout the war consisted of huts made of bamboo and palm leaves. The prisoners slept on two long platforms fixed about two feet from the floor. Sometimes these huts had to be erected in paddy-fields which were often flooded in the rainy season.

The food was not only unsuitable but inadequate. A typical breakfast consisted of porridge or rice and a mug of tea. For lunch a small portion of dried fish and rice. The evening meal was again the eternal rice, vegetables and tea. On this diet heavy manual labour was demanded.

Food supplies were often irregular. For the greater part of the time they were brought up by barge on the Kwai Noi River or by lorries on a road which was frequently impassable. Thus a regular service could not be maintained. The Japanese were unable to keep the rations up to the official regulations authorized by their own High Command. Rice was often of poor quality and contaminated. Meat, fish, sugar and salt, the latter an essential item of any diet in tropical countries, were issued in very small quantities, and often there were periods when they had to live entirely on rice and a little salt. Red Cross parcels did help, but usually the Japanese deliberately held up the distribution on all kinds of pretexts, some of which were just further examples of petty tyranny.

From the Thai end, work began at Bahn Pong. The working parties made their laborious progress under the most appalling conditions of hardship and brutality. They were frequently beaten, sometimes unmercifully, by the Japanese guards. Bill said that, at first, a few of the quick-tempered ones struck back, but the reprisals were so savage that they found it better to submit, although this was often very difficult. Those who fell sick received scant consideration. The Japanese view, made clear right from the start, was that sick men held up the progress of the railway, and those who did not work required less to eat. Cholera, dysentery, sleeping sickness and hookworm took a fearful toll.

The Japanese High Command ordered that a prescribed percentage of the prisoners at each camp had to form the working parties. To make up the quota totally unfit men had to be carried or driven out. If a sick man could do no more than break a few stones in the course of a whole day, then this was a contribution to the work. It was of no account if the effort proved too much, and he dropped dead beside his pitiful labours.

Those who did stay behind at the work camps were allowed to rest in camp hospitals, which were often rough bamboo huts. The main camps which were at Chungkai, Tamakhan, Nong Pladuk and Thanbyuzayat had base hospitals. They were staffed by doctors and orderlies, the actual number being decided by the Japanese commandant. The very sick were evacuated from the camps to these hospitals by sampan or motor lorry.

Many lives could have been saved if, instead of the continual strain on constitutions weakened by heavy labour, the Japanese had provided a few simple mechanized aids. To a large number of men death came as a merciful release after a long nightmare of torment and indignity, and their bodies were enclosed in rice sacks and buried or cremated on hastily erected funeral pyres.

It is a criminal indictment of the Japanese administration that, although large quantities of medical supplies were sent by the Red Cross, after hostilities were over an abundant and wide variety of medical stores—every kind of drug and surgical instrument, according to Bill—were found stored in Bangkok. The Japanese permitted only very small amounts to be issued to the Allied doctors. Bill was loud in his praise of these men but for whom thousands more would have died. They carried out most difficult operations with instruments they had improvised with skill and infinite patience. Sometimes the Japanese guards indirectly supplemented the meagre supply of drugs. They preferred the services of the Allied doctors to their own and were able to procure more than sufficient drugs to treat their own particular illnesses.

I told Bill of a Japanese bank official in Bangkok, with whom I had become friendly and who admitted quite frankly that he believed the accounts of the atrocities committed by the guards. As a young officer he had been struck more than once by a superior. It was the code of the military class and one had to accept it. He, in turn, did not hesitate to take it out of his subordinates. At the same time he couldn't understand, and neither could many of his compatriots, why such a large Allied force had surrendered at Singapore. Japanese soldiers would have been exhorted to fight to the death, and if exhortation had not accomplished the desired result then other methods would have been employed.

He went on to say that the enormous number of prisoners captured was something that the High Command had not expected. There were 75,000 of them, and this presented them with a serious problem. They had to get them out of Malaya, where they would always constitute a threat, and so they were forced to send them to Thailand. This had special advantages. Escape was impossible, for the nearest Allied troops were about 1,000 miles away, and so they were put to work on the strategic railway, to help Japan.

Bill listened in silence. Then he grinned. "And I don't think that if the boot had been on the other foot, that bastard would have expected any mercy!"

Their engineers and surveyors had worked out the route the railway track was to follow. This was from Bangkok to Bahn Pong, then to Kanchanaburi, across the river, then up the valley of the River Kwai to the Burmese border at the Three Pagodas Pass. For centuries the Siamese have associated this pass with the invasions by the Burmese. From this pass the railway would pass over the watershed into Burma to join an existing line at Moulmein.

It was a most ambitious project, for not only had the Siamese and Burmese engineers decided to call off the project in the past, French and German engineers had also made detailed surveys and had abandoned the idea on the grounds of the enormous cost involved, as well as the difficulties. It was therefore a challenge to the Japanese engineers as well as the High Command. They would succeed where the inferior Siamese and Burmese, as well as the much vaunted French and Germans, had failed.

To supplement the efforts of the prisoners of war, thousands of coolies were brought over from Malaya. These were designated 'hired labourers' and paid a wage. They were unable to withstand the fearful conditions and they died like flies.

Camps were spaced out along the Kwai valley. The Siamese peasant farmers built rafts of long bamboos which they floated down the Kwai. It was the job of the forward parties at the bases to dismantle these rafts and use the bamboos to build the huts.

Paths were hacked out of the dense jungle. Embankments and cuttings had to connect with those from camps up- and downstream. Ropes and the combined efforts of several prisoners uprooted the trees and bamboo clumps, and, to ensure that no one slacked, the norm for each man was one square metre a day. The earth and rock were chipped, dug out by pick and shovel and carried away in small baskets. Sometimes the track was laid on an embankment or in a cutting prepared by the prisoners. Solid rock had to be blasted or chipped by hand until the obstacle was removed. Crowbars and sledgehammers were used to make the bore holes for the explosives, and as these had to be about three feet deep, it often took two men a whole day to complete only one.

For the construction of bridges and waterways, wood was on hand in the jungle. Heavy supports were floated downstream. As there was no power-driven machinery, the supports had to be sawn by hand to the required length. The track climbed and descended. There were steep gradients, and these added to the difficulties.

On the whole, the Japanese engineers were more considerate than the guards and, as was to be expected, superior in intelligence. Sometimes they endeavoured to get rations increased, for they realized that starving men were incapable of much physical effort, but were not always successful.

There was an inevitable sameness about the work which was made more frustrating when it was carried on after the customary hours with the aid of flares. When sections of the track were completed, working parties followed with sleepers and rails. One ghastly method of calculation, according to Bill, was one life per sleeper.

One camp was named by the men 'Monkey Bend Camp' because of the continual chattering of the monkeys in the area. This camp was reached by the working party in four days' marching, which brought them past the Wanlan Viaduct. A Thai railway engineer at Kanchanaburi asked us to look out for this particular spot. He considered that it was one of the most difficult and dangerous constructions, and he marvelled at the skill of the men who built it. Apparently a part of it was laid on a ledge cut out of a steep cliff. Some of the upright wooden supports were over sixty feet high and embedded into the rocks lower down for support. Bill's comment on the unsolicited praise was that the building of the viaduct resulted in a fearful loss of life. He had no desire to see it again. At Monkey Bend Camp the work was speeded up, the prisoners being made to work all hours of daylight. Morning and evening meals were eaten in darkness.

Bankao Camp was the next one on the up-country march from Chungkai, and the discipline here was much more severe. The Japanese commandant was a particularly unpleasant individual. The rule that every prisoner, irrespective of rank, had to bow to all guards was rigorously enforced.

When the rails had been laid as far as Wang Yai, which was the next camp, the Japanese lost no time in putting that section of the track to good use. Supplies were sent up by train. This marked the half way point. Thousands of prisoners had been forced to march from Kanchanaburi, while a convoy of sampans had been used to bring large numbers up the river.

The Japanese revealed the practical side of their nature in their dealings with the Chinese. Very early in the campaign they realized that they could not intern such a large number. In any case the economy would collapse. They used them to help with supplies and also used their vast numbers of sampans for transport. There were numerous cases of atrocities committed against them by the Japanese.

Bill had retained a vivid recollection of Wang Yai camp. Another name for it was Tarso. Most prisoners at one time or another passed through this camp, which was continually extended as more prisoners flocked in, for Wang Yai was a kind of junction. The railway line had been pushed as far as this point. The camp could also be reached by boat up the River Kwai, although this was a hazardous journey. Another route was by a rough road from the River Mekong.

What Bill considered to be a particularly callous treatment occurred on the occasion of the cholera epidemic at Dha Khanun, which soon assumed most serious proportions. The Japanese ordered that fences be erected to isolate the prisoners. Then they were left to look after themselves as best they could.

The working parties at the Burmese end were mostly Australians and Dutch. Bill had naturally been delighted to see large numbers of his compatriots, and within the next couple of days found two of his friends. According to him, they had all had a rough time, but these two were in good shape. They told him that they found the Dutch good comrades.

A special ceremony was arranged by the Japanese to celebrate the linking up of the two halves of the railway. A small locomotive steamed slowly up the gradient, pulling three of the trucks. Two Japanese flags flew from the funnel, and bunting streamed from the trucks. Japanese officers, wearing their long swords, sat proudly, if uncomfortably, in the trucks.

Then, a few days afterwards, the Japanese senior officer awarded a day's holiday, and invited the prisoners to organize a memorial service to honour the men who had died in building it. The senior British officer consulted his colleagues, and they agreed to take part provided that they were left to organize their own memorial service without interference. This condition was accepted.

Bill recalled that it was a most impressive and moving parade, and it gave him a high regard for what he called our "spit and polish". "I had to admit your chaps could lick any army in putting that over. Half starved and in rags, they came to it like a crack regiment on parade. And the eyes of the Japs nearly popped out of their sockets. They'd never seen anything like it. As for me, I marched as I never thought I could!"

The senior British officer led the parade to the burial ground, followed by the Japanese, who were led by a colonel.

There a huge crucifix made from a tree was in position. The British padre conducted a brief service. Then the commander of each unit laid a wreath at the foot of the cross. The Allied prisoners were surprised to see the Japanese colonel advance to the cross and salute their dead. I asked Bill whether his gesture was appreciated. "At the time a few of us thought that it was a decent gesture, but most of us wanted no part of it. After all they were responsible for thousands of our chaps dying. Looking back now over twenty years, I'm glad in a way that he acted in the way he did. Probably he thought that it was war and that he had a job to do, but at the same time wanted to honour our dead in some way."

Bill said that he found it difficult to forgive them for their attitude to the bombing. Just before the completion of the railway, bombing was intensified, particularly at the Burma end, when trainloads of Japanese soldiers and supplies began to move from Siam to Burma.

The Japanese commandants were approached by the British senior officers and asked if they could erect a large white triangle on a blue background to show that it was a prisoner-of-war camp. This request was refused, and as a result many lives were lost. As nearly all the camps had been built alongside the track or sited near the bridges or other strategic points, the prisoners were exposed to grave danger.

They were told to shelter in the bamboo huts. In one raid on the Nong Pladuk area they were ordered to remain in their camp. This was situated among sidings where ammunition, petrol and store trains were protected by anti-aircraft guns. Some ninety-five Allied prisoners were killed and 300 wounded.

From this time there was a general drift towards the south. Those who had been working on the Burma end, as well as the sick and the dying, either left or passed through Wang Yai on their way to Chungkai and Kanchanaburi.

In March 1944, there was an improvement in the general conditions. There were several reasons for this. The Japanese were not only surprised but alarmed by the publicity given in the press of the Allied powers, as well as some neutral states, to their inhuman treatment of prisoners of war. There were threats of a day of reckoning. The wave of fury which swept over those countries whose nationals were involved made the Japanese camp commandants have misgivings. The Japanese High Command were anxious to change their reputation even at this late hour; moreover they had been stung by the charges that their much vaunted Bushido was a sham and that their treatment of the prisoners was not that of a civilized country. Then the high total of deaths for 1943 had caused some concern in Tokyo.

The prisons were now concentrated in five main camps. These were Tamakham, Kanchanaburi, Tamuan, Nong Pladuk and Nakon Pathom, and it was more easy to maintain supplies and some semblance of organization. The traders were able to come to the camps and trade with the prisoners.

Unfortunately, Japanese remorse proved only temporary. From May 1944 to the capitulation of the Japanese in 1945 working parties from the main camps were set to work in groups. Some worked on maintenance; others on cutting down wood for fuel, building roads through the jungle and setting up defence posts.

The Allies were stepping up their bombing, and working parties were hard put to it making good the damage, filling in the craters, re-making the cuttings and re-laying the rails. Bill said that when the planes had passed over and he saw the extent of the damage he could have danced with joy. The Siamese end was getting its share, but, as the planes appeared to know where to bomb, there was a feeling that some Thais were passing on information. There was now considerable traffic passing along the railway, and this provided the planes with a double target—the railway and the trains. However, prisoners suffered further privations through the increased use of the track. As so many were sent out on working parties, the numbers at the main base camps naturally declined. The traders saw that their visits were not so profitable and came less frequently, with the result that rations were reduced.

The years of imprisonment were not without their light moments, and, apart from the entertainments organized at the camps, the men could see a humorous side of what Bill called Japanese disorganization and excess dignity. On the Allied side, he had met some wonderful men who, by their force of character and general conduct, he would never forget. There were a few he never wanted to see again. These were the vampires, as he called them, who made a profit out of the misfortunes of others, but he thought that they were few in comparison with the large numbers of thoroughly decent fellows.

Basil Peacock's book *Prisoner on the Kwai* and Russell Braddon's *Naked Island* bear this out and, incidentally, show the amazing fortitude and resilience of both men in captivity.

I saw Bill several times after our visit to the cemeteries. When I left Thailand, he was still making his annual pilgrimage to the Railway of Death.

The Political See-saw

During the last years of absolute monarchy, and from the inception of a constitution and government, two great figures in Siamese politics were to leave an indelible mark on the history of their country. For fifteen years the pattern of their political lives was interwoven, the fate of one during this time bound up with that of the other. Together they were the main architects of the new order which smashed for all time the institution of absolute monarchy which had endured for 1,000 years. What was to come in its place tore the alliance of these two men to shreds.

Both had meteoric rises, and both came from humble circumstances. In each case the victory and resultant supreme power for the one was to be the downfall and ignominy of the other. One was never to rise again, and has been in exile in China for the past twenty-two years, only just escaping arrest through the good offices of the British and American embassies in Bangkok, who remembered with gratitude his wartime services to the Allied cause during the Japanese occupation, when he was Regent of Thailand and 'Ruth' of the underground.

An unwritten bond between them, a solemn oath was to spare the one from dishonour and opprobrium. It is likely that it saved the other from the vengeance of the Japanese. The pact was to send the former, Field Marshal Pibul Songkram, to the pinnacle of power, where he was to dominate the Thai scene and much of that of South-east Asia for a quarter of a century; and when he finally fell and fled the country, never to return, the other, Pridi Panomyong, was to prove magnanimous and forgiving and to send an open invitation from his exile in Yunnan. "Come over here and join me, old pal Pibul!"

Both men in their way were great patriots, but they had conflicting conceptions of patriotism. Pibul's patriotism was allied to a high ambition. He saw himself as the leader of a greater Thai Empire. Pridi was the complete socialist, his life dedicated to giving his country democratic rule, raising the standards of living, promoting the welfare of the people and reducing the powers, as well as abolishing the abuses, of the privileged classes. Both men were absolutely fearless and possessed high intelligence. While Pridi was more brilliant, Pibul was more astute.

Unfortunately for Pridi, it was the monarchists and members of the privileged classes who were to prove his deadly enemies. He had incurred their enmity by the very *coup* which had robbed them of much of their power. They were to support Pibul because, as a member of the army *élite*, he was to help to preserve what remained of it.

Although the year 1932 is given as the first time an attempt was made to overthrow the absolute monarchy, there had been an earlier attempt in 1912, during the reign of King Vajiravudh or Rama VI, when a group of army officers and civilians plotted to capture the King and force him to grant a constitution. If he refused, they were going to replace him. The conspiracy was well in hand when one of the conspirators betrayed everything to the King's brother, Prince Chakrabongse, who was at that time Chief of the General Staff. The Prince acted swiftly. The conspirators were thrown into prison. When Prince Chakrabongse told him that the number of those who sympathized with the conspirators ran into several thousands, King Vajiravudh realized that there was obviously considerable dissatisfaction with his reign.

He allowed Prince Chakrabongse to deal with the conspirators. The Prince displayed extraordinary clemency. There were no executions and no witch hunts. A promise was made to introduce a more liberal régime. It was actually given out that there would be a constitution, but nothing came of it.

In the late Twenties, a group of young Siamese intellectuals spent some years studying in France and became imbued with revolutionary ideals. Their leader was Pridi Panomyong, a brilliant law student. Studying at the artillery school at Fontaine-bleau, and already showing considerable promise, was another young Siamese student—Pibul Songkram.

In 1928 Pridi and his fellow students returned to Bangkok and formed the People's Party. It was composed of Pridi's civilians and some army officers. In great secrecy, a *coup* was planned. The leaders took that fateful oath that never at any time in the future would one of the brethren harm another.

On 24th June 1932 the conspirators struck. The King accepted a constitutional monarchy and granted a constitution which was largely Pridi's work. A provisional assembly of seventy members was appointed by the People's Party. The office of Prime Minister was given to Pya Manopakarn, a former chief judge. Pridi took on the post of Minister of Finance.

There were two courses open to Pridi. One was to proceed with caution and introduce his reforms gradually, for the change in the social order had been so sudden and drastic—the princes were barred from politics—that the people had not been able to grasp the true significance of what had happened. The other was to carry through his reforms regardless of opposition. Pridi was an energetic, impetuous man, only 30 years of age. He decided on the latter course of action. But already there was a split in the People's Party. The right wing, which consisted mainly of officers, had always been a little suspicious of the young intellectuals, and they were resolved to keep the revolution within definite bounds.

Pridi's plan included the nationalization of agriculture and commerce. On this the cabinet split. Pya Manopakorn denounced Pridi as a communist and prorogued the Assembly. Pridi's friends advised him to leave the country. He went to France.

The army and the civilians at once saw the threat to the revolution and formed a united front. They ousted Pya Manopakarn, replaced him by Colonel Pahol and allowed Pridi to return from exile. An independent and international commission cleared him of charges of being a communist.

The monarchists, however, were not finished. Prince Boworadet led what was to be known as the Royalists' Insurrection. Supported by army units and others who opposed the changes, they marched on Bangkok. In four days Colonel Pahol completely crushed the revolt. Boworadet fled the country. Six of the leaders were sentenced to death and over 300 to terms of imprisonment.

Pibul took over the leadership of the powerful army group.

Pridi was still standing firm by his proposed democratic reforms, Pahol kept the balance between the army group and Pridi's socialists. He made Pridi Minister of the Interior, and Pibul Minister of Defence. In order to dispel any suspicion of his political views, Pridi introduced a law banning communism. It was as Minister of the Interior that Pridi earned universal respect by his handling of the judiciary and the police and the improvements he brought about in the penal laws and prison administration.

In 1936 he travelled abroad. The energy and passionate sincerity of this young man of 34 made such a favourable impression on heads of foreign governments that, on his return, Pahol made him Foreign Minister. In this post he acquitted himself brilliantly. He negotiated treaties of friendship and was able to persuade those countries which possessed extra-territorial rights in Siam to abandon them. Siam was now unfettered and free.

He founded the University of Moral and Political Sciences, and his students called him 'Mentor'. His popularity was tremendous. He was the idol of the intellectuals and the hope of the peasants.

In 1938 Pibul became Prime Minister. Pridi was again Minister of Finance. The war clouds were gathering, and Pibul saw that a strong government was absolutely necessary. He was popular with the officer class. Handsome and of cultured appearance, of great personal charm and a stimulating personality, always immaculately dressed, he had a big following. He took over the posts of Defence Minister and Minister of the Interior. Later the Foreign Office followed, and by 1940 he was in virtual control of the Government.

On 7th December 1941, the Japanese Ambassador demanded the right of passage for Japanese troops to Burma and Malaya. There was little that Pibul could do. Britain, once the ruler of a mighty empire, had been hurled out of Europe. Mr. Joseph Kennedy, American Ambassador to Britain, had informed his President that she was finished. Marshal Pétain had said that Britain would have her neck wrung like a chicken.

The legions of the swastika were victorious everywhere and the Bangkok Nazis were active propagandists. Pibul allowed the Japanese to pass.

More defeats followed quickly. Two of Britain's finest battle-

ships, the *Prince of Wales* and the *Repulse*, symbols of the might of
the Royal Navy which had been much admired in Siam for over
a century, were sunk by Japanese planes. The fearful havoc at
Pearl Harbor stunned the Siamese.

Pibul was a realist and a great opportunist. Then, during the
eight years leading up to World War II, the Japanese had been
making friendly overtures to the Bangkok government. While
some of the ministers, including Pridi and Direck Jayanama, were
in favour of allowing the Japanese no more freedom than that
required for the passage of her troops, Pibul went further. He
asked for an alliance. He gave Pridi the post of Regent and sent
Direck to Tokyo as ambassador, thus removing all opposition.

Pibul was convinced of a Japanese victory. And so he declared
war on Britain and the United States. The old name of Siam was
changed to Thailand, which means 'Land of the Free'. But the
new name had a mixed reception among the Siamese, and after
the war there was a move to revert to the old one. When the
Thai Minister in Washington, Mom Seni Pramoj, who had
achieved an outstanding reputation at Oxford, where he had won
the coveted Birkenhead Prize, received the official declaration of
war, he placed it in a drawer. This action was to bring big dividends after the war was over, and the Allies victorious, for
technically Thailand had never declared war on the United States.
Seni Pramoj broadcast from San Francisco to the effect that he
did not recognize Japan's puppet government led by Field
Marshal Pibul and was forming a Free Thai Movement. This
broadcast was relayed to the Far East, where it gave support to
Pridi's attempt to form a similar activity. As Regent, he was
playing a double and dangerous game. He took the name of
Ruth and had some hair-raising escapes.

Thus, while Pibul was supporting the Japanese, Pridi was
working against them. The members of his underground slipped
out of the country and made their way into China, establishing
an escape route by which others, in rapidly increasing numbers,
joined them. Others remained in Siam with Pridi's knowledge
and built airstrips and helped British airmen who had been forced
down. Pibul must have been well aware of his activities, but made
no attempt to stop him or harm him in any way, although by
late 1942 the Free Thai Movement within Thailand numbered
about 50,000 men, including high-ranking officers of the armed

forces. They were waiting for arms and equipment to be supplied at an opportune moment by the Allies.

I have asked Thais in different parts of the country why Pridi was not betrayed by Pibul and was astonished to be told by several of them, all influential men, that he knew all about his clandestine activities, but both men were great patriots and made a pact which ensured that one or the other was on the winning side so that, no matter the final result, Thailand would be able to cut her losses.

The day in September 1957, when Pibul fled the country, I remembered these conversations when I read Pridi's open message to his former rival, displayed in headlines in the newspapers, "Come over here and join me, old pal Pibul!" This after Pridi had been living in exile for ten years!

Again I put the same question to several Thais I knew, and found that there was support for this theory. Even die-hard monarchists admitted that there was something in it and went on to agree with the others, who declared that although the followers of each of the two great figures fought savagely, for two opposite ideals and opposing forces were represented, both Pibul and Pridi never forgot that they had both been students together and were the main architects of the People's Party and the subsequent revolution which abolished the absolute monarchy in 1932.

Be that as it may, their conduct presented a violent contrast during the Japanese occupation. Pibul's dream was of a greater Thai Empire and this required disciplined subjects.

In 1956, in an up-country town, Pibul arrived to open a new branch of his political party—the Seri Mangansila Party. He loved fast cars and handled them with ease. He was driving. I watched him jump out of the car with the energy of a much younger man. We shook hands and chatted for a few minutes. I was the only foreigner among the vast crowd. After the ceremony he got back in the car, and, amid lively banter from his close supporters, he drove off. I formed the impression that he was popular. When I returned to the capital, I described the visit to two women in their thirties who had graduated at London University and who were on the staff of a College of Education. They were politely scornful. They told me that during the war Pibul had insisted that they all greeted each other with "Heil Pibul!" and that women had to wear hats and stockings. Again copying Nazi propaganda, newspapers and streamers carried the exhortation "One country, one Leader Pibul!" The chewing of betel-nut was forbidden on the grounds that it was unsightly and degrading, and betel-nut trees were cut down.

Three of their colleagues joined us, and they bore out what I had been told. I asked if these regulations were resented. They admitted that they were but often caused some amusement. In any case they had to be obeyed. However, wherever I went I found that Pibul, the strong man of Thailand, had a large following.

In Korat I found support for Pibul's wartime measures. Two army officers and a dentist, who were about the same age as Pibul, said that in 1942 it appeared certain that Japan was going to emerge the victor, and Pibul realized that it was necessary for Thailand to be a disciplined nation in readiness for the greater rôle she would have to play in South-east Asia. "The stakes were very high, he staked all and he lost!" was their verdict.

When the tide began to turn, he started to build a new capital in the north-west. It could be defended against the Japanese, but would also serve as a stronghold for the Allies in Burma. The Japanese were not taken in and began to ask awkward questions.

In July 1944 Pibul resigned. It was now beyond doubt that an Allied victory was imminent and that Thailand would have to answer to the Allies for her actions. She had broken the non-aggression treaty signed with Britain in 1940. In 1943 she had taken control of four Malay and two Burmese states. Her active collaboration with Japan had helped towards her victories in Malaya and in the passage of her troops through Burma to the eastern gates of India.

Pridi would be more acceptable as head of the nation. He issued a proclamation disavowing Thailand's declaration of war, Kuang Abhaiwongse became Prime Minister, but he stepped down a year later in favour of Mom Seni Pramoj, whom Pridi had recalled to take over because of his high standing with the Allies. Pibul was placed under arrest to await trial as a war criminal.

The terms of the subsequent Peace Treaty were lenient. Thailand was to return the Burmese territories; to sell to Britain at a fixed price $1\frac{1}{2}$ million tons of rice for distribution to India, Singapore, Malaya and Burma. She agreed not to build a canal across the Kra Isthmus without Britain's approval and to sell

9

rubber, tin, tea and rice at prices fixed by an international committee. Britain and India agreed to support Thailand's membership of the United Nations.

Pridi was the idol of the country. He went ahead with his social reforms, impatient at the delay caused by the war. At the elections of January 1946 his candidates won by a large majority. Kuang once again took over the Premiership.

Pridi had great plans for Thailand. He saw her rôle as leader of the future independent states of South-east Asia. It was unfortunate that he tried to accomplish too much too soon. Kuang resigned, for he felt that he was being controlled by Pridi. He founded his own party, which became known as the Democratic Party. Pridi's followers urged him to take Kuang's place. Pridi preferred his position of Regent but accepted. His first step was to present the Assembly with a new draft constitution. It differed from that of 1932 by providing two legislative chambers in which members of the Upper House or Senate were elected by the lower house.

Pibul was set free, the court ruling that the legislation against war crimes was invalid since it was retrospective. It is very likely that Pridi knew what the verdict would be, for he was one of the greatest lawyers in the country. In any case, he was the most powerful man in Thailand and could have swayed the judges had he wanted to. Pibul retired to private life.

A few months afterwards an event occurred which set the political see-saw in motion. The young king Ananda Mahidol was found dead in bed. He had been shot through the head. Pridi was suspected of complicity in the murder. Regicide had been common enough in Thailand. It had often been an instrument of state policy. During the 400 years of the Ayudhya era, there had been thirty-three kings, one-third of whom had either been murdered or had murdered rival claimants. The assassins included a mother, brothers and high officials of the state who pushed the claims of one who would be more useful to them.

Pridi's enemies saw an excellent opportunity to get rid of him. His plans for the nation's economy had frightened the wealthy and privileged classes. Freedom for political parties, freedom of speech and a free press, no restrictions on electioneering; all this would seriously weaken their positions. Much of the storm against him was manufactured by his enemies. Its aim was to discredit

Pridi. The rumours that he was involved in the murder spread, although others, too, were named. A few months later, embittered by the attacks and thoroughly disillusioned, he resigned and retired from public life.

The new Prime Minister was one of his supporters, Admiral Dhamrong Nawasawat. He had been a member of the 1932 revolutionary group and was very popular. Unfortunately, he was not the strong man the Government needed so much at this difficult period. The régime was to prove insipid and corrupt. On 8th November 1947, the army took over by a well organized *coup*. Resistance was useless for tanks and machine gun nests were in position at all strategic points. Dhamrong fled the country. Pibul had made a come-back but decided to keep in the wings. Kuang took over as Prime Minister. Pridi's party was ousted, and he fled the country.

In order to gain support at home and abroad for the *coup*, stories were circulated of the corruption which existed and of an alleged plot by Pridi to turn the country into a republic. The old rumour of his complicity in the murder of the king was revived and, to give it added weight, it was said that there was a plot against King Phumipol, who had returned to Switzerland.

Kuang had been in office for only six months when there was another *coup*, again bloodless. Four army officers 'invited' him to resign, which he did when he realized that refusal would lead to bloodshed. Pibul then took over.

In 1949 there was yet another *coup*. Pridi returned from abroad and, supported by the Royal Marines and detachments of the navy, made an attempt to overthrow the Government and bring back the civilian members. Although the *coup* was well-organized, and the leaders had even planted a fifth column among Pibul's government, it failed, but it came very near to success. The army commanders just managed to take over the tank battalions before Pridi's forces could seize them. Once again Pridi fled the country.

The Thais were deeply shocked by the extent of the fighting and the severity of the reprisals. Previous *coups* had been bloodless affairs, the losing side accepting the position gracefully. This time the police under Police General Phao acted with great cruelty. For some months they hunted suspects. Six of Pridi's former cabinet ministers and deputies were shot while in police custody, and several hundred suspects were thrown into prison. Phao formed a special riot squad of over 1,000 picked men stationed in Bangkok, and increased the strength of the ordinary police force to deal with any opposition. A purge was made of the navy. A number of officers were dismissed and the marine corps disbanded.

Pibul delegated much authority to Phao and was later to regret it, for he was building up one who was to be a powerful rival.

In June 1951 another *coup d'état* was to cause terror among those who had not forgotten the horrors of the last one. This time the navy sought revenge for the defeat at the 1949 *coup* and subsequent persecution.

A number of very important guests, including diplomats and service chiefs, accompanied by their wives, were assembled at the royal jetty on the Chao Phya River. The occasion was the presentation by the United States of a dredger, the *Manhattan*. Two Thai naval officers kidnapped Pibul at gun point and ordered him to board a launch. Others covered the guests. Pibul begged them all to keep calm and to make no attempt to rescue him. The launch took him to the battleship *Ayudhya*, where he was confined in a cabin. Leaders of the *coup* asked for negotiations with representatives of the army and police, with a view to the setting up of a new and more representative government, but this was refused.

Phao's newly-formed riot squad had been given an opportunity for a trial of strength. The Chakri memorial bridge was closed, thus isolating the *Ayudhya* from the naval bases and the sea. Savage fighting broke out in the capital. For two days the issue was in doubt. Then the air force, under the command of General Ronapakas, and which had remained neutral, joined forces with the army and police. They used their new planes, supplied by the United States, and bombed ships and naval installations.

An ultimatum was sent to the naval authorities that, unless Pibul was released, the *Ayudhya* would be bombed. Immediately on the expiration of the very short ultimatum a plane scored a direct hit on the *Ayudhya*. With characteristic courage, Pibul dived overboard and swam to safety. The *coup* had failed. It was rumoured that Pridi had taken part, but this was denied. The navy's prestige was now at a very low ebb, and it has never yet recovered. A further purge of the officers was made, and some were sent to prison.

When the country heard of the enormous casualties in the two days of fighting, there was much bitter comment. Over a hundred civilians had been killed, 500 wounded, some very seriously. Service casualties were known to be heavy, but the numbers were not revealed. Phao's tough measures increased the widespread resentment. Sympathizers were mercilessly tracked down. Abroad it was felt that the oft-repeated description of Thailand's *coups* as bloodless was becoming an illusion. The last two had been brutal affairs.

Phao was promoted to higher rank, and an army officer, who had taken a leading part in defeating the coup, now loomed large in the public eye. This was General Sarit Thanarat, who was soon to become Commander-in-Chief of the army.

Pibul's position had been weakened by the *coup*, and he was quick to realize that, in order to strengthen his own position, he would have to play off Sarit against Phao, but both men were not deceived by his tactics of divide and rule. In 1951 they joined forces to consolidate their position and to remove what remained of opposition to the army. This particular *coup* was known as the 'radio *coup*' because it was reported simply as a *fait accompli* over the radio by representatives of the army and police, who declared that the 1949 constitution was abrogated, the present assembly closed and the 1932 constitution reimposed with the Government-appointed upper half of the assembly.

Following the practice of previous *coups*, the leaders declared their support for the constitutional monarchy and gave as their reasons the spread of communism in Thailand and the world situation. Pibul remained in office as Prime Minister, but he had received an unpleasant jolt.

In 1952 the Government appointed the upper half of the Assembly. As was to be expected, nearly all those elected had proved their loyalty to Phao and the army during the recent revolt. At the general elections to elect the lower half, Kuang and a large number of his followers refused to stand and the government party, the Damatipat, scored an easy victory. From 1952 to 1955 there was no opposition.

In the spring and summer of 1955, Pibul made a triumphant world tour. He returned to Thailand with his pro-West sympathies increased. He brought back with him one British Institution which he had admired. This was Speaker's Corner in Hyde

Park. He informed an astonished Assembly that Bangkok would have similar facilities for criticism and that he had earmarked a section of the Pramane Grounds for this purpose.

Pibul promised that very soon the nominated half of the Assembly would be replaced by deputies elected in a popular franchise.

Soon after his return he realized that he could no longer keep the peace between Phao and Sarit. He hoped that the general elections due to be held in 1957 would give him a bigger majority in the Assembly. Phao decided that at the present time his own interests would best be served by a close association with Pibul.

The February elections gave Pibul a narrow victory over the Democratic Party. Then in the following weeks the storm burst. There were furious accusations that the elections had been rigged. This time the opposition could not be silenced. There were demands for Phao's dismissal and exile and the resignation of Pibul. The usually well-controlled and admirably self-disciplined university students marched to Pibul's official residence to demonstrate. Yet it appears more likely that Phao was responsible for the rigging.

Sarit acted one jump ahead of the police. Another *coup*, with the army in complete control, was announced on the radio and in the press. It was bloodless. I saw the tanks moving into position and the soldiers at their battle stations. Phao was escorted out of the country and he took his fortune with him. He died in Switzerland in 1960.

Pibul bowed to the inevitable, but he was very bitter over what he called his 'betrayal' by those he had trusted. He climbed into his fast new Citroën and drove to the little harbour of Trad. Here a motor boat was waiting. It took him down the coast and he went to Pnom Penh. For a month he stayed in Cambodia, awaiting the outcome of the *coup*, then he flew to California.

At the Rotary Club the following week the members were discussing the *coup*. A tall, handsome Frenchman was explaining to a small group what, in his view, had brought about Pibul's downfall. Then to emphasize his remarks, he lapsed into his own language "*Il a bien mérité de son pays!*" The others nodded approvingly. Pibul had deserved well of his country.

I found myself contemplating Kuang Abhaiwongse at lunch, and I wondered how he had managed to survive the rises and falls of the political see-saw, and could walk anywhere without danger and be liked by those of all parties. And then the only possible explanation dawned upon me. Kuang had never upset the balance of power. He had never become so strong that a rival party had to stage a *coup* to bring him down. And he was a most likeable man.

The same month that Field Marshal Sarit took over, I was taking a group of local government officials from the Highways Department for English conversation. They were all extroverts and so friendly towards each other and to me that the lessons were often both a tonic and an entertainment.

They asked me what I thought of Sarit. I replied, diplomatically, that he was obviously very popular and that I hoped that his health would stand up to the stresses of office.

"What's the matter with him?" asked a tall, jovial-looking individual, whose rings and stripes on his shoulders indicated high rank. As he was always smiling, it was difficult to know when he was serious or joking.

"I heard that he was suffering from cirrhosis of the liver," I replied.

There was a roar of laughter from them all. Once again my leg had been successfully pulled.

"You mean—hobnail liver," they shouted.

Sarit was very popular. He assured Britain, the United States and other S.E.A.T.O. powers that there would be no change in foreign policy and that the monarchy would be respected as before. Pote Sarasin formed a caretaker government, and new elections were fixed for the end of the year. The enormous police force was reduced in size and much of its equipment transferred to the army.

During the first few months following the *coup*, Sarit started off by following a democratic policy. At that time he owned some left-wing newspapers, and for a time they were anti-American. This was partly due to Pibul's pro-American policy, and Sarit was anxious to convey the impression that the new government was not going to be a continuation of Pibul's ministry. The elections were fair, and a pro-Western government was returned.

Towards the end of the year he took over the office of Prime Minister, got rid of those ministers on whom he could not rely

for absolute loyalty, assumed special emergency powers and
rounded up suspected communists, whom he interrogated himself. Some arsonists were arrested and executed.

One case which made headlines concerned a young student
named Superchai. He had been discovered in a hide-out he had
built in a durian orchard in Dhonburi. The durian fruit is a luxury
in Siam, but the smell is particularly offensive. On the earth walls
he had pinned pictures of Mao Tse-tung and Ho Chi Minh. He
also had the works of Karl Marx and Lenin. I did not think that
one who so openly proclaims his political views could be a
menace. However, Sarit dashed to his hide-out and questioned
him. The young man freely admitted that the pictures and books
were a souvenir of a visit to Moscow. He was immediately
executed. Communism is not taken lightly in Siam.

Sarit handed over power to General Thanom Kittikachorn,
and left for England and the United States for medical treatment.
In his absence, Thanom had banned communist propaganda in
the press and removed known communists from the teaching
staffs at the universities. Sarit went much further. He forbade
travel to Communist China and ordered Chinese schools to teach
the Siamese language, but he was careful to keep on good terms
with official Chinese associations to win their support. Here he
was indirectly helped by the Tibet invasion, for this alienated
much of the sympathy which the Chinese minority felt for
Communist China.

In spite of his illness, he worked with a tireless energy. It was as
if the doctors in the United States and Britain had told him that
his days were few, and he was determined to make Thailand more
powerful and stable than she had ever been. At the same time, the
excesses in his private life were amazing. For this vigorous,
colourful personality had a weakness for lovely girls, and he now
indulged it with abandon.

His popularity did not suffer on this account, nor were the
details of his private life kept secret. In a land where polygamy
and concubines had for centuries been accepted as a normal way
of life, Sarit's conduct was not considered so unusual, although,
when the whole story became known after his death, it proved
too much even for the sensual, pleasure-loving but tolerant
Thais.

Even when he cleaned up Bangkok and closed the massage

establishments, brothels and opium dens, no one appeared to object. They knew that the closure was only temporary and, in any case, these went on underground.

In foreign policy he was a realist, believed in strong measures and was very critical of S.E.A.T.O. In August 1960 there was a sudden *coup* in sprawling, land-locked Laos. A parachute battalion commander, Captain Kong Le, who had fought brilliantly against the Pathet Lao forces, seized power and ousted the pro-Western government. He believed that a policy of neutralism and co-operation with the Pathet Lao could save Laos from a bloody civil war. He offered the leadership of the Government to Prince Boon Oum, who declined. He then approached Prince Souvanna Pouma, the President of the National Assembly. Souvanna accepted, provided that the Assembly gave him a vote of confidence. This prince also favoured neutralism, declaring that this would make the Western and communist powers understand that they could not use Laos as a base for military operations.

Communist agents infiltrated and organized cells. Procommunist propaganda was broadcast. Sarit regarded this as evidence that Kong Le was siding with the Pathet Lao and called on S.E.A.T.O. to act.

In Laos there was utter confusion. The cabinet in Luang Probang would not return to Vientiane for fear of arrest by Kong Le's parachutists. Poumi Nosavan flew to Savannaket to organize an army to recapture Vientiane. Sarit supported him and urged the United States and S.E.A.T.O. to equip his forces to march on Vientiane and drive out Kong Le.

Laos was split. In Vientiane there was the neutralist government of Prince Souvanna, backed by Kong Le and Pathet Lao sympathizers. In the south there were the remnants of the pro-Western government led by General Poumi Nosavan and the Royal Laotian troops.

Sarit remained firm. He wanted support for Poumi. He was ready to intervene before the Pathet Lao could make Laos a satellite of Hanoi and Peking. He distrusted Prince Souvanna, whom, he believed, was influenced by his half brother, Prince Soupanouvong, leader of the Pathet Lao. Sarit bluntly asked the United States if she would support Poumi in his efforts to maintain a pro-Western government. However, it was believed by the S.E.A.T.O. powers that Souvanna was the only one who could form a united government and prevent civil war and the resultant escalation.

In December 1960 General Poumi recaptured Vientiane. Souvanna's government having fled, a government under Prince Boum Oun was approved by the National Assembly. Kong Le and Souvanna regrouped in Xieng Khoung, and, with the support of the pro-communist Pathet Lao forces and with equipment from communist countries, they made a successful counter-attack, forcing the Government forces to cease fire.

In May 1961 a fourteen-nation conference met in Geneva to bring about Laotian neutrality. Owing to internal disputes, it was not until June in the following year that agreement was reached. The three princes agreed on a coalition under Prince Souvanna, and a new Geneva agreement to guarantee Laotian neutrality was signed on 23rd July.

There was another *coup d'état* in April 1964, led by the rightist General Kou Prasit and Police General Siho. The object was to oust Souvanna, but the King of Laos insisted that he remained in office. There was bitter fighting on and around the Plain of Jars, between the Government forces and the Pathet Lao, assisted by the North Vietnamese troops, and Kong Le's neutralist forces fled from the plain.

During these years Sarit raged at what he called America's vacillation. His newspaper, *Sarn Seri*, deplored the negative policy of the United States and its peace-at-any-price attitude. The *Siam Rath* and the *Kiattisak* pointed out the danger confronting Thailand and the rest of Asia once the communists have taken over Laos.

The general view put forward by the Siamese Press was that much of the bloodshed and the continued threat to the security of Thailand could have been avoided had America acted promptly at the time of the Laotian crisis of 1960.

Sarit approached the Russian Ambassador for trade talks and cultural exchanges, and the move aroused some anxiety in Washington. In Bangkok his ministers were talking openly of Siam breaking with S.E.A.T.O. and following a policy of strict neutralism. S.E.A.T.O. was described as "A paper tiger".

The arrival of American troops in Siam did much to alleviate the fears of the Bangkok government, as did also Dean Rusk's declaration that the U.S. obligation to Thailand under S.E.A.T.O.

"does not depend upon the prior agreement of all other parties to the treaty, since the treaty obligation is individual as well as collective". For this meant that the British or French could not veto treaty action in defence of Thailand, but confidence in S.E.A.T.O. and the mighty American nation had been rudely shaken over Laos.

Elsewhere Sarit had displayed admirable statesmanship. In June 1962 the International Court of Justice had awarded the disputed Khao Phra Viharn, in eastern Thailand, to Cambodia. The Khao Phra Viharn was a temple, situated on the edge of a cliff which marked the boundary between the two countries and more accessible from the Thai side. It had only a sentimental appeal, but the award sparked off a wave of nationalistic fervour. Sarit insisted that all accept the findings of the court, although he, like them, disagreed with the verdict. Thailand would lose the prestige it had acquired if it failed to meet its obligations under international law.

He rallied the nation behind the monarchy. On Army Days I have seen him kneeling before the King in token of respect. Thailand was brought closely into the Western alliance, but managed to preserve her independence of action. The West realized that Thailand could not be taken for granted but was a sovereign state to be consulted.

Sarit died in December 1963. In the six years which had passed since his seizure of power in October 1957 he had done much for Thailand. The Laos problem still remained, but, if it had not been for Sarit's dogged efforts, the situation could well have been more serious. His insistence had led to the arrival of American troops at Udorn in the disaffected north-east provinces, which is only twenty-five miles from the Laotian border. Britain, Australia and New Zealand also sent forces.

He was the first minister to attempt to do anything for the north-eastern provinces. Sarit overhauled the agricultural policy. He made Bangkok a prosperous city and encouraged foreign investments. More schools and universities were built.

Very soon after his death a scandal of such magnitude was uncovered that it rocked the Government. It was declared that he had salted away a fortune estimated at about 120 million dollars. Clearly Sarit had not taken seriously the forecasts by the American and British doctors of an early death. American-aid officials were red-faced when it was revealed that their aid programme had helped to build his fortune.

It was stated that he had first, second and third wives and hundreds of concubines, whom he treated most generously with gifts of houses and cars. His sexual appetite was insatiable, his virility, according to reports, prodigious. The Press had a bumper season as more details were disclosed. Sarit had kept a court such as Thailand had not known for a century. Apart from his sex activities, he had developed a great financial empire. His second wife, Vichitra, was one of the principal shareholders. His half-brother Saguan ran the State Lottery. Another brother ran a very profitable gold shop. One of the more popular newspapers published the accounts of some twenty interviews with his minor wives. Sarit's most fervent admirers began to wonder if his services to Thailand were worth the colossal sums he had paid himself.

There was some anxiety over a possible clash between the military leaders, but King Phumipol stepped in quickly. He appointed General Thanom Kittikachorn, who took over without difficulty. One result of the reconstitution of the Government was the appointment of a Minister of National Defence. Pote Sarasin resigned from his post as Secretary-General of S.E.A.T.O. to lead the new ministry.

Shrewd but honest, General Thanom Kittikachorn was thoroughly alarmed by the implications of some aspects of the scandal. He ordered Sarit's assets to be frozen and hoped desperately for the disclosures in the Press to cease. The Press was more outspoken than it had been for many years and was particularly critical of the Government. However, his own reputation for integrity had a calming influence upon the country, and gradually the storm abated.

One significant feature of Sarit's administration was that the power clique, composed of the senior military chiefs and senior state officials, who had governed the country since the inception of constitutional monarchy in 1932, remained roughly unchanged. It was the mixture as before. The political see-saw was not rocked.

During the years 1932–60, 200 ministers had served in twenty-nine cabinets. There had been seventy-eight military officers. Twenty-one of Pibul's former ministers continued to serve under

Sarit. The same political pattern was revealed. Power remained in the hands of the powerful, exclusive circle. Only the leadership had changed.

Thanom Kittikachorn had taken office for a brief period in 1958. The profiteers had been unable to buy him, and he was glad when Sarit relieved him of his position. He became Deputy Prime Minister and served Sarit with loyalty.

His rival was General Praphass. Sarit had been a shrewd judge of the abilities and weaknesses of his immediate subordinates and he knew how to handle them. He arranged a marriage between Thanom's son and the daughter of Praphass in order to bring the two families together. He realized that he had come to power largely on account of the rivalry of Pibul and Phao, and he did not want similar circumstances to arise. Praphass had been a member of the triumvirate which had ousted Pibul.

Praphass is a highly intelligent, energetic and capable man, and an ambitious politician. Where Sarit had allowed his friends to join in the profiteering, Praphass was not so accommodating, and this attitude did not endear him to his followers. With Sarit dead, there was no unifying influence. Praphass was becoming Thanom's rival.

Thanom was not prepared to grant a constitution, and the military régime continued. There were more rumours of communist plots and threats of *coups*. The Bangkok government appeared to devote more time to these problems than to the growing unrest in the north-east provinces. Towards the end of November 1964 and the beginning of December, ten officers of the armed forces, including one air marshal, were arrested on charges of sedition.

The following year the draft of a new Constitution, on which work had been in progress for four years, was submitted to the authorities. The patience of the democrats was indeed sorely tested, and one wonders what Pridi must have thought in far off Yunnan. For Pridi and King Prajadhipok had worked one out in a matter of months.

Praphass, who also held the office of Minister of the Interior, declared that some of the provisions were too liberal and, if adopted, would weaken Thailand's security, for she would be open to exploitation by her enemies. He did not specify which countries he had in mind.

A committee of the Constituent Assembly was appointed to study the draft, but it was stated in October that there would be no promulgation that year, and the position was to remain unchanged even in 1968. On 8th December 1967 he stated in a Press interview that no Americans would be used for counter-insurgency action in Thailand. "United States Special Forces detachments are helping in the training of the Royal Thai Army but they are forbidden from participating in operations. We do not want Americans involved in combat against the communist terrorists and guerrillas. This is a Thai government responsibility and we will carry out the suppression ourselves. American aircraft will not be allowed to bomb any Thais even if they are terrorists."

He was answering allegations that American forces were bombing terrorists in north-east Thailand, as well as piloting helicopters and ferrying Thai troops into action. Praphass was also replying to allegations that American troops were becoming involved in the north-east provinces, just as they were in the early stages of the campaign in Vietnam. He declared that the 35,000 American forces "are in Thailand to support the war effort in Vietnam, and are not here in connection with the anti-terrorist drive".

As Deputy Premier, he is second to Thanom Kittikachorn, and, with his two offices as Minister of the Interior and Commander-in-Chief, he has tremendous power. Only three years ago it was stated quite openly that if this ambitious politician thought that a *coup* would be successful, he would lead it, but he realizes that the time is not propitious; moreover a failure would mean the end of his career. And so he keeps other claimants and rivals out of the running, particularly General Kris Sivara, the Commander-in-Chief of the First Army. This particular general is popular in the country and is well liked by foreigners.

We have not seen the end of *coups*, but none of the possible leaders can be sure of support at the present time. This may explain why the political see-saw is temporarily at rest.

···⚓···

I had my first introduction to police, prisoners, courts and prisons very early during my stay in Thailand. One morning I was strolling through the town of Chachoengsao when I noticed two policemen standing guard with fixed bayonets outside a large iron cage. There was a small crowd with them. Inside the cage were three men. Their wrists were manacled. I was about to walk on, for I felt a slight sense of intrusion, when one of them called out to me. He was grinning broadly. The policemen smiled. It was as if all were trying to tell me that it was not as bad as it appeared. Certainly, everything looked very casual. The prisoners were smoking and relatives were passing food through the bars. There is a strong acceptance of the inevitable among the Thais, as well as a high degree of fatalism.

Two armed policemen came to the cage. The door was opened and one of the prisoners walked out, placed his manacled hands together in a friendly greeting to me, acknowledged the good wishes of his friends and relations and walked between the two policemen to the courts a few yards away.

There were armed policemen on duty here, at the foot of the steps and at the top. I looked inquiringly at the one who appeared to be in charge, and he opened the door and ushered me in. The prisoner gave a delighted chuckle. It was unusual to see a *farang* in the court, and he appeared to be both amused and pleased that I had come to see him sentenced. He positively beamed at me.

The judge sat at a high table. To his right was the furled flag of Thailand. There was an atmosphere of quiet dignity in the court. The swearing of the oath was a more elaborate and prolonged procedure than in England. The voices of judge and lawyers were seldom raised during the proceedings which followed.

The case I was listening to concerned a burglary. These are very common all over Thailand, but particularly in Bangkok, as a large number of foreigners know to their cost. I have been told by some of them that the Siamese *kammoy* (burglar) is the most cunning, fearless and nimble burglar in South-east Asia. Foreign residents are advised against trying to apprehend them, as they will use a knife or a revolver to avoid capture. I had surprised one when returning in the early hours from a social event. For a second or two we stared at each other across the bed, then he appeared to spring backwards through the open shutters. I ran to the shutters to see him pick himself up, apparently unhurt, although this amazing leap had carried him into space and on to the ground twelve feet below. He darted down the lane.

Some amusing accounts of their exploits have appeared in the press. In some cases, everything portable has been taken away, even the sheets and blankets from under the sleeper. It is said that the *kammoy* enters the room and burns the leaves of a species of the oleander tree, which gives off fumes. These have the effect of a drug. However, there have been occasions when foreigners have been stabbed, and some have died. It is usual to leave electric lights on outside the house throughout the hours of darkness, for then the *kammoy* would be visible to anyone passing. Shutters are also closed and bolted. In spite of these precautions, they appear to have an amazing record of success, although often it has been established that they have worked in co-operation with the servants.

My convict did not appear to be unduly dismayed by his sentence. For the next two years he would be able to plan his future exploits.

Chachoengsao is the capital of the province or *changwad* of the same name. In addition to the law courts, it has a provincial prison.

The judicial system of Thailand has well-established procedures. There are Courts of the First Instance, which are sub-divided into twenty-eight magistrates courts or *kwaengs*. The *kwaeng* has limited civil and minor criminal jurisdiction. The *changwad* or higher court's jurisdiction here is unlimited. There are civil and criminal courts with exclusive jurisdiction in Bangkok and

Dhonburi, and central juvenile courts for those under 18, also at Dhonburi.

The Uthorn is the Court of Appeal. It deals with appeals on judgments delivered in the Courts of First Instance. Appeals from judgments of the Uthorn are decided by the Dikka. This is the Supreme Court of Thailand. This court also has semi-jurisdiction over general election petitions. Its decisions are absolutely final.

The manacling and chaining, the armed guards, the public exhibition in cages suggest a harsher penal code and ill-treatment by prison wardens than is the actual case, although to foreigners it must appear degrading. I have passed several large prisons. Two were familiar landmarks, and I drove past them regularly. There was always the sentry high up in the central watch tower with his machine gun trained on the exercise yard or cells. Armed guards were stationed in look-out towers and vantage points. I visited one prison in the capital and one up-country. In both cases the rapport between the prisoners and wardens appeared to be satisfactory. While it is certain that in the event of a break-out the guns would blaze from the watch-towers, then, provided that the rules were obeyed and these were reasonable, the prisoners could work out their term of imprisonment under fair conditions. There was no evidence of cruelty for cruelty's sake.

In the provincial towns the prisons are on the primitive side, although the surroundings were often quite pleasant. Inside the grounds were attractive with flowering shrubs looked after by the prisoners. I have watched parties returning from work. They were chained and manacled and escorted by armed guards. As they marched through the prison gates, some of them would joke or call out a cheery greeting to the guards.

For those convicted of more serious crimes, the régime was more rigorous. Their movements were restricted by chains on wrists and ankles. They were allowed to do handwork, and I thought that some examples of their work showed skill and talent. I was told that there was a programme for prison reform but that it had only made a small start in Bangkok. When built, new prisons in the provinces would possess more modern amenities.

It is a little disconcerting to enter a police station in the capital and be confronted by a huge cage with several of the round-ups of the day or night inside. The cage is one large communal cell and is easily supervised. I have been surprised to find Westerners in these cages. They are, of course, subject to Thai law.

One, an Englishman, had sworn at a policeman and also threatened him. He appeared to be making the best of the unusual surroundings and company. We chatted between the bars for a few minutes, then he continued what he had been doing when I arrived, which was giving a lesson in English to his cell mates! Two were *kammoy*, one was a pimp, another a painted she-man, and two were thieves. My compatriot was due to be bailed out in the early hours. In the meantime he was hoping to annoy the police lieutenant. As I left, he appeared to be succeeding.

On another occasion—I had been unlucky twice in the same month with parking offences—two Frenchmen were in the cage, but they were too drunk and happy to tell me why they were there. The noise was deafening. I don't think that the lieutenant and his squad had heard French songs sung with such volume, alternated with maudlin sobs which rose to vibrant crescendos. They were obviously fascinated, for they had all gathered around the bars. They were disappointed when three embarrassed compatriots arrived to take the drunks home.

Foreigners have not always been tried by Siamese or Thai courts. British courts were set up in accordance with the Anglo-Siamese Treaty of 1855, which granted extra-territorial rights to Britain. Similar treaties were also concluded with the United States and France. At that time, Siam was anxious to avoid unpleasantness with any of the great powers. Moreover, there were comparatively few foreigners, except in the case of Britain, whose nationals included thousands of Chinese, Indians, Burmese and Malays. Here any loss of sovereignty was offset by British judges taking over the difficult duties of interpretation and discipline. The British courts were known as consular courts until 1902, when they were called 'His Britannic Majesty's Courts for Siam'.

When France annexed Annam and Cambodia and Britain seized Upper Burma, there was a sudden rush into Siam of foreigners who were not subject to Siamese law. Siam thereupon remodelled her courts with the help of foreign judges, and then eventually took over. The British maintained consular prisons in the compounds of their consulates and even carried out their own executions.

The first international court in Siam was set up at Chiengmai in the north. This was as a result of the Anglo-Siamese Treaty of 1883. A British consular officer was empowered to sit in on any case involving a British subject. He could examine the witnesses, offer any suggestions and advice and draw up a report for the Appeal Court. If necessary, he could retire to the consular court and try himself all cases where British subjects were defendants.

The British Consul General in Bangkok sat with a representative of the Siamese Ministry of Justice and gave judgment on all appeals. By a further treaty with Siam in 1909, this system, with certain revisions, was adopted all over the kingdom. Appeals were decided by the Siamese Court of Appeal, which sat with a European adviser. These advisers had been working in Bangkok since the days of King Chulalongkorn and were mostly French. The law was Siamese, but where this could not be applied, then English law was administered.

These international courts continued until World War II, with a foreign adviser, sometimes British, sitting with two Siamese judges. Then, with extra-territoriality, they came to an end, although Thailand continued to employ legal advisers.

As far as Siamese subjects were concerned, the criminal code was harsh. Since the end of World War II there has been some improvement. Until the *coup* which ended absolute monarchy, the method of capital punishment was cruel. The condemned man, or woman, was taken to the place of the crime and made to sit on the ground. He was then bound to a post which had a cross piece for the support of his back. The arms were roped at the elbows to the posts. His outstretched legs were tied around the ankles to a post between them.

Long chains were fixed around his wrists and held by armed policemen standing on either side of him. Then the executioners— there were usually three—began a kind of ritual dance which always delighted the huge crowds. It consisted of a dance with rhythmic steps towards the condemned man, waving their swords, rushing at him, and just when all thought that the blow would be struck; they would retreat backwards to perform the traditional dance all over again. This was done several times. Then the first executioner would make a dash and deliver the first stroke which was intended to decapitate. It rarely did. The duties of the other two were to finish off the job. The execution was often bungled, for the executioners were supplied with alcoholic drinks. Too much liquor impeded their judgment and the unfortunate wretch was horribly mangled. This method of capital punishment was replaced with death by shooting.

The police have exercised undue influence over the courts, particularly during the reign of Police General Phao. Then their conduct was a scandal. In 1956, the power of the police rivalled that of the army. It was equipped with planes, tanks, helicopters, parachute battalions, armoured cars and heavy machine guns. The total force numbered nearly 50,000. Ten thousand were stationed in the capital and about 20,000 in the north-east.

Wherever I went that year, I was warned of the imminent clash between the army and the police. Few were prepared to bet on who would emerge as victor. It was well known that General Phao had ambitions to be Prime Minister. However, Field Marshal Sarit was one jump ahead, and the following year Phao was exiled. The police were then reorganized.

The enormous cost of this force was largely met by the smuggling of opium, brilliantly organized by Phao. He was an intelligent, fearless and resourceful man, as well as unscrupulous and ruthless. He promoted police officers to a special *corps d'élite* for their services to him, not to the state, for often the two interests clashed. This corps were known as *asawins* or knights.

The actual smuggling of opium was largely in the hands of this corps. They travelled to the north, where they bought up large stocks of illicit opium. These were sent to Bangkok, where the value was assessed by the Excise Department. The *asawins* then received a percentage reward. Then the load was shuttled back and forth between the capital and the north, and the reward was again claimed. The cover story put out by Phao was that his special agents had tracked down the smugglers' hide-outs and followed them to their caches of raw opium. Unfortunately they had escaped, which was not surprising, since they were in Phao's pay and were employed on the same mission again. However, the opium had been seized.

On one occasion I went by bus to the frontier at Arundh-pradet. We were delayed for two hours, while the bus was searched and the driver and all passengers questioned. Then, for some reason no one appeared to understand, we were not allowed to travel to Angkor Wat but had to go to the Cambodian town of Battambong. The search appeared to be thorough. Huge baskets of fruit were unloaded from the roof and tipped on the ground. Household goods had a similar fate. I asked two of the passengers if it had been found. With a cynical grin, they whispered, "We're taking it with us!"

Another time, I was travelling to Bangkok from Korat when the bus was stopped by armed police. The roof was covered with merchandise, which was heavy and bulky. Everything was unloaded and searched. Then two of the police accompanied us to Bangkok. Valluya and Vichit, to whom I described the incident later, said that there was little doubt that the opium was on the bus, and that the police were escorting it to Bangkok, where it would be collected. They said that one favourite hiding place was under a false roof. The searches were merely a pretence. After Phao had left the country, amazing accounts of the years of smuggling were reported in the press. It was stated that the police organized the export of the drug to Singapore, Hong Kong and Saigon.

When I was first invited to visit an opium den, which I knew was not licensed, I thought that it was inviting trouble. My friends laughed and told me that it was under police protection. I visited two in Bangkok, one of which was very large, and three in the provinces. I was offered a pipe in each place. I did not like the first, and when I declined the others, I was not pressed.

There was no visible sign from the outside that they were opium dens. I thought that all of them were squalid. Bunks were fixed round the walls of the rooms and some in the middle. They were all occupied by men naked to the waist, for it was very hot. They were lying on their backs, their heads and necks supported by wooden pillows. I watched several of them open small tins and hook out a small globule of the drug, which they heated in a flame of a small coconut oil lamp and then inserted into the bowl of the pipe. After this they sat back and inhaled deeply. Between the bunks, pimps threaded their way, stopping and whispering. More hangers-on stood around the rooms weighing up the human cargo, in quest of likely prey. Small girls, aged only 8 or 10 years, brought trays with tiny teapots and cups to those who asked for them. There was never any attempt to molest them.

The addicts just wanted their dreams. Some were being massaged. I watched these men working. They obviously knew their job, unlike the pretty dolls of the massage establishments. The addicts all appeared to find it soothing. Lines disappeared, if only temporarily, from faces which told of the stresses and struggles of life. Several were very emaciated and looked indescribably weary, as if they had reached the end of life's tortuous journey. Perhaps they would find it in a wooden bunk in a wooden shack as long as they could find the price of a pipe. Others looked happy and contented and were making it a social evening with their friends, for, as if by some telepathic signal, they reached for their pipes and the tiny lamp.

I have heard that there are some sumptuously furnished and decorated clubs, but these are very exclusive. Most of the addicts are Chinese.

In July 1959 Field Marshal Sarit banned opium smoking. The ban was heralded by the public burning of some 9,000 opium pipes from licensed houses on the Pramane Grounds. The unlicensed places presumably hid their pipes. However, it was not stamped out. Poppies continue to grow in the north. The hill tribes cultivate their patches of land. Smoking continues underground, and, what is worse, it is being replaced by heroin which is more difficult to detect.

Apart from opium, Police General Phao took his squeeze from brothels, gambling houses, private cinemas and other dens of vice. He was accused of having bank notes forged in Hong Kong and circulated in Bangkok. Money was extorted from merchants, who were intimidated and beaten up.

The faked elections of 1957 were an example of police corruption and evil. Phao's hired thugs beat up political opponents, intimidated the Press, forged election lists, printed and used illegal ballot forms and sent out flying detachments to vote in place of those on regular voting lists. All carried the written and dreaded authority of the master.

The full extent of the corruption and crimes will never be known, but much came to light after his departure, when numbers of police officers stood trial. Most of his *asawins* had left the country with him. Two police generals were convicted of complicity in the murder of four former Cabinet Ministers. A 'mass' murder trial was opened in August 1958. Police officers admitted murdering and burying political opponents, including a deputy; others to murdering the director of a company publishing two newspapers who had refused to sell his shares to Phao. The press printed details of the trials, with particularly gruesome details of some of the murders; of bodies trussed up and then taken to the middle of the river and sunk, of trips into the jungle, holes dug and bodies buried. Witnesses admitted receiving generous payments from Phao for their part in their murders. Numbers of those considered to be politically dangerous had been murdered by the police. Their relatives had been too frightened to protest. Now that Phao was out of the way, they came forward with harrowing stories.

The trials caused widespread consternation. It was difficult to realize that such appalling crimes could have continued, been hushed up for so long, that, under the smiling surface of everyday life, extortion, cruelty, murder and false imprisonment were rampant. The socialists and democrats were shocked, although many had been suspicious for the past few years. Others admitted that they had been threatened with similar fates. The trials were an object lesson to those of both parties. Without organization, unity or funds, their causes could have little chance of success.

However, Pibul's introduction of free speech on the Pramane Grounds, on the lines of Speaker's Corner which he had so much admired during his visit to England in 1955, was partly responsible for the outburst of fury against Phao and subsequent disclosures. Unfortunately, it ended not long after it had started. It was found to be too explosive for Thailand. The Thais have yet to appreciate democracy.

The police one finds on traffic and patrol duties appear to be reasonable enough, although I have met those who are officious. They are poorly paid, and a large number supplement their earnings by spare-time work. I knew three who were taxi drivers. Many receive commissions from owners of night clubs, brothels and massage establishments for introducing clients. However, they can be very helpful when the car breaks down, or when the motorist wishes to enter a stream of traffic from a side road.

It is not difficult to bribe them. On one occasion I left my car outside a shop while I went inside to pick up a sewing-machine. In less than two minutes I was back to find a policeman writing out a ticket. He had obviously seen me arrive and seized his opportunity. I told him what he knew quite well, that I had simply been in and out, and I called the Chinese shopkeeper to support my story. This infuriated him. The frightened shopkeeper withdrew. With an ingratiating smile, he held up the ticket. The smile was instantly replaced by a scowl when I accepted it.

The number of accidents each day in Bangkok is appalling. One morning I sat in a café in New Road and watched the slow-moving stream of traffic flow by. I counted thirty-five cars with the tell-tale flat brown undercoating on repaired or renewed panels. I have seen accidents all over the capital, but very few of them have been more than collisions, largely due to careless driving or defective brakes. Outside the capital, I have come across dreadful sights, when buses have collided head-on. It is quite common for the drivers to vanish, if they are able to, before the police arrive.

However, for minor traffic offences a small consideration will settle the matter. Taxi drivers are considered fair game. The policeman pockets the driver's licence. He can go to the police station or have it back on the spot.

There is much enthusiasm for learning English, even among the lowest ranks, and classes are well supported. Proficiency in this subject can be an aid to promotion.

The commissioned officers are generally well-educated and of smart appearance. When the king drives through the streets, they are out in force controlling the crowds, and they look impressive in their khaki uniforms.

It is unlikely that the police will ever again be as strong and oppressive as they were under Police General Phao. Much of their varied equipment, which was more suitable for an army, has been taken away. Their main source of wealth, which was the smuggling of opium, has gone. Then it is doubtful whether the people would permit a renewal of the tyranny and evils of those days.

Schools and Universities

One morning I was driving through a jungle town when a lorry in front of me pulled up. I noticed that all the pedestrians had stopped. Some were standing to attention. All vehicles were stationary. The Thai national flag was being hoisted very slowly up the flagpole in a school playground. When it was at top mast, some of the pedestrians and drivers bowed.

The entire school was assembled. The pupils were very smart in a uniform which is simple and obligatory throughout the kingdom. Boys wore white shirts and khaki shorts. I was about to drive off when the actions of one of the teachers attracted my attention. About a dozen boys were lined up in front of him. He was measuring the distance between the hem of the shorts and the knee. Apparently there was a regulation distance. I watched the assembly of a girls' school. They looked very attractive in white blouses, blue ties and blue skirts.

At Petchburi a week afterwards, I attended a celebration in honour of Army Day. Among the distinguished guests were head teachers of local schools. Teachers enjoy a high prestige in Thailand. The term *acharn* or teacher is an honoured one.

Education in Thailand today has made enormous strides, particularly during the past fifteen years. There are some magnificent schools in up-country towns. Thailand has eight universities. The latest, in Chiengmai, was opened three years ago.

As in England, the monks established schools before state education became general. The education provided was free, but the pupils were required to perform certain monastic duties.

Apart from a few private schools, no education was provided for girls until the introduction of state education this century.

Hand blackboards were used for writing. Writing books were made up of palm leaves, and the pen was a stylo. It was not until the seventeenth century that paper was introduced. This was made from a leaf called a *khoi* and was of two colours, black for use with white chalk, and white for use with black lacquer.

In 1828 an Englishman, Captain James Low, introduced Thai characters to print his grammar for foreign students. Nine years afterwards another English missionary, Dr. Bradley, brought his printing press to Bangkok to publish the Bible in Thai. French missionaries in Bangkok commenced printing about the same time.

In the middle of the nineteenth century, French and American missionaries opened private schools. For many years they had little success, in spite of King Chulalongkorn's decree of religious toleration in 1878, which was actually an encouragement to Thais to send their children to these schools where they could learn English and French in addition to their own language. At first the missionaries had to bribe pupils to enrol. The excellent schools run by the Roman Catholic and Presbyterian missions all over the country today are a testimony to the courage and persistence of those early missionaries.

King Chulalongkorn started a palace school with the object of training future civil servants. The pupils were chosen from among the sons of princes and nobles, for the offices of the crown were hereditary. He had been disturbed to find that few of the existing holders of these sinecures could read or write.

He sent his many sons to England, Denmark, the United States, Russia, Germany and Japan to study the educational systems of these countries, as well as other subjects.

More schools were opening in the *wats* at this time. These were the centre of community life, as the saffron-robed monks were closely identified with all progress in education. In 1880 the first girls' school was opened. By 1886 thirty-five schools were in session all over the country. In 1887 King Chulalongkorn established a Department of Education, which in 1889 comprised some five departments, namely Education, Central, Museum, Hospital and Ecclesiastical.

In 1890 the advent of the railway was to bring more pupils

flocking to the schools. In many areas the villagers worked along-side the saffron-robed monks, building more schools or extending the existing ones. In 1892 the first teacher-training college was opened, and an Englishman was appointed principal. The first training college for women was opened in 1913.

The king called for a report from his minister in London on the English educational system. It was implemented the following year and became the basis for the Siamese national system. It was divided into primary, secondary and higher education, with provisions for vocational education, preparation of textbooks, training of teachers and local administration. Later some of the features of the Japanese system were adopted. This followed on a report from one of his advisers who had been sent to Japan.

In 1909 the first steps were taken towards making education compulsory. Small committees were set up in every village. These consisted of the abbot, the headman and the doctor. In that year there were 12,000 *wats* where classes were being taught by 30,000 monks to some 200,000 children.

There was, however, a disturbing fluctuation in the number of teachers in state and private schools. Funds were never sufficient to pay their salaries. Even a poll tax levied locally did not produce enough revenue, and the funds allocated by the Government could not meet the needs of an ever-increasing school population. These difficulties did not arise in the *wat* schools for the monks were fed by the local community; moreover their vows forbade them to take money. There was no problem in connection with the missionary schools.

In 1910 King Chulalongkorn, who had done so much to bring education within the reach of so many, died. Six years afterwards, the school which he had opened as a palace school for training civil servants became Siam's first university and was inaugurated as Chulalongkorn University.

State schools were increasing, and it was becoming apparent that they would eventually take the place of the *wat* schools, although they would continue for some time to work in close co-operation with the monks. Village groups had been making progress; a more regular system of taxation was enforced, and in 1921, before the law of compulsory education was passed, there were 5,050 village groups and 2,311 schools. The temple buildings continued to be put to the maximum use.

Compulsory education could only be enforced as facilities became available, and in the sparsely populated and remote areas these remained inadequate for many years. The revolution of 1932 gave it impetus, for the new constitutional government had promised to set up a fully elected parliament as soon as half the population had completed five years of primary education, or within ten years, whichever period was the shorter.

Education in Siam was making rapid strides; more new schools were being built, the number of trained teachers was increasing each year. Then the outbreak of World War II and the resultant depression brought progress almost to a standstill. When conditions improved, the development plans received a fresh spurt. Financial support was provided principally by the United States, and also by other countries, as well as organizations of the United Nations.

The Ministry of Education experimented with pilot projects, advisers from abroad were invited to Bangkok. Leading Thai educationists travelled extensively to study educational techniques in other countries.

Today the national education system consists of twelve grades. The first seven are at the primary level, and are called Prathom 1–7. Then follow five secondary grades known as Mathayom 1–5. A secondary school is one which accepts pupils who have completed the primary stage and provides a five-year academic course in preparation for university entrance. A vocational school accepts pupils in the same way, for a three-year non-academic course.

These schools have many unsolved problems. The chief one concerns the curriculum. There is still a prevailing contempt for manual labour, even in its higher forms. Consequently agriculture, woodwork and metalwork courses do not receive adequate support. Even if they did, the future is very uncertain for those who complete their training in these vocational schools.

Most openings in trade subjects are almost entirely blocked by the Chinese minority. I have been into scores of small towns and watched the Chinese metalworkers at work. I have seen whole streets of them, their wares displayed on the pavement, while, inside the shop, grandparents and children were working at some stage of the article. The skills have been handed down from father to son. I have had water cans made, water cylinders fitted

with taps, perforated pipes, guttering for rain-water to flow into
the storage tanks, lids to keep out the dust and leaves, and all
made to a design, and I have marvelled at the excellent workmanship. They operated a ring, for the price of standard articles was
the same in every shop. Then the Chinese are prepared to work
very long hours for very little money. Thai governments have
ordered that the Thai language should be taught in Chinese
schools, but this has actually helped them in trade.

I committed my first indiscretion in this field very early in my
stay, when, in company with some Thais, I visited a metalwork shop to have a simple fountain and water supply made for
an ornamental pond in my garden. It was well done, and the price
was absurdly low. On the way home I drew the attention of my
friends to the quality of the workmanship. To my surprise, they
were scornful. It was undignified labour. The worker had just sat
there banging away, working hard for very little. Yet I felt that
there was also a certain amount of envy.

Much the same is true of woodwork. Chinese shops will
quickly and cheaply make almost anything to design, if they
cannot satisfy your demands from existing stocks. Or they will
drive miles to the shop of another compatriot to obtain an
article. I wanted a cabinet made to house a wireless set, gramo-
phone pick-up and records. Late one night I heard voices and
opened the door to find a father and two sons with the completed
article. They had driven down from Bangkok with it, loaded it
on a sampan and ferried it across the river. It was beautifully
made of hand-polished teak. They insisted on wiring it up for me,
although I had the idea that in their minds, Beethoven's 'Emperor'
Concerto was not the best test of the pick-up's reproductive
quality. The sons wanted cymbals, gongs, pipes and booming
basses!

However, the Ministry of Education is aware of the need to
encourage and develop pride and dignity in craftsmanship, as well
as to foster an interest in the simple basic mechanical skills.
Exhibitions and competitions are organized and receive wide
publicity. As a long-term policy, this might well result in a
changing outlook.

Employment in fields requiring technical knowledge and
know-how has boomed in recent years. The armed forces with
their jeeps, bridges, jet aircraft and radar; farming with its

increased mechanization; the enormous expansion in communications, all provide openings which did not exist fifteen years ago, but they also need men of higher mental calibre to fill them.

The position of the private school in Thailand is almost unique among the countries of South-east Asia and the Far East. There are about 150 schools controlled by the Roman Catholic mission. They have a total school population of some 75,000. Thirty-six are controlled by the Ecumenical Mission, which are mainly Presbyterian but also include the Church of Christ and Baptist denominations. Over 21,000 pupils attend these schools.

In Bangkok four Roman Catholic schools have established a national reputation. These are Mater Dei, St. Francis, St. Joseph's and the College of the Assumption. Pupils include royalty and the most illustrious families in the kingdom. The present king, Phumipol, was educated at Mater Dei, his queen, Sirikit, at St. Francis Convent. Cabinet ministers and senior bureaucrats, including those from the Ministry of Education, also send their children to these schools, which is an eloquent tribute to the reputation they have built up.

The large and spacious College of the Assumption was opened in 1885. Mission schools are not only confined to Bangkok. I have come across them in the provinces. Hilary and Jacqueline, when aged 10 and 12, attended an excellent missionary school up-country. This mission was opened a hundred years ago and consisted of a collection of wooden huts. When I left Thailand it was being replaced by magnificent brick and stone buildings. The headmaster had served the mission for many years and left to start a new one elsewhere. High officials of the Ministry of Education were among the large crowd who had assembled to honour him.

In this kingdom of the saffron robe conversions to the Christian faith are very few, despite the large sums of money spent on the missions. Of the converts, a large percentage lapse. I knew a headmaster and a doctor who had been educated right through to university. When I first met them they told me that they were Christians. Just before I left Thailand I came across them lecturing to large audiences on Buddhism!

The Catholics are well aware that, during the past century, their schools and hospitals have thrived and met an urgent need, but that their religion has not had the same success. However, they believe that their missions serve to bring people into contact with the Church and Christian teaching and that eventually some may find their way over to them. The Protestant missions take much the same view. In Pitsanulok an American missionary admitted that if success was judged by conversions, they might just as well close down, but they knew that they were wanted and that they were appreciated.

I have discussed the question of converts with missionaries of all missions, both in the capital and in the provinces. All that I have met are dedicated. They have told me that they are here to stay, to make the missions a tradition and an institution. In this way they could always be at hand to be of service and satisfy a need. They are hopeful of a trend developing towards the creeds they follow and preach. I cannot see this happening. Buddhism gives the Thai inspiration, comfort and assurance. It is compassionate, friendly and uncomplicated.

There are about 2,000 private schools all over the country which are not operated by the missions. The mission schools account for about 10 per cent or one-third of the pupils in private schools. Islamic schools, 6 per cent. Here the mosque replaces the *wat*, especially in the Moslem-Malay provinces. Chinese schools form 21 per cent. Private schools, run for profit, make up the remainder.

The Vajiravudh school, named after the king of that name, is modelled on the lines of Eton. I have attended two of its Speech Days. In each case the king presented the awards. It is a magnificent building, well-equipped, has a graduate staff and is one of the outstanding schools in the kingdom.

There have been frequent allegations in the press of *pae-chia*, by which head teachers in state schools will favour the admission of a pupil on payment of a bribe. The same charge has been made against the principals of mission schools, although here the bribe has no doubt been passed to the Church. Unfortunately these allegations are not without foundation.

A German junior technical institute, established in 1959, and working in close contact with the Ministry of Education, provides a three- or five-year course for young Thais in engineering. The standard reached is equivalent to that of a German technician who has completed an apprenticeship in the engineering trade. It has been a very successful experiment. Thailand is in desperate need of technicians, and more schools of this type are required.

In all private schools, both missionary and commercial, the Government has adopted an enlightened and generous policy. It has made grants of land. It subsidizes the fees and staff salaries. The fees are very moderate, starting at about six pounds a term in all day secondary schools, regardless of size and prestige. All private schools must follow the same syllabuses as those taught in state schools, which are drawn up by the state, and they must be subject to state inspection and control.

There are frequent demands that the National Education policy be revised in accordance with the needs of the nation and that standards at all levels be improved. In 1963 Field Marshal Sarit, Thailand's leader, pointed the finger at the shortcomings in the national education system. He declared that out of a school population of 3 million, 600,000 had either failed or had not reached the prescribed standards of their fourth or final year.

Actually, in spite of Sarit's strictures, progress during the eight years leading up to his outburst had been quite remarkable. The number of schools had increased by 25 per cent, teachers by 50 per cent, and the number of pupils from 3 million to 4,100,000. In the ten years from 1958 all branches of education have made outstanding advances, and the situation in 1968 was most promising.

Unfortunately, too many pupils leave before completion of the course, and the examinations system, by which pupils who fail one of the grades are required to repeat it the following year or until they pass, holds up progress and results in a wide age range in some classes, which is frustrating and educationally unsound. In some schools I have visited I have found this range to be as much as four years.

Thailand is desperately short of teachers. The very low salaries, and not enough teacher-training colleges are responsible for this shortage. Teachers are trained for primary or secondary work and paid accordingly. A large number of teachers are untrained and paid at a lower rate. However, with the provision of more teacher-training colleges as well as a more realistic salary structure, Thailand's teaching force is already increasing in numbers, and the quality of the new recruits is steadily improving.

While some schools are housed in fine brick and stone buildings,

Learning the alphabet in a school in the north-east

A school fair up-country

Thailand's newest university at Chiengmai; (*left*) the science laboratory and (*below*) the Council Buildings, used for ceremonies

with modern equipment and excellent amenities, many are of timber construction, and a large number are of the open sala type. There are some very dilapidated and inadequate buildings in the north-east.

Many schools are closed during the dry season because of the shortage of water. In many cases this could be avoided. I have seen water gushing from the gutters and drain-pipes on to the ground. Some of these schools have enormous roof areas, and the quantity of water wasted is immense. The drainage pipes are intended to feed into tanks, but these have either not been supplied or have been used for another purpose. It would appear that all that is required is for a simple directive to be sent to the head teacher, requiring him to make arrangements for the conservation of water. Much will depend upon the district education officer. I have seen underground and above-ground reservoirs constructed in the compounds of many schools, with the result that there has been no wastage.

In this happy country, there is a strong tendency to avoid being firm with one's subordinates. I have been in schools where, on occasions, two or more teachers have been absent. In the staff room there were often a large number of teachers off duty. When I have asked the head teachers why they have not taken over the classes of their absent colleagues, they have replied: "They will think that I am unkind!" This benevolent attitude to each other may be a most commendable trait, but I am inclined to the view that it is not conducive to progress.

Chulalongkorn and Thamassat are the Oxford and Cambridge of Thailand, and the annual football match between these two universities is one of the social events of the year. The parade of the students, with band majorettes and cheer leaders, is modelled on American university life.

There is also a fine Buddhist university in Bangkok. All universities have Americans and Europeans among their professors and lecturers. Last year there were twenty-four at Chulalongkorn, and half this number were Americans.

A magnificent university was opened in the beautiful city of Chiengmai, in northern Thailand, in 1963. This represents a tremendous advance, for, prior to this, students from all over the kingdom had to concentrate on the capital.

It is very unusual for the young men and women students to pair off. They usually go about in small groups. The teaching staff is treated with great respect, but an unpopular professor or lecturer can find that life can be made difficult by these polite and pleasant students.

Until quite recently they have not taken an active interest in politics. Their marches and demonstrations in protest against the rigged elections of 1958 came as a surprise to the nation but it showed that they could easily become a powerful force politically in future *coups*.

An inquiry into 'Public Opinion among Thai students', conducted by the University of Thamassat in 1957, after the *coup* which sent Pibul and Phao into exile, included students of this university, the Medical, Agricultural and Education Universities and the Technical Institute. It revealed that less than 1 per cent believed that Communism offered the best future for Thailand. Over 75 per cent favoured democracy, and the majority supported neutralism as the foreign policy. About 85 per cent considered that the results of the 1932 *coup*, which ended the absolute monarchy, were mainly good. Between 60 per cent and 75 per cent thought that they showed the "beginnings of democracy". Corruption, and a system in which there was no real democracy, were considered evil.

Over a third asked for more industrialization. Both dictatorship and communism were strongly opposed. It is quite likely that trends would differ in another year, according to the political calm or unrest, but even then these views are not without significance. The Bangkok government obviously attached some importance to the students' views and has not forgotten the demonstration. In March 1962 the Minister of the Interior announced the setting up of a university police corps to protect property and maintain law and order.

The highlight of university life is the day when the young graduates kneel before the king to receive their degree. During the past ten years the number of university graduates has soared. This is one effect of the country's current prosperity. An increasing number of parents are now able to keep their children on at school.

America and other foreign countries, as well as organizations of the United Nations, Colombo and other Treaty powers, award fellowships by which the successful candidates can study for a year or more overseas. America grants the majority and is a favoured country for fellowships and exhibitions granted by the United Nations and other organizations. The Government also subsidizes large numbers of students for overseas study. The result is that Thailand has an educated *élite*, already of an impressive size and growing each year, which could well influence public opinion. Should the spectre of unemployment raise its head, this *élite* could also be a prey to political parties.

I have met many foreign teachers in the capital and up-country. They appear to enjoy their work, whether it is teaching in the schools or universities. The students of all ages are charming and a pleasure to teach. I have visited schools all over the country, have taught in several and found it all a most pleasant experience. I have rarely come across problems of discipline. The students stand to attention when you enter the room. They clasp their hands together and bow over them when you hand them back their homework. They are gay and amusing. Education in Thailand is still regarded by students and parents as a great privilege.

————————•⚜•————————

The up-country town of Chachoengsao is situated on the banks of the Bangpakong River. It has a population of about 24,000. The Chinese minority accounts for 6 per cent of this figure, but this very small percentage was much in evidence as I was to see every day during my stay.

The shopping centre was a collection of Chinese shops. As I walked through the town, I would pass several coppersmiths and tinsmiths, and all were busily engaged in producing their wares, a large variety of which were on view in front of the shops. There were several jewellers, silversmiths and goldsmiths sitting in their little glass-screened cubicles, always with the tiny flame in readiness. Elderly Chinese women, in white blouses and black trousers, would be gossiping outside tailor's shops, while inside the men were working. I always received a beaming smile from one intelligent-looking matriarch, whose six sons, all handsome and industrious, ran three businesses between them, two of which she knew I patronized. Clouds of steam floated upwards from Chinese laundries, where, again, the menfolk worked while their mothers or aunts filled the large irons with glowing charcoal. I would receive a gentle smile from a grave-looking Chinese chemist, whose mixtures of herbs and roots prominently displayed in glass jars would cure anything and make everything possible, including paternity at an age when no longer believed possible.

The discreet and understanding Chinese hotels were dotted around the town. I shall always remember the day I stopped outside one of them to study the Chinese concepts in large embossed gilt plaster. A window was flung open, and a young, attractive, dark-eyed Chinese girl grinned impishly at me and shouted some words which, of course, I did not understand. Unfortunately, the shoppers did, and a gale of laughter blew up and took volume as it swept across the square. A *samlor* stopped, and the son of the ironmonger, recently returned from Australia, stepped out. He, too, was laughing. "She wants to know if you will be the first to have her virginity for today!" he said in his soft-spoken, musical English.

Then into the market, where the wares were stacked on long stone tables. Spaced out at intervals sat the vendors, all Chinese women, except in the meat section, where men sawed and hacked at the sides of fat pork. Huge quantities of fish of many varieties, some still twitching; blue, red, black and a mixture, had been stacked in baskets or lay on the bench. There were pyramids of pineapples, stocks of bananas, durians, mangosteens, litchies, papaya, oranges and other fruits, and the ubiquitous sacks of rice. A profusion of wild and cultivated flowers, with exotic colours and enormous stems, were stacked across the benches. There were wild orchids, lotuses, tuberoses and roses.

Fingers deftly flicked the abacus, and the total sum was sung out, with more smiles.

There were many restaurants, and all had their clientèle. Here chickens were fried over charcoal braziers, or eggs, fish and noodles, and ready in record time.

Marian usually did much of the shopping. With her fair hair and blue eyes, and being the only Westerner, she was at first a nine-days' wonder when she came into the market, and no attempt was ever made to overcharge her. Mouths opened in smiles to reveal gold or gold-filled teeth as the women gave her the morning greeting and inquired after all of us. Outside a *samlor* boy, always a Thai, would wait to take her home. The same scene was repeated at Korat, Lopburi, Nakornsawan, Chiengmai; in short, all over Thailand.

The villages and small towns have their Chinese temples, which are quite small buildings when compared with the *wats*, and decorated with huge Chinese concepts in gilt, while there is an abundance of red.

One favourite walk took me past one of these temples. Sometimes I was in time to see the priest arrive. This one was tall and scholarly-looking, dressed in brown robes. He had a soft but resonant voice. The little temple was always full.

And, of course, there was an opium den, a wooden building with no exterior sign to proclaim its identity. I went in several times, was always treated with courtesy and friendliness, and on the first two occasions was offered and declined a pipe. After this they did not attempt to persuade me to smoke.

The Chinese work very hard. I have had suits made in a couple of days, shoes that fitted like a glove. Indeed, I have never worn such comfortable shoes. I wore one pair for four years in Thailand and still use them. They were made in less than a week.

In walking through Bangkok, one literally bursts upon Chinatown, and the contrast is so sudden and violent that it is like entering a different city inhabited by different people. There are Chinese restaurants, Chinese goldsmiths, with the day's quotation recorded in white chalk on a black board. One comes across Chinese cinemas and theatres with their huge hoardings and lurid posters as high as twenty feet. From daylight to the early hours, music blares stridently from loudspeakers. Every shop has a radio and uses it to drown the others. Interspersed between the goldsmiths, the grocers and the furniture showrooms, Chinese hotels stand out clear and distinctive. I watched half a dozen lovely Chinese girls, all wearing cheongsams, emerge from a goldsmith's and, with superb carriage, walk briskly and purposefully across the road into their hotel. They appeared to be secretaries from Chinese business houses. There was pride, industry, independence and prosperity among the Chinese minority here, as elsewhere in Thailand. They walked as if they belonged and had a place in this country.

The money-lenders and money-changers, who had their offices in different parts of the town, but mainly in this quarter, were well-patronized, and I was told that they were fair-dealing. They charged the lowest rate of interest; the Siamese money-lenders, especially the women, lent at a higher rate. The Indians were said to be extortioners.

Thais in different walks of life have told me that they do not like Indians. They have a favourite comment—if we go into the jungle and meet a cobra and an Indian, we shoot the Indian.

There were newspaper shops, selling Chinese newspapers and a variety of Chinese magazines, the covers of which attracted your attention immediately by their gaudy colours and the fearsome characters and scenes they portrayed. There were those which risked a brush with the censor, for sex was portrayed near naked and proud. Chinese garages and service stations, Chinese factories, Chinese banks, Chinese companies—the Chinese minority largely controls the nation's economy.

After a study and the close observation of some years of the relationship between the Thais and the Chinese, I believe that on the whole they get on amazingly well together in the towns and the villages, and that many of the occasional outbursts of anti-Chinese sentiment are officially inspired.

Historically, both nations have a close affinity with each other. The original homeland of the Thais was in the Yunnan plateau in south-west China. From the sixth century onwards they migrated into South-east Asia. The first Siamese kingdom was established in the northern part of present-day Thailand, with Chiengsen as capital. In the thirteenth century the Mongols over-ran South China. The Siamese came south in ever increasing numbers, overwhelmed the Mons, moved the capital to Sukhothai and continued their southern drive. They defeated the Khmers and over the years adopted much of the culture of the Mons and Khmers, and later the Chinese. About one-fifth of Thailand's population is composed of Chinese, Cambodians, Malays, Lao and hill tribes, such as the Karens, Meos, Yaos and Akhas. Today, Thailand has more Chinese than any country of South-east Asia. There are over $3\frac{1}{2}$ million, and nearly half the population of Bangkok are Chinese or of Chinese descent.

When Ayudhya, the former capital, was at the height of her glory, which was towards the end of the seventeenth century, they were well liked. They were more submissive than the settlers from the West. They came without family connections, married Siamese girls, and their descendants were assimilated. During the past 300 years this intermarriage on such a vast scale has resulted in the mixed blood of a very high percentage of the Thai population. Many leading Thai families have Chinese blood. The Chinese observe an apartheid today, which is becoming stronger because of the persecution they suffered during the Fifties and an awareness that they are being used as political pawns. The great Chinese Republic calls to them, and, whenever it does, the Bangkok government becomes uneasy. Yet the occasions when Peking has made a direct appeal to her Chinese nationals in Thailand are very few. Her propaganda is directed at the whole country, but the Government is inclined to the view that it is an exhortation to the Chinese minority to take action. However, these appeals are usually followed by allegations that a Chinese fifth column is at work in the capital.

There have been a few riots and disorders in Bangkok, but in the towns and villages the Chinese food seller, with his incredibly heavy burdens suspended from the cross bar over his shoulders, has continued to call on all and sundry without the slightest fear of personal attack.

One has only to attend a Chinese funeral, marriage, theatre, even some hereditary custom in family life, to realize the strength of these traditions and ties. There is nothing secret about them. The Chinese in Thailand proclaim their nationality to all. Their processions hold up the traffic, and everyone accepts the inconvenience. When they celebrate the Chinese New Year, an exclusively Chinese event, the life of the country slows down. The shops are closed, and it is an unfortunate Thai or foreigner who has not stocked up.

They have their own schools, where they teach their pupils the concepts of the language, the history of their very old nation, and they pass on their culture. Occasionally the Government announces that spies will be placed in Chinese schools, but what good this action is expected to achieve, especially after an open warning, is something I have never been able to establish.

Apart from the persecution of the Chinese minority during the reign of King Vajiravudh, Siam did not consider China to be a danger right until the end of World War I. That enormous country was in the throes of internal convulsions brought about by internecine warfare. Bangkok imposed a few labour laws but rarely enforced them.

However, after World War II, Siam, now Thailand, adopted a different attitude. China under the Kuomintang was one of the Allies. Thailand was uneasy as to the implications of her wartime collaboration with Japan. She lost no time in recognizing the government of Chiang Kai-shek. Even when he withdrew from Formosa and the Kuomintang collapsed, Bangkok maintained her relations with Taiwan.

There was a demonstration very soon after the war, when the Chinese flag flew alongside those of the Allies. The Thai flag was conspicuous by its absence. Riots continued for over a week. The Chinese government lodged a vigorous protest against the repressive measures of the Bangkok police and threatened to veto Thailand's application to join the United Nations. The Government was immediately conciliatory. The rights which the Chinese had lost in 1939 were restored. They were granted the same privileges as other aliens. Chinese schools were allowed to reopen, and a quota of 10,000 annual immigrants was allowed.

In 1947 the Thai-Chinese Friendship Society was formed. Pridi became a leading member. The following year Pibul was Prime Minister, and his government imposed more restrictions. He attached more importance to a threat from the Chinese minority than from communist subversion among the Thais. He warned the Chinese Press against such propaganda and anti-government views. This was followed by a drastic reduction in the immigrant quota, to 200.

In October 1949, the Chinese communists proclaimed their victory in mainland China. Pibul advised the Chinese in Thailand to refrain from all political activity, but here he was careful to avoid offending Taiwan or Peking until the situation was clear. By a brilliant diplomatic move, he made it clear that he looked upon the Chinese minority as anti-Chinese, rather than anti-communist, and thus avoided confrontation with Russia and other communist states.

The same month, Mao Tse-Tung proclaimed at Peking the People's Republic of China, and later he denounced the persecution of the Chinese in Thailand and called for assurances that it would cease.

In 1951 Moscow and Peking stepped up their propaganda in an all-out drive to swing Thailand to neutralism. Both nations launched an appeal to writers, teachers and Buddhist monks, but with little result. Among Chinese everywhere, the prestige of the young and powerful People's Republic was soaring. To them she had fought back in Korea against the United States, the mightiest nation in the world, and her Western allies. The old mystic appeal of China exercised a disturbing and restless influence upon the Chinese in Thailand, as well as among the Thais.

However, in Bangkok there were two camps; the supporters of the new régime and those whose sympathies lay with the Kuomintang. Police General Phao decided to take advantage of the split. Announcing the discovery of a communist plot—such discoveries were to be commonplace and a feature of the policy of future governments—he ordered the mass arrests of Chinese. There was a witch-hunt amongst Chinese societies, firms and schools. The Un-Thai Activities Act of 1952 was passed, by which anyone who had any connections with a communist organization or attempted to proselytize was given a prison term of from five to ten years.

Phao, through extortion, made vast sums out of the Chinese. He took large bribes from Chinese merchants and even did a deal with the Chinese communists. If they could pay they were left alone, but a 'squeeze' was put on the rank and file.

In January 1953 Peking proclaimed the inception of the Thai Autonomous People's Government in Yunnan. Peking had repeatedly been provoked by Bangkok and could hardly be blamed for some measure of retaliation. The propaganda called on Thai-speaking people, not only in Thailand but in South-east Asia, to throw off the yoke of American and Nationalist Chinese imperialism.

In 1954 Pridi broke his long silence, denounced the Pibul government and appealed to all Thais to unite.

Thailand was represented at the Bandung Conference in April 1955 by Prince Wan Waityakorn, one of her most brilliant diplomats. He had discussions with Chou-en Lai, who invited him to Peking. He assured Prince Wan that China had no designs on Thailand, and that the Thai Autonomous Republic had no significance outside China; further, that Pridi was not engaged in subversive activities. China was prepared to enter into negotiations over the question of citizenship for the Chinese minority in Thailand along the lines of the treaty reached with Indonesia, in spite of the absence of diplomatic relations between China and Thailand.

The report of these discussions made a profound impression in Thailand. Pibul's opponents were not slow in pointing out that Thailand was losing all chances of better relations with Peking through too close an involvement with the United States.

On his return from his world tour in 1955, Pibul's policy was less restrictive. The communists arrested in the alleged November 1952 plot were put on trial, and the Thai cabinet ministers went about red-faced when it was revealed that among those arrested there were more Thais than Chinese. Pibul was obliged to take Phao off Chinese affairs.

The Bangkok Press, both Thai and Chinese, took full advantage of the abolition of press censorship to attack S.E.A.T.O. and the United States. It was stated that Thailand was an American satellite, and this threatened her traditional good relations with China. Burma, Indonesia and Cambodia were cited as examples where neutralism brought in handsome dividends. Pibul's government, surprisingly, did not hit back, and the Press continued to enjoy their freedom.

When Pibul fell and Sarit took over, more repressive measures against the Chinese minority were imposed. Several Chinese were executed for setting fire to buildings. They were denounced as communists. Sarit interrogated them in person, and the death sentence was carried out promptly. It is more likely that they were arsonists than communists. There is a well-established practice in South-east Asia for shops, warehouses and buildings to be burnt down when the insurance is due. It has become too easy to blame communists and communist subversion for unexplained crimes and incidents in Thailand. The Peking government warned Sarit that they could not stand idly by while their nationals were slaughtered. Then Sarit was not convinced that he would have the support of the United States if he was too aggressive towards China.

The anti-communist rôle which Thailand has adopted for so long is largely responsible for the absence of official relations with the People's Republic of China. Many Thais do not support the official view. At official functions in honour of Taiwan and attended by S.E.A.T.O. and the Western powers, influential Thais have said to me, "Just think, all this for a China of 10 million souls, and we ignore the real one with over 650 millions."

Sarit alternated between policies of repression and *rapprochement*. In 1960 he was considering an eventual take-over of all Chinese shops and all commerce. If this was intended as a sop to the nationalists it fell on deaf ears. It was declared impractical, and he had the good sense to abandon it. The immigrant quota was kept at 200 annually, and every immigrant was required to invest or deposit about 1,600 pounds as a proof of financial independence, as well as payment of a residence permit and poll tax. These

measures kept the Chinese population in check. Thirty years ago
the quota was 100,000.

There is little doubt that some of the Chinese societies, guilds
and associations are under the influence of Peking. The largest,
the powerful Teochiu Association, owns schools and a cemetery,
and it was well known that it was controlled by Peking for some
years. Chinese associations look after their fellow countrymen.
They set up schools, hospitals, run their own employment
bureaux and support those in need. It is small wonder that the
bonds between members of the Chinese minority are close.

Total bans on all goods from the Chinese mainland have been
enforced on the grounds that the income from them was used to
finance the activities of Chinese agents in Thailand. But at times
there has been an outcry that the ban increased the cost of
living.

There have been demands in the press that the Chinese in
Bangkok be required to reside in Chinatown. The official attitude
towards the Chinese in Thailand is at times perplexing to the
foreigner. Laws and regulations are made, and then ways are
found around them by the very people one would expect to
support them. The host country and the guests appear to come to
terms with a simplicity and nicety which compels some measure
of admiration. For example, Chinese companies, factories, banks,
shipping firms and other concerns invite influential Thais to serve
on the board of directors. These include army generals, police
generals, even cabinet ministers. Then usually all is well. The
farmer brings his rice to the mill, which he knows is almost
certain to be owned by a Chinese, and is content.

Far more Chinese in Thailand support Peking than Taiwan,
and the Bangkok government is well aware of it, just as they know
that the position is exactly the same with the overwhelming
majority of the Thais, and even among the cabinet ministers.

Where so many foreign observers misjudge the situation is by
assuming that China's propaganda is directed principally at their
nationals in Thailand. China wants Thailand to break with the
United States. She urges Thailand to be neutralist or, better still,
to move over to her camp. Her fellow Chinese or 'near Chinese'
in Thailand can do little on their own. They are too closely
watched. In any case they require no open outside propaganda.
(The propaganda and subversive activities which Peking organizes

against Thailand are referred to in the concluding chapter of this book.)

The Chinese minority is an obvious target for communist infiltration and subversive activities. It is also a convenient scapegoat for failures of government policies and plans, a ready excuse for repressive measures over the whole country and for stricter security control. It has always provided a bargaining factor for American aid.

Yet, apart from the occasional outburst of anti-Chinese feeling, it is generally conceded that the Chinese have achieved a well-deserved and honoured place in Thai life. On the whole, both Thais and Chinese maintain an easy and friendly relationship.

Of all the states in South-east Asia, Thailand has been the most successful with the Chinese population, and she has the largest of them all. Strife and clashes in the future cannot be ruled out, but there is unlikely to be a repetition of the savage persecution which prevailed during the régime of Police General Phao. It would not have popular support. The United States would oppose it, and Peking might decide that it called for stronger action than a mere protest.

For centuries the Chinese have been coming to Thailand, bringing their skills and trades, their manners and customs with them. Over this vast passage of time, their roots have become embedded in all aspects of Thai life. The Thais and the Chinese are likely to go on living and working together throughout their national lives.

———————•❖•———————

There must be few visitors to Bangkok who do not make the journey to Angkor Wat in Cambodia. We had heard much about this former lost city before we left England.

"Angkor, as it stands, ranks as the chief wonder of the world today, one of the summits to which human genius has aspired in stone." So wrote Osbert Sitwell.

Soon after we had arrived in Thailand, my imagination was fired by an illustrated talk given by a Frenchman who had recently returned from a protracted stay, and we decided that we could not put off the visit any longer. It is a convenient and short journey by air, but we allowed ourselves to be influenced by the pleas of Hilary and Jacqueline to go by road. Apparently three of their classmates at their school in Bangkok had travelled in two cars. We did not learn until much later that they were jeeps.

Unless there has been a considerable improvement in road conditions, I strongly urge the tourist to make the journey by plane, and so avoid the strain on the nerves as well as the wear and tear of the car.

We made a very early start and drove through the deserted streets of the capital, to take the road which skirts Ayudhya and goes on to Saraburi. We had not gone very far when the car rocked violently while negotiating a log bridge. I thought that it was the movement of the logs. When we had cleared the bridge, the car was still difficult to handle. One of the tyres was flat. There was a large gash where a huge nail, which had been loosened by the weight and movement of the cars crossing the bridge, had torn into the tyre. We changed the wheel and drove on.

We were forced to make frequent and sudden diversions into the jungle because of road repairs or bridge-building. I had been warned to look out for the Washboard Stretch, so called because its surface was corrugated. Here the motorist is advised to travel at a minimum speed of fifty miles an hour in order to ride the corrugations.

All went well until it was necessary to slow down and take a right-hand diversion through the jungle again. Then the reduced speed made it very difficult to control the car on that surface. Clouds of red dust made us close the car windows until the stifling heat made us open them and swallow more dust.

We had no difficulty in leaving Thailand and were fortunate in being given an easy clearance and friendly welcome at the Cambodian frontier. The frontier authorities can sometimes be difficult, especially when relations between their country and Thailand are strained or if there has been an epidemic of smuggling.

There were more road diversions from the frontier onwards, and sometimes we had to drive on a rough jungle track for more than two miles before rejoining the main route only thirty yards from where we had left it. The red dust penetrated everywhere. It got into our luggage and coated our changes of clothing, and we arrived looking the worse for wear. We booked in at the 'Grand Hotel'. It has a superb situation with magnificent views.

After a quick shower and a meal, we set out and had not gone far when the awe-inspiring and majestic vastness of Angkor Wat rose up dark and forbidding, its outline standing out in bold relief against a blue sky. In front of the main building stretched a huge moat, and behind rose the tall towers of Angkor.

In an area of some fifty square miles are the ruins of 600 towers, temples and buildings of the great capital of the Khmers. This great empire produced a 'master race' which was the scourge of the Orient for 600 years. It shone with a grandeur unsurpassed by that of Babylon.

It stretched from the South China Sea to the Gulf of Siam and comprised all of present-day Cambodia, parts of Thailand, Vietnam and Laos. This empire was supported by slave labour. The warrior race subdued whole nations and brought back hundreds of thousands of slaves to quarry the rock and build their great edifices. The Khmers farmed the land and built a wonderful irrigation system, which ensured that there would be an ample supply of water. They raised huge armies and navies and trained large numbers of war elephants. The figure has been put as high as 150,000. The population was about 25 million. Angkor was the capital. Later Angkor Thom was developed as the city proper, and its peak population was over a million. In Angkor Thom, such architectural masterpieces as the Bayon, a temple with 200 stone faces, the Royal Palace, the Baphoon, the Elephant Terrace and the Terrace of the Leper King were constructed. Angkor Wat is the celebrated temple, often described as the eighth wonder of the world, and is built outside the city walls.

For centuries stories had circulated of the lost cities, but it was not until 1861 that the jungle revealed its secrets to an incredulous world. In that year a French naturalist, Henri Mouhot, was hacking a path through the dense jungle when he came upon the ruins of huge temples and enormous faces in stone. He spent several days there, and his astonishment grew as he came across scores of temples, palaces and galleries, all in ruins. Huge trees had burst through the thick ornate ceilings and roofs and had continued to grope their way upwards. Roots as thick as a man's thigh, and over thirty feet long, twisted and twined around the walls of vast buildings. Trees had taken root in the ceilings of towers and palaces. There were courtyards and halls. He saw hundreds of giant statues, some of which had overturned, and massive blocks of stone.

According to historians, the Siamese, who were the Khmers' vassals, attacked Angkor in 1431 and pillaged the capital. The Khmers succeeded in driving them out. A year later the city was deserted. The Khmers had disappeared without trace. The mystery has never been solved.

Several theories have been advanced, and each has its supporters. It is said that there was an uprising of the enormous slave population which had lived under conditions of great cruelty. According to another, the people had finally turned away from a religion which worshipped a god-king and which maintained a wealthy ecclesiastical hierarchy, who, in turn, supported the privileged upper classes and a class society. The upkeep of the magnificent and ornate temple buildings was a crushing burden imposed on the masses. Gradually they had been turning to the compassionate and democratic Hinayanist Buddhism, whose teachings made

Shipping the pottery in Bangkok

Visitors to Angkor Wat

Temple dancers in the Inner Courtyard of Angkor Wat

them yearn for peace. And so the Khmer kings could no longer rely upon the blind obedience and loyalty of their subjects. There is also the theory that the Khmer kings themselves were influenced by Buddhism and became less warlike. A less charitable conclusion is that a life of luxury and corruption had demoralized the Empire. One theory, which has some historical foundation, is that the Khmers were tired of having to resist the constant attacks of the Siamese and other rampaging states and moved their capital. Then there is the theory that a fearful plague was responsible.

Angkor Wat is the largest of thirty vast and varied collections of buildings. There are nine towers. It gives the impression of being even larger than it is because the galleries and towers are mirrored in the waters of the moat. Masses of pink lotus flowers on the water give a fragile beauty to the reflections. The moat is huge. Each of its four sides extends for about a mile. The walls of the central sanctuary are more than half a mile in length. It rises in three stages to a central cluster of five towers, the tallest of which reaches a height of 220 feet above the ground. Each tower is surmounted by a lofty pinnacle, shaped like a bursting lotus bud.

Three Buddhist monks were walking very slowly over the great causeway, their saffron robes lifting gently in the breeze. I was curious and followed them. I had not heard of a *wat* in the sanctuary, and I concluded that they were on a pilgrimage. And then I saw them disappear into one. It consisted of several wooden buildings, some with yellow roofs. This was their *wat*. It did not make too violent a contrast to the antiquity on all sides, for it was humble and unobtrusive. It was a reminder of the brotherhood of monks whose forebears had walked in the streets centuries ago, as well as a testimony to the permanence of Buddhism.

I rejoined my family, and we climbed up to the outer gallery of the main temple. All around us was an amazing sight. As we moved from terrace to terrace, from gallery to gallery, and stared down into innumerable courtyards, we saw in stone the story of the Khmer Empire unfolding before our eyes. Massive faces in stone stared at us from pillars, walls and terraces.

The sanctuary is so vast; there are so many rooms, and visitors move from one to another to admire more treasures, that for minutes one is entirely alone amid the silent and extensive ruins.

The effect of the solitude was to endow the figures with an identity, almost life itself. They were exquisitely carved. Temple dancers were everywhere and in fantastic abundance. They smiled at us from frames of fretted stone, they garlanded the towers, they were half hidden on the walled galleries. There were the large-breasted courtesans of Indra. Gods, demons, three-headed elephants, nine-headed serpents, and again more temple dancers, appeared wherever you walked. Yet, although we came across the same figures hundreds of times, they were not replicas of one pattern. Their faces were different, thus showing the individuality of the artists.

It was obvious that large numbers of artists were employed on this massive work, not only over the years but at the same time. We came across huge rooms which were schools of art and workshops. One enormous frieze, which spans the entire exterior of the temple, is a quarter of a mile long and is filled with life-size human figures.

The friezes and reliefs depict a most amazing variety of scenes, and many are striking and vivid, as well as rich in detail. These include war scenes. One, which I found particularly unpleasant, depicted a naval battle where a sailor had fallen overboard into the jaws of a crocodile. There is also the age-old attempt to win the elixir of eternal life. In this case the heavenly gods and the evil spirits combine to search for the elixir which lies at the bottom of the sea surrounding Mount Mandara. In the motif, a water god in the form of a snake, which must have been of prodigious length, is coiled around and around the mountain. The gods and demons pull at each end of the serpent, churning up the sea. When the mountain is about to disintegrate under this enormous pressure, the god Vishnu transforms himself into an enormous tortoise and supports the entire weight on his upper body. Amid the churning, strange creatures come from the sea. Among them is the girl Vishnu later marries. He finds the elixir of life at the bottom of the sea, foils an attempt by the demons to steal it and returns with it to the sacred mountains of Meru.

The everyday life of the ordinary Khmer is preserved in perpetuity by a series of reliefs, showing the building of the wooden huts, fishing and rice cultivation. The simple life of the peasants in these parts has not changed much over the centuries.

We walked back over the long causeway. It is 380 yards long, and on either side is a Naga serpent balustrade. The Naga snake is the water god. This balustrade is supported on massive stone blocks, and, where the line is broken to allow passage to one or other of the buildings, the snakes raise their heads with their hoods flared.

At the hotel that night we were told that the number of figures of men and animals exceeded 20,000. I was not surprised for I was sure that the elephants I had seen ran into several hundreds. The scenes from the Hindu epics of the Ramayana and Mahabharata extended for 700 feet.

We spent the next day wandering leisurely through the ruins and finding more wonders. The work of Nature left undisturbed was in this case a little fearful. Twisted and knotted roots of banyan trees framed the faces of gods, and the enormous pressure of the enfolding roots had split the faces. Where there was an opening, the probing root had found it. On some figures the roots were plaited like snakes in an embrace, then they flattened out to disappear under the sweeping arms of another tree.

We stared down in wonder at huge water tanks and at the steps which led down to them. Here elephants by the hundred had come down to bathe.

We climbed once again into one of the galleries for a last look round. Two elderly peasants, a man and his wife, climbed slowly and breathlessly up the steps. They stopped just in front of me, and I would have liked to have taken their photographs, but there was a dignity about them both, a desire for privacy, which made them completely unaware of the presence of others. Each held in withered, gnarled hands a bunch of flowers. The wrinkled, deeply-lined face of the man smiled encouragingly at his companion. She nodded. They continued on their way. In a few minutes they were back. Hilary whispered to me, "What have they done with the flowers?" Jacqueline went up the steps and disappeared. Then she reappeared and walked over to her sister.

We all went in. Against some fallen pieces of stone which had been fashioned into a crude form of shrine, the flowers reposed. I had the feeling that this very old couple did this often. It was their pilgrimage, and I found myself wondering what sorrow they shared which made them do this, or whether it was just an impersonal gesture of worship. The previous day I had come across smouldering sticks of incense, but I had not seen anyone light them. There were no people about, and there were no flowers.

The next day we drove to Angkor Thom. We walked over a causeway bordered on each side by stone giants. Their faces are uncompromising, even threatening. Beneath their arms they hold up a huge stone naga, the sacred serpent which girdles the earth. The multi-cobra heads rear up under the fan of joined heads. Each serpent forms a balustrade for the causeway, which leads to the south gate of Angkor Thom. There were fifty-four giants in each balustrade. This made a total of 540. Some are damaged; there are signs that others have crashed into the moat, but the causeway has a menacing appearance. The giants in their squatting position are between six and eight feet high.

Beyond the causeway we found the object of our visit. This was the Bayon temple. We entered a labyrinth of narrow galleries. Climbing from terrace to terrace we came to the top. Here we gazed up at 200 huge faces on fifty stone towers.

I looked at the central sanctuary and recalled what I had been told the previous night by a commercial artist staying at the hotel. The slaves who had built this place under the orders of King Jayavarman were strangled and buried under the walls in order that their spirits might guard the temple. The guardian monk had his tongue cut out so that he could not reveal the secrets of the temple, including where the treasures were buried.

We left the Bayon and came upon the Great Square of Angkor Thom, where the court attended the royal functions or watched entertainments, and then we made our way to the terrace of the Leper King. The king is represented as a life-sized figure of a man without sex organs and is seated on a stone slab. It is reputed to be either a statue of Yasovarman, who founded Angkor, or of Jayavarman, creator of Bayon, but a more authoritative source declares that it is not a king at all, but a judge in Hell, and that it bears no evidence of leprosy.

That evening I stared across at Angkor Wat from my bedroom window and marvelled at the work of construction. Those huge blocks of stone must have weighed several tons, yet they were moved into position with only primitive hoists. Block fitted so perfectly to block that there was no need for cement, although the Khmers had invented a vegetable glue which was very strong.

The French restoration teams have worked wonders. When they cleared the jungle, the protection which the trees and vegetation had afforded the buildings for centuries was removed. The sandstone began to disintegrate from the attacks of a water-borne bacilli. The archaeologists were able to prevent further disintegration by dismantling the ruins, where necessary, and reconstituting them on a strong concrete base, surrounded by drainage pipes. In this way, they were able to treat the affected parts with antibiotics.

What was life like in this city of the 'master race'? They left records in the form of inscriptions on papyrus and wood, but the heat and humidity have obliterated them. Fortunately there is an account of a mission made by Chou Ta-kuan, who was sent to Angkor in A.D. 1292 by the Chinese Emperor, Timur Khan.

He writes of a magnificent city, where the roofs of gold shone in the sun. The window-frames were of gold, and on the buildings of lesser importance the roofs were of copper. The magnificent public buildings were of yellow porcelain. Huge columns supported the terraces, and were sculptured with many *garudas* (Hindu demi-gods, part man, part bird). The galleries had been lavishly designed and decorated. He tells us of thousands of dancing girls in the palace grounds, and that in the royal processions the king was preceded by hundreds of these girls, followed by wagons drawn by goats or horses, with golden harness.

The large numbers of parasols were decorated with gold, and had golden handles. The king stood on an elephant, so that all could see him. He wore armour with golden jewellery and pearls around his neck, ankles and wrists, in such abundance that they almost weighed him down. The elephants' tusks were gilded. "In the King's palace there is a golden tower, on top of which the King sleeps. In the tower is the spirit of a nine-headed serpent, Master of the Earth, and the whole Kingdom. This serpent appears in the form of a woman with whom the King sleeps."

The communities were class-ridden. Some of the wealthy Khmers had more than a hundred slaves. Only the very poor had none at all. Social status was judged by the size and style of the house. The higher orders were allowed to use tiles, the lower ones had to make do with thatch for their roofs. When high officials rode through the streets, they drove in palanquins with golden litters and four gold-handled parasols.

Chou Ta-kuan was puzzled by some of the customs. Apparently the people bathed too often, and this he considered responsible for certain illnesses. "There are women who urinate standing. It is ridiculous!" Funeral processions included flags, banners and the playing of musical instruments. As the *cortège* proceeded on its way, grilled rice was thrown. Mats were used instead of coffins, and the body was left in some desolate spot outside the city to await the dogs and vultures.

He writes of the high prestige enjoyed by the educated classes, the annual custom of presenting a jar of human gall to the king, and has high praise for the system of irrigation with artificial tanks and canals, as well as the methods of cultivation. It is a detailed and descriptive report and ranges over a wide sphere. There is mention of the peculiar ritual of the Buddhist monks in deflowering young girls.

Chou Ta-kuan describes the sparkling scenes on festival days. There were firework displays, wild boar hunts, pavilions decorated with flowers and lanterns. His reference to the ceremony of Washing the Buddhas and to the thousands of saffron-robed monks who walked through the streets every morning with their alms bowls is some indication of the spread of Buddhism. That the omnipotent king-emperors allowed this, suggests that they may have become more democratic and humane, abjured the old cult, and accepted the teachings of the Enlightened One.

But no one knows the story of the last days. With the disappearance of all human life, the jungle and the wild beasts took over. These included elephants, tigers, panthers, rhinoceroses, bears, crocodiles, deer and monkeys. The Khmer Empire, which had lasted for 600 years, disappeared, and remained concealed for another 450.

As one gives a final glance at the Giant Causeway, one has the feeling that these ranks of giant figures, with their fixed and forbidding stare, guard the secrets.

All visitors to Thailand who intend staying there several months should visit the south. This region is quite unlike any other part of the kingdom. Here one finds the Moslem Malay provinces. Here is Islam in Thailand.

It is quite a shock to find that three out of every four children do not speak Thai and attend Islamic schools, that Friday, and not Sunday, is the holy day. Here is polygamy, for the religion allows men to have four wives. Boys wear the fez and chat to each other in the Malay tongue. Girls walk with averted eyes. They are aloof, but they are allowed more freedom than in Islam countries. The muezzin calls the faithful to prayer.

As you drive on, you pass *wats* and yellow robes and realize that this is Thailand. You drive past a farm and are surprised to see pigs. But this is a Chinese settlement! Not far away is Moslem land, and there pigs are an abomination. It takes some time to get one's bearings. However, in spite of so many features so blatantly Islamic, the Moslem community appears to live harmoniously with the Thai and Chinese, the latter whom they greatly outnumber.

In Bangkok there is an 'Islamic Adviser to the Thai Government', watching over the interests of the Moslem minority—there are nearly 2 million of them—and working in close contact with the different ministries. For the Bangkok government attaches great importance to the establishment of smooth relations with those in the south and is taking an active interest in their welfare, although observers maintain that it has been long delayed and has only been prompted by the political situation.

Malays have settled in the south of Thailand for centuries. In 1474 the ruler of Kedah was a Moslem prince. Towards the end of the fifteenth century Islam had spread all over modern Malaya and into Siam's four southern provinces of Yala, Pattani, Naradhivat and Satul. Buddhism appears to have had sufficient support to halt the northerly thrust.

The Siamese kings extended the same tolerance to Islam as to Christianity. They gave financial assistance towards the building of mosques. As a step towards assimilation, and to assist integration throughout the educational structure, as well as to offset the appeal from Malaysia, a new university, the Songkla Nakarina or University of the South, is due to be opened in the near future at Haadyai, while a College of Education and Arts is being built in Pattani.

The Moslem communities are well organized. In addition to the very active Thai Muslim Women's Foundation of Thailand, founded in 1955, there are some 200 Moslem societies. They provide homes for orphans and help the needy. Yet assimilation and integration have been very slow in the past. As I assessed it during my visit, any marked advance in these directions is still a long way off. The Moslems stand fast by their old customs and traditions. Young Moslems must do their service with the Thai colours, just as ordinary Thais, but the fact that four out of five speak Malay, and not many of them speak Thai, does not promise well for the development of close bonds between Thais and Moslems. The Moslems are not oppressed. It is possible that they enjoy a slight advantage over the Buddhists. Both creeds are, of course, subject to the laws of the land, but the Moslems have the protection of the 1945 Decree of the Patronage of Islam, as well as the 1947 Act concerning the mosques. In Courts of the First Instance, where Islamic law is observed, one of the judges is a Moslem. When two Moslems are in dispute over an inheritance, the Islamic law is applied.

The inhabitants of the Moslem Malay provinces have a deep respect and affection for the Thai monarchy. In March 1968 there was much enthusiasm, as well as demonstrations of loyalty and devotion, in the provinces, when the King received a white elephant. This animal has no sanctity where Moslems are concerned, but they realize that it is sacred to the Buddhists, and so they provided a fitting and elaborate setting to the ceremony.

There have been outbursts against the Government. The Malays are inclined to resent Thai rule. Fundamentally, there is little affinity between the two races. Many Moslem Malays would prefer union with Malaysia. Critics maintain that the Government could have been more active in the past with development schemes. The provinces are under-developed, but the potential is high.

The strategic geographical importance of this region places it in a favourable position in any negotiations with Bangkok. It extends for roughly 600 miles to the Malaysian border and is lapped by the Gulf of Thailand and the China Sea on the east; in the west it is flanked by the Tennasserim range of mountains which borders part of Burma. The region is irrigated by six rivers. The mountain range renders jungle encroachment impossible. There are areas of great natural beauty; pleasant valleys, sandy beaches with tall limestone rocks, white and gold pagodas, the sombre mosques and the background of the purple mountains.

Songkla lies at the entrance to a large inland sea. It was to this port that King Prajadipok travelled in 1933 at the time of the Royalists' Insurrection. The inland sea is protected from the ravages of the ocean by a strip of half-submerged jungle land. In parts it is very beautiful, dotted here and there with tiny islets. On the opposite shore stands the town of Pattalung, which lies on the main railway line to Penang.

Songkla had a long and colourful history as a hide-out for Chinese pirates, who resisted all attempts by the Siamese to drive them out. They were magnificent seamen, resourceful and intrepid. In the end they turned from piracy to trade, became law-abiding citizens and founded settlements.

Pattani was formerly an important town. It had been forced to accept Siamese and Malayan overlordship for years, but it had made several attempts to gain independence. Its decline was due to the rise of Singapore and to faster ships.

Southern Thailand has the heaviest rainfall of the country, with rain falling almost the entire year, the amount ranging from 60 to 120 inches. The population is mainly concentrated in the town of Pattalung, Pattani, Chumporn, Nakornsrithamarat and Suratthani. Overall density is low.

It is the principal rubber-growing area in the kingdom. Rubber was first introduced from Malaya in 1901. It got off to a very slow start, and forty years afterwards only about 35,000 acres had been planted. In the years following the end of World War II there was a big expansion. The Thai government realized that they had a valuable export market. The acreage was doubled, then further increased. In 1965 the output was nearly 200,000 tons, which placed Thailand third among the world producers of rubber.

It was in the rubber plantations that I had my first experience of resentment over the alleged incompetence and apathy of the Government, although I suspected that a little more local efficiency might have helped production. A Chinese overseer was explaining to me the various stages in the growth of the trees, for I had told him that I knew absolutely nothing about rubber, other than what I had read. He said that more than double the existing acreage could be put down to rubber and that the yield would be increased if terraces were used. Two outstanding needs were more efficient management and replanting with better trees. Apparently half the trees were uneconomic. There had been gross neglect. The plantation owners had to wait until 1960 for the passing of the Cess Act which made funds available for replanting. The new trees take six to seven years to mature. He had a strong admiration for the methods further south—in Malaysia. I had read a report on rubber production and costs, and it showed that Thai rubber costs 50 per cent more to produce than Malaysian rubber. However, even under existing conditions, the output has shown a tremendous increase in recent years. Rubber is second in export to tin.

There are rich deposits of tin in the island of Bhuket, as well as other parts of the peninsular region. The output two years ago was 20,000 metric tons, all of which were exported. Two-thirds of this yield is provided by several hundred Chinese-worked mines, the remainder comes from those owned by British and Australian companies, where modern techniques are employed. Again I heard talk of frustration and further instances of government apathy, but it would appear that there is an answer here. The Thai National Economic Board admits that the mines have not been working up to full capacity, but points out that, according to the International Tin Agreement, Thailand can only produce an allotted quota. This simple explanation is not easily understood by the Chinese owners and workers.

The yield of wolfram has increased considerably during the past ten years, but the board has had to control the production in view of the falling prices on the world market.

The wealth of the Moslem Malay provinces has yet to be explored. The initial resources are extensive and varied. In addition to tin and wolfram, they include iron, copper, manganese and alluvial gold.

It is a most fascinating region. Broadly speaking, the Moslems and the Chinese practise their own form of apartheid. The former follow the teachings and laws of the Prophet, although they are not always as strict in their observances as in Arab countries. The Chinese hold fast to their much more ancient customs and preserve their very old traditions. However, this apartheid is accepted and respected on both sides. Each people holds its separate festivals, ceremonies and functions as its forefathers did. The Thais watch it all with interest and with a tolerance which is a characteristic of the race.

The Bangkok government has been deeply concerned over the political situation in the provinces. The emergence of the independent Islamic state of Malaya was watched with some anxiety. The Thais had become used to having the British as their neighbours, both in Malaya and Burma. The defeat of the Burmese in 1826 by the British had put an end to the repeated invasions of her territory. Malaysia was an unknown quantity. They appeared to derive undue comfort from the realization that Tunku Abdul Rahman, Prime Minister of Malaysia, had a Thai mother. There was much sentimental talk of the ties which were bound to exist because of this connection.

If Malaysia were involved in a war with Indonesia, which country has the largest armed forces in South-east Asia, and were defeated, then Thailand would have a mighty Islamic Empire right on her borders, which could exert much influence upon the Islamic minority in her country. This fear is never far from the minds of her politicians.

Then China, as always, is feared. If the Chinese minority took over the entire economy of the south, they too could bring pressure to bear on the Government. They could even use as a pretext the defence of the Islamic religion, if it suited their policy.

The communist threat is not underestimated. It never is in

Thailand. When, after the end of the emergency in Malaya, the Central Executive Committee of the Malayan Communist Party failed to take over Malaya by force, they fled to the Moslem Malay provinces, where they soon established easy relations with the inhabitants. They are Chinese, and their leader, Chin Peng, is a veteran guerrilla fighter. An American adviser in the rubber plantations pulled my leg good-naturedly when talking of this formidable character to me. "And you Limeys gave him the O.B.E. and put him in the Victory Parade through London!" It was true, but Chin Peng had rendered valuable assistance against the Japanese during the war.

Chin Peng set up his headquarters in the Betong salient. He has established the Malaysian People's Liberation Army and organized the training. It is said that he has arranged an educational programme, which includes lessons in the Chinese language and history. Chinese businessmen and workers help to finance these activities, either voluntarily or by coercion. M.P.L.A. has achieved only moderate success on the Malaysian side, even less in the Moslem Malay provinces. It is important to remember that the Malays and the Chinese are split by cultural and political differences which cannot be bridged by communism.

They retain their differences even when small numbers of Malays are won over to Chinese communism. This was shown when a M.P.L.A. camp was overrun by security forces, and it was discovered that there were two kitchens, one for the non-pork-eating Malays, the other for the Chinese. There were separate sleeping quarters. Signs and instructions were in both languages. M.P.L.A. has eventually realized that the Moslems are difficult to indoctrinate, and now concentrates on the Chinese. But even after ten years' propaganda, the number of known communists is estimated to be less than a 1,000, mostly Chinese. It would appear that the Moslem Malay provinces are not fertile ground for communism and that the threat has been exaggerated.

The affinity between the Moslem Malays in the south and their brethren across the border is too close to be easily disrupted by Chinese agitators and infiltrators, although they are well-trained at their job. The Federation of Malaysia is too occupied with its own internal problems to make any emotional, mystical or militant appeal to fellow Moslems in another country with which it has long been at peace. In any case there is little to be gained by such action. Large numbers of those in the southern provinces are well content with their lot.

Over the centuries, the Moslem Malays of Thailand have made an important contribution to the economy and prosperity of the kingdom. They are excellent farmers and fishermen. Their settlements are to be found all over the south and are well run. Although they are more heavily concentrated in Pattani, Yala and Naradhivat—for these regions formed the old kingdom of Pattani, ruled long by queens—they have settled and flourished in Bhuket, Trang and Ranong. Former prisoners of war found homes in the province of Nakornsrithamarat.

This is indeed a most complex and difficult part of Thailand to administer and must prove a veritable headache. But it is rich, and with development schemes it would yield big dividends.

With abundance of fish in the sea, rivers and lakes, ample provision for cattle, fertile lands for agricultural crops, its beautiful and varied scenery and the vast mineral resources, I thought that southern Thailand could be as fair a region as any in the kingdom.

Signposts to the Future

———————— ··✥·· ————————

Thailand has the strongest economy in South-east Asia. During the past ten years its growth has averaged 6½ per cent. Her currency is firm. Her population is soaring. A hundred years ago it was 5½ millions; fifty years ago it had increased to 8½ millions. In 1950 it was 18½ millions; in 1960 25½ millions. The Thai Technical and Economic Commission forecasts 45 millions by 1980.

With an area of 198,000 square miles, it is about the size of France. The average food consumption is high when compared with other countries of South-east Asia. In agricultural growth alone, it leads the countries of Asia. Farm production has increased by 90 per cent in the past ten years.

Extensive plans are in hand for the improvement of crop yields in her commercial and subsistence farming. Large-scale irrigation projects will harness the vast resources of the Mekong basin. Railways and roads are being extended. An excellent network of roads links Bangkok with the provinces. Communications between the up-country towns are being improved.

Her powerful friend, the United States, guards her frontiers and continues to pour vast sums of money into the country. And yet there is unease where there should be confidence and security, restlessness where there should be an atmosphere of tranquillity. It may well be that the boom has developed too quickly or that the changes have been too sweeping and too sudden. It is doubtful whether the Thais appreciate the implications of the political issues involved. Here some are real, while others are misrepresented to suit political forces and motives. There are two Thai-lands. One is Bangkok; the other is the rest of the kingdom. The wages and working conditions of the farmers in the north-east have not improved to any appreciable extent. The professional classes are little better off than they were fifteen years ago.

Large sums of money have been invested in the hotel industry and in building blocks of luxury apartments. In 1960 there were about ten first-class hotels. Today there are twenty-five. The hotel industry depends upon contracts from American forces; much of the luxury accommodation on American personnel and other foreign residents. Bangkok housing has enjoyed an unprecedented boom. Land fetches astronomical prices. A shutdown of even a few of the American bases would throw thousands out of work.

A process of Americanization is spreading over the country. The development and modernization of some towns during the past ten years has been quite spectacular. The massive American bases have created problems for the Bangkok government. Although they have given a measure of security to the country, they have made the capital vulnerable. If America pulls out of Thailand, these bases, with their strategic highways, could well constitute a threat, both internally and externally. Prince Bowora-det led the Monarchist Revolution in 1933 from Korat, when it was quite a minor town. In any case, Bangkok will have to reckon on the growing importance of some of the provincial towns.

American jeeps speed all over the country. Their planes sweep the skies, their motor launches patrol the huge Mekong. Their soldiers drive through the streets, eat in their restaurants, spend lavishly in the numerous night clubs and clip joints which cater especially for them. To the average Thai the ordinary American private soldier is a man of wealth.

Trucks, jeeps and utility vans, sporting the emblem of the clasped hands and the Stars and Stripes, can be seen in quite small towns. Officials of the American-Aid Programme travel from province to province or work on projects at different centres. Their field experts advise on agriculture, irrigation, fishing and the social services. The Peace Corps—one of America's finest exports—does a splendid job in outlying areas.

The American impact upon education is tremendous. One day, I went into an up-country school to borrow a pair of pliers and a hammer for emergency repairs to my car. The headmaster handed me a box of tools, each one with the imprint of the American flag. Typewriters, chemical apparatus, refrigerators, dynamos and generators were similarly adorned. The pupils were left in no doubt as to the identity of the donor.

Thousands of Thai teachers and students have received free study fellowships to universities in the United States and have returned with American degrees. As British universities require higher entrance qualifications from their candidates, many young Thais who pay their own expenses opt for American universities, which also recognize the Thai Bachelor degree as a step to the Master's. This recognition is not granted in Britain. One drawback to the system is that American university degrees are given far too easily, when they should be awarded to an intelligent *élite* only. The Thais are well aware of the low prestige value of some American degrees, but as they have admitted quite freely to me, "They are easier, we get them more quickly, and the graduate allowance is the same whether we are graduates from Oxford or Arizona." On one occasion I shocked a high official of the Thai Ministry of Education with examples of two highly intelligent school teachers who had passed their Secondary Teacher's Certificate but had later been rejected for Chulalongkorn University to study for their B.A. They were awarded an American fellowship and returned with a degree. This particular case showed that it was easier for a Thai national to obtain a degree from an American university than from his own. It may have been an exceptional case, but it revealed a deplorable situation where degrees from any university are concerned.

From their studies in the United States, they bring back with them American customs which they try to incorporate into the Thai system or structure, sometimes with a fair degree of success, although these additions are alien to Thai culture. One example here is the parade of the students of Chulalongkorn and Thammasat universities, complete with bands, majorettes and cheerleaders, on the occasion of the annual football match. I have not, however, met anyone who has been able to introduce the militant P.T.A. into the schools. Some things are not for export!

If a school in a rural area decides to form a Young Farmers' Club, then some enthusiast from the American-Aid mission will arrive promptly, complete with films, film strips and literature. Of course, the club will be modelled on the lines of the American

4H (run on the fourfold aim in improving head, heart, hands and health).

Hospitals, schools, waterways, roads, irrigation works, agricultural, mining, industrial and technological projects and undertakings—America directs, or is involved in them all. Thailand owes much to the American-built highways for the improvement in her agriculture.

Are the Americans liked by the Thais? I think that there is no doubt that they are. It is difficult to dislike these friendly and generous people who visit a teacher-training college, draft out syllabuses—even if they are forgotten as soon as they leave—present the college with motor coaches to take the students to practising schools, hand out a few fellowships and a goodly supply of expensive equipment and help them so much in various ways. It is true that other countries also make contributions, but America is way out in front.

And the United States is determined that Thailand shall be aware of the extent of the aid. I have listened to American speakers addressing the Rotary Club and Anglo-American associations, discussion groups and clubs on the subject of American aid and its increase over past years. Newspapers carry photographs of official functions, where a Thai cabinet minister or other official is receiving from the Head of U.S.O.M. or other aid mission some item of equipment. It is broadcast on the radio. It is featured on television.

All Thais look upon the U.S.A. as a powerful and enormously wealthy country. American films have done much to encourage this outlook. They are not only shown in the capital. I have seen trucks drive into up-country areas, and American officials rig up portable screens and give film shows watched by large crowds. For the intellectuals, U.S.I.S. (the United States Information Service) offers an excellent library. Some of the books have a strong political and pro-American bias. Americans are the most demonstratively patriotic of all nationals in Thailand.

The proud place which Britain occupied for over a century has been taken over by America. Britain's contribution to Thailand's economy is small and in any case receives little publicity. She has not recovered from the humiliation of Suez. Here American prestige soared. I was in the Bamboo Bar of the 'Oriental Hotel' in Bangkok at the time of Suez, listening to a news broadcast.

13

Valluya, Vichit and two others were with me. The voice of the American announcer for the Thailand news service was angry and blatant: "Eden asked for two days' delay, but General Eisenhower was adamant. Get out and stay out!"

My young Thai friends looked embarrassed. "Thou shalt have no other country but me!" said Valluya sarcastically, looking at the radio with distate.

"Why don't the British go ahead?" an elderly Thai asked me politely.

Before I could reply, his friend interrupted him: "They told the British that they would smash their economy. France couldn't go it alone!"

Two Frenchmen sitting in the lounge jumped to their feet, glared at everyone in the lounge, as if looking for Americans, and stalked out into the street.

American friendliness is more easily understood than British reserve. A handful of British residents and Thais, all graduates of Oxbridge, meet for an annual reunion dinner. "The *élite* of Thailand!" said one Cambridge graduate to me. I doubt whether he was as impressed as he appeared to be. There might have been some truth in the claim twenty years ago. Then, eleven out of twelve Directors-General of one Ministry were Oxbridge graduates. Today, more than half are graduates from American universities.

However, the traditional liking and respect for the British and the British way of life persists, particularly among the older generation. Today there are 1,000 young Thais studying in British schools and universities.

The Thais have supported America over Vietnam, and in 1968 sent over 25,000 Thai soldiers there. Yet, although the Thais may like the Americans they meet, and the majority of those who have visited the country have pleasant recollections of their stay, there is a widespread distrust of the American government and American policy. Allegations that the South East Asia Supply Corporation, which has strong links with the American Central Intelligence Agency, financed Phao in his drive against political suspects were believed and aroused widespread resentment.

I listened to a talk given by an eminent Thai historian. He acknowledged Thailand's debt to America, then went on to examine critically what he called her uncertain and conflicting policy. He said that she could be absolutely ruthless where her own interests were concerned. She had betrayed Laos and was responsible for the chaos existing in that country today. Tracing her actions over the past years, he said that she could have saved Dien Bien Phu, that France implored her assistance, but she refused. In spite of her uncompromising opposition to communism, there was evidence of American ships discharging freight in Hong Kong for shipment to Red China. The deaf ear she had turned to the appeals of the Jews up to the outbreak of World War II encouraged Hitler to go ahead with his policy of liquidation. He concluded by saying that American policy was often quite unpredictable to foreigners, and that he did not think that she would confront Peking or Moscow over Thailand. I have heard the same sentiments expressed elsewhere.

President Johnson's decision to meet the Vietnamese representatives in Paris was unjustly termed another American 'climbdown', but the description was another example of Thailand's suspicions of her formidable ally.

The view of the man in the street in Bangkok is that Thailand may have to pay a heavy price for her line-up with America, but that American withdrawal would put her in a most critical situation. She would be in a most vulnerable position if she found herself with a thousand-mile common frontier with a communist state. In any case, Thailand is not an easy country to defend. She has a common boundary with Malaysia in the south, and is bounded on the west and north-east by Burma, and to the north and north-east by Laos and Cambodia. She has no common boundary with China. The Chinese province of Yunnan is separated from the Thai northern border by a narrow stretch of Lao and Burmese territory.

The Thai Armed Forces have been increased. There are 100,000 army regulars and conscripts, a trained reserve of double that number, an air force of 20,000 and a para-military and counter-insurgency force of about 60,000. All able-bodied men between the ages of 21 and 30 are required to serve two years with the colours, seven years with the First Reserve, ten years with the Second Reserve and six years with the Third Reserve.

It has been Thailand's official policy to encourage the Americans in their belief that there is serious communist infiltration. The result is that the communist threat has been exaggerated out of all proportion. There has always been a touch of the dramatic in the reports of subversive activities. Agents have been dropped by parachute, or helicopters have made landings in deserted places. Here, it should be remembered that Thailand's frontiers are very easy to cross and that communications are so inadequate in some parts of the disaffected north-east that anyone coming down in a deserted place is likely to remain undiscovered. There have been midnight trips across the Mekong. Communist cells have been 'discovered' in amazing places. The men of the saffron robes have made "private but frank admission of their political views". And so the sensational stories circulate and are too easily believed.

One can only view with dismay the conflicting pronouncements by the Bangkok government concerning the political situation in the north-east. In February 1968 the Prime Minister declared that terrorists were everywhere, including the west. The following month he stated that not a single life had been lost in the north-east during the past eight months. Critics of the Government say that too many ministers have never been outside the capital and are therefore completely out of touch.

Despite massive propaganda and vast sums of money from the People's Republic of China and Moscow, the number of known communists in the north-east in 1968 was officially stated to be about 1,400. The communist campaign in Thailand has always been alien. The leaders are non-Thai. Communism in Thailand is not united, not dedicated and not permanent. Peking propaganda suffers from a wearisome monotony. There is the continual attack on the presence of American forces and the Bangkok government, which is declared to be an American puppet. The Thais are warned to protect their womenfolk from the 'lecherous Americans'.

In 1965, Peking realized that progress was very slow, and stepped up its propaganda. The Thai Independence Group and the Thai Patriotic Front were formed. The following year, a League of Patriotic Youth of Thailand was established. The headquarters in each case was Peking. The alarm bells began to ring furiously in Bangkok, but the threat was not viewed with much anxiety. There has always been the danger that the Bangkok government would 'cry wolf' too often. The obsession with communism is mainly responsible for the present military régime. 'Leftish' views are promptly labelled communist.

There is always the threat of attack from outside her borders, but at the present time China is fully occupied with internal problems arising from her cultural revolution. I have been told by quite a few Thai observers that the People's Republic cannot count upon internal unity. The Thais understand the Chinese mentality.

It is extremely unlikely that a situation comparable to that of North Vietnam could arise. The Thais are deeply loyal to their royal family. Buddhism is centralized under the king. Then the country is not divided. Moreover, it has never been colonized and has none of the problems which confront the newly dependent states.

Two years after Sarit's successful *coup*, I was sitting in a café in Roi-Ed, a province deep in the north-east, when a Thai army captain asked if he could join me. He said that he had been explaining the necessity for a road diversion to a group of farmers and peasants and that they had declared that they had not heard of Field Marshal Sarit. Before many minutes had passed he had seen the amusing side and was laughing heartily, but he admitted that he could not take that story back to Bangkok. The 'Old Man' would not laugh! He said that the King and Queen were much loved and that the Thai peasants were not politically conscious.

The possibility of unrest among the students and the young intellectuals cannot be ruled out, although some foreign observers have maintained that this class is politically apathetic. This, in my opinion, is quite wrong. The Bangkok government does not dismiss them so easily. It was the demonstration of some 2,000 students of Chulalongkorn who lowered the flag to half-mast in memory of a dead democracy, then marched on Pibul's official residence as a protest against the rigged elections, that sparked off the 1957 revolution. They demanded fresh elections, with students on the vigilance committees. The same year, Mom Seni Pramoj, former Prime Minister and brilliant lawyer, denounced the students of Thamassat University for publishing an ideology hostile to Thai traditions. It may be of significance that the Rector of Thamassat is Minister of Defence, and the Rector of Chulalongkorn is Minister of the Interior. In March 1962 it was announced that a university police corps would be set up.

There has been a great increase in the university population and the number of students going on for higher education. The young intellectuals are consequently growing in numbers, and they are coming out into the open with their views. There was indignation and disgust over the disclosures of corruption and immorality following the death of Sarit. A large number of the 'intellectual school' felt that Thailand had been made to appear ludicrous, and Thai democracy a mockery in the eyes of the world. Those who have studied abroad, and the total runs into thousands, take a long time to settle down on their return. They are restless, resent privilege and feel that their education has fitted them for better posts than the ones they are forced to take.

They could well support a democratic movement in Bangkok. However, a strong force of police, including a special detachment of riot police, watches all agitators in the capital. The students and young intellectuals would need unity and a wide measure of support for any uprising to be successful.

They are unlikely to disseminate in the north-east provinces and the Moslem Malay south any revolutionary ideals they may have acquired through their studies and travels in the West. However, they are subjected to continual propaganda at home. The Russian form is shrewd, simple, but exercises an insidious influence. It does not ask for an alliance, but calls on them to agitate for a neutralist policy and a withdrawal from S.E.A.T.O. It criticizes an educational system which is unable to make use of their qualifications and talents. It dwells on the existing privileges and corruption which rob them of equal opportunities and a fair chance.

Propaganda is also directed at writers, artists, journalists and professors, but, in general, the extreme form sent out from Peking has been avoided. Yet Russia admits ruefully that she has had little success. Not all Russians encountered abroad are the reticent tight-lipped type one reads about. Two very jovial officials from a Russian trade mission were telling me of their experiences in Thailand, when two Roman Catholic priests joined us. I thought at first that it was an odd mixture, but all were soon on friendly terms. The elder Russian, who had been an artillery officer in World War II, gave his views with the air of a man who had given much thought to the subject, and had arrived at a judgment, which to him was final.

"You can't do much with these people. They're too light-hearted; they don't take life seriously. Your people have been working among them for over a hundred years. They've worn you down. What have you got to show for the money and effort? How far did Japan get? Peking has tried hard enough. So have we. They will go on taking all the money America cares to give them. And they'll change when it suits them. Then it will be from the inside, not from without."

One of the priests made the conventional, diplomatic comment, "There's a lot in what you say," but it was obvious that he and his colleagues were impressed.

Although Thailand is too prosperous at the present time for communism to take root, the 'Red Menace' has always provided an excellent excuse for the sudden imposition of repressive measures, including press censorship, and a periodic round-up of suspects. The Government attaches a degree of importance to the Press which foreigners find difficult to understand, for the circulation is so small. In Bangkok there are about twenty-five daily newspapers, of which two are in English and four in Chinese. The total circulation is under 250,000. In the provinces, there are thirty-seven weekly papers, many of which are short-lived.

The Government has always been suspicious of trades unions. Sarit declared that they provided scope for subversive activities. The Central Labour Party had a brief history. In 1949 it affiliated with the World Federation of Trades Unions. Later it was banned. Pibul organized the Thai National T.U.C. and gave it a grant. The leaders were police and army officers, and the members were composed of agricultural workers, fishermen and *samlor* drivers. When Pibul returned from his world tour, approval was again given to the formation of trades unions and the right to strike, but little progress was made. It was rather like unions of workers controlled by their employers.

The monarchy reinforces the Government. Only thirty-six years ago Thailand was ruled by an absolute monarchy, and since its abolition it has had to struggle to maintain a figurehead role. Leaders of successful *coups* have lost no time in affirming loyalty to the king, who has recognized the *coup* and thus encouraged early recognition by foreign powers. Under these circumstances, and in the light of history, political evolution has always been slow and often corrupt.

Pridi Panonyong was a great democrat, although in too much

of a hurry. His name still makes a great appeal to democrats, which is quite remarkable when it is realized that he has been in exile since 1949. Over the years he has behaved with great restraint towards the Bangkok government when he could have embarrassed it. His democracy never had time to get off the ground. It was beset with ill-fortune. His three Prime Ministers after the war, Kuang Abhaiwongse, Seni Pramoj and Tawee Bunyaket were soon out of office and at one time or another were blamed for Thailand's post-war difficulties and for the loss of face sustained by the enforced return of the territories seized by Pibul. Democracy, then, has never been given a real trial in Thailand. However, Pridi is now 68 years of age, and any political activity under his leadership would have to be effected in the not too distant future.

Both Pridi and Pibul had roughly the same ambition. This was a great independent region of South-east Asia under Thai leadership, or a greater Thai empire. Under Pibul, the militarists had seen how co-operation with the Japanese had paid big dividends. For in 1943 Thailand had taken over four Malay and two Burmese states. Had the Japanese been victorious, Pibul would have seen the dream of a greater Thai empire realized. It is possible that Pridi, in his home in Yunnan—a name which has a mystical appeal for so many Thais, for it was their original home-land—still dreams of his independent South-east Asia. A considerable number of them have emigrated to be with the former 'Mentor'.

There is evidence of a militarist and militant trend among the younger Thais. Posters showing young Thai soldiers at battle stations may appear incongruous among a people known for their gaiety, tolerance and avoidance of responsibility and worry. But the Thais are more complex than this. As individuals, they are proud and independent. They are easily provoked. If they are struck, then a knife blow is a reflex action. The Thai peasant's sense of honesty is unsurpassed.

I was very surprised to be told by the senior boys of one school I visited in my first year in Thailand that the army was their choice of career. I asked the same question at ten other schools and received the same answer. I have been impressed by the armed forces' manœuvres, particularly the parachutists.

The political situation is always uncertain in this delightful country. The leaders appear to be afraid of democracy, particularly the American brand. However, it appears certain that America would wish to see a more liberal régime in a country which has been under martial law since 1958, especially if the Vietnam war is concluded satisfactorily.

I had thought of calling this chapter 'Stars and Stripes over Siam'. The independence they so proudly maintained for centuries has been lost in as many years. Those who clamoured for non-alignment only a few years ago, and cited countries which received possibly even more American aid than Thailand, although they followed a neutralist policy, now realize that non-alignment did not save Indonesia, Burma, Ceylon, Nepal and Cambodia from internal subversion, infiltration and, in the case of Burma, attacks by the Red Guards.

At present there is a strong desire for the Americans to stay. It is true that there are occasional outbursts of anti-American feeling, but this is not new. It has been going on for over fifteen years. In 1956 in Bangkok, I remember reading a spate of articles in which the writers complained of American arrogance and defiantly proclaimed that Thailand would never be the forty-ninth State. This particular attack was sparked off by two soldiers from J.U.S.M.A.G. (Joint United States Military Aid Group) injuring a pedestrian through careless driving. The Americans are well used to these sudden storms. Usually the culprits are promptly flown home, and all is quiet until the next incident. The fashion today is to remind them that Thailand is not an American colony. However, it would be unwise to regard the sensitivity of the Thais as of no account.

There are Thais who want the country to be free of Americans, but are alarmed at the possible consequences of their departure. When asked if they would be prepared to sacrifice the material benefits of alignment with the United States for the emotional benefits of complete independence, reaction is mixed. Life has been made too easy for so many. Indeed, the inhabitants of Bangkok have never had it so good. America has spoilt them. They do not want to think about a future which for many has fears.

I have often wondered whether these pleasant, friendly people feel deeply about social injustices and inequality, and whether there are many among them who are prepared to agitate and work to bring about reforms. The many *coups* are no inspiration, for here the object is not to improve the lot of the people but rather to serve the interests of the few. I have asked several well-educated young Thais, whom one would expect to be in the pioneer or leader class—why don't you do a spell in the north-east? or the Moslem Malay south? Valluya's reaction was that the Government should give a more vigorous and inspiring lead. She was probably right, but I felt that consciences were not easily disturbed. For example, it is significant that doctors average one per 1,000 inhabitants in Bangkok and one per 25,000 up-country, and that half the total nursing force is in the capital. My experiences in the north-east taught me that there was not so much apathy and idleness on the part of the workers but insufficient energy, strength and will power because constitutions were undermined by disease and inadequate diet, as well as lack of medical care.

"Politics? Politics up here? That's all Bangkok worries about up here. Food, medical care, water and fertilizers for the crops—these are the things we think and talk about here," said an elderly abbot to me. His voice was quiet and composed, but I detected a slight bitterness. He had lived many years in the region.

Thailand's foreign policy would be largely determined by America's conduct of affairs in South-east Asia. Another fiasco like Laos, or a retreat from Vietnam, could result in a clamour for neutralism. If, however, the rest of South-east Asia turns communist, Thailand is certain to follow. Neither event is imminent.

As far as internal problems are concerned, there are three schools of thought, only one of which is at present playing the dominant role. This is the powerful militaristic school or the 'coup group'. The second is the socialistic, or followers and admirers of Pridi and his disciples. The third is the intellectual school. The latter, as yet, does not realize its strength and has no known leaders, but these would quickly emerge in any uprising, and here this could be spontaneous. It is possible that the latter two might combine against the militaristic group.

The long-awaited constitution was finally promulgated on 20th June 1968. General elections were scheduled to take place 240 days later.

The months following the granting of the constitution and subsequent elections will be critical for Thailand. Any attempt to manipulate it, to rig the elections, or to postpone them on the pretext of the military situation, or for the die-hard military group to buy out the civilian party, could well result in a show-down. The young intellectuals, who appear to be apathetic over such concrete problems as the plight of the farmers in the north-east provinces, would take a different stand over the intangible ones of theory and democracy. So would the socialistic school. Disorders would not be confined to Bangkok. If they assumed serious proportions then the likelihood of foreign intervention is highly probable.

It is likely that the Government is aware of the dangers, and that the constitution will be safeguarded. In any case, the leaders are faced with possibly the most crucial period since the end of World War II. This prosperous country could well remain the jewel of South-east Asia, or, with her neighbour states, disappear behind a bamboo curtain.

Index

A

Akha Tribe, 23, 167
American Central Intelligence Agency, 194
Ananda Mahidol, King, 38, 90-91, 92, 93, 94, 95, 130
Ananta Throne Hall, 34
Angkor Thom, 176, 180
Angkor Wat, 174, 175, 176, 180-82
Annam, King of, 84
Anuwongse, Prince, 79
Arundhpradet, 148
Ayudhya, 28-31, 33, 74, 107
Ayudhya, 132

B

Bahn Pong, 111, 115, 117
Bamboo Bar, 109, 193
Bangkao Camp, 119
Bang Pa In, 86
Bangkok, 12, 13, 34-43, 47, 51, 82, 89, 93, 124, 158, 161, 166, 183, 202
Bangkok Post, 12
Bayon, 176, 180
Bhuket, 63, 75
Boon Oum, Prince, 137, 138
Borneo Company, The, 19, 22
Borom Piman Palace, 38
Boworadet, Prince, 90, 125, 191
Bowring, Sir John, 81
Bridge on the River Kwai, The, 112
Buat Nek, Festival of, 56
Buddha, The, 18, 21, 54, 56, 98, 104
Buddhism, 42-3, 67, 81, 99, 100-102, 106, 177
Buddhist Era, 98

Buddhist Monks, 51, 66, 71, 76, 103-8, 154, 182
Buddhist Nuns, 107
Buddhist Society of Thailand, 107
Burma, 28-9, 30, 33, 78, 110, 129, 187
Burney, Captain, 78-9
Butr, 92, 93, 94, 95

C

Cambodia, 73, 84, 139
Chachoengsao, 50, 143, 165
Chakrabongse, Prince, 87, 124
Chakri, General, 55, 73
Chaleo, 93, 94, 96
Chao Khun, 100
Chao Phya, River, 35, 55, 132
Chiengmai, 17, 18, 19, 20, 21, 24, 147
China, 30, 68, 78, 80, 87, 136, 173, 187, 188
Chin Peng, 188
Chou-en Lai, 170
Chou Ta-Kuan, 181-2
Chula Chakrabongse, Prince, 102
Chulalongkorn, King, 34, 83-5, 144
Chulalongkorn University, 161, 192, 197
Chumporn, 75, 76
Chungkai, 109, 113-14
Cochin China, 79
Courts of the First Instance, 144, 184

D

Dararasmai, Princess, 17
De Chaumont, Chevalier, 31, 35
Decree of the Patronage of Islam, 184
De Gaulle, General, 68-9
Desfarges, General, 33

Devil's Discus, The, 95
Dha Khanun, 119
Dhamma Yutta, 81
Dhamrong, Admiral, 93
Dhonburi, 33, 73, 145
Dikka (Supreme Court), 94
Direck Jayanama, 127
Duong Van Min, General, 71
Dusit Maha Prasart, 37

E

Eisenhower, General, 194
Elephants, 20, 21, 22, 27, 30
Eton, 80

F

First Buddhist temple in Europe, 107
Floating Market, 36
Forbidden City, 37
France, 31, 32, 33, 81, 84, 146
Free Thai Movement, 127
Friendship Highway, 60, 61, 64

G

Galyani, Princess, 90
German School, 159

H

Hanoi, 65
Ho Chi Minh, 64, 68, 136
Hua Hin, 89
Hué, 70, 79
Hong Kong, 149, 195

I

Indonesia, 171
Isarasunthon, Prince, 75
Islamic Adviser to the Thai Government, 183

J

Japan, 85, 109, 110, 113, 127
Jars, Plain of, 138
Jayavarman, King, 180
J.U.S.M.A.G., 201

K

Kanchanaburi, 109, 111, 113
Kao Phra Sumen, 103
Karen, tribe, 23, 167
Karl Marx, 107, 136
Karma, 109
Kennedy, Joseph, 126

Khamu, tribe, 23
Khao Phra Viharn, 139
Khmers, 167, 175, 176-7, 181-2
Khon Khen, 62
Kite Fighting, 51-2
Kong Le, Captain, 137, 138
Korat, 24, 60-62, 129, 191
Korea, 169
Kra Isthmus, 114, 129
Kris Sivara, General, 142
Kuang Abhaiwongse, 129, 131, 134-5
Kuomintang, 168
Kwai Rivers, 112, 113, 115, 117, 119

L

Lahu, tribe, 23
Landon, Margaret, 80
Lampang, 16, 117
Lampoon, 16, 17
Lannathai, 17, 27
Laos, 64, 84, 137, 138, 139
Lawa, tribe, 23
League of Patriotic Youth of Thailand, 196
Leonowens, Anna, 15, 80
——Louis T., 15, 19, 20-21
Leprosy, 25
Le Van Kim, General, 71
Lisu, tribe, 23
Lopburi, 31
Louis XIV, 31, 32
Loy Krathong, Festival of, 54-6
Luang Prabang, 73, 137

M

Maha Berien, 105
Mahayana, 66
Malacca Straits, 110
Malayan Communist Party, 118, 195
Malaysia, 185, 188, 195
Malaysian People's Liberation Army, 188
Manhattan, 132
Mao Tse-tung, 136, 169
Mekong, River, 62, 70, 190
Meo, tribe, 22, 167
Missionaries, 31, 32, 78, 80, 81-2, 83
Monkey Bend Camp, 118, 119
Mons, tribe, 27
Moslem Malay provinces, 159, 183-9, 198
Mouhot, Henri, 176
Moulmein, 110

N

Naked Island, 121
Nakornpanom, 41, 65
Nakorn Sawan, Prince, 89
Nakornsrithamarat, 185, 189
Nang Toronee, 18
Narai, King, 31, 32, 33
New Road, 35, 152
Ngo Dinh Diem, President, 65-6
Ngo Dinh Nhu, 71
Nirvana, 38, 100-101
Nongkai, 61, 62, 63
Nong Pladuk, 116, 121
Nuns, Buddhist, 107

O

Opium, 22, 24, 75-6, 78, 79, 81, 148-150, 166

P

Pae-chia, 159
Pahol, Colonel, 89, 90
Pai-si, 103, 104
Pathet-Lao, 68, 137, 138
Panomyong, Pridi, 15, 89, 90, 91, 92-3, 94, 96, 123-32, 141, 169, 170, 199-200, 202
Pattani, 184, 189
Peace Corps, American, 191
Pearl Harbor, 127
Peking, 167-9, 172
Penang, 77
People's Party, The, 125, 128
People's Republic of China, The, 169, 171, 196, 197
Petchburi, 153
Petchburi Road, 41
Phao, Police General, 64, 68, 94, 95, 100, 131-2, 133, 134, 148, 149, 150-151, 152, 170, 194
Phaulcon, Constantine, 31-3
Phetraja, King, 103
Phi Tong Luang, tribe, 23
Phra Phum Chao Thi, 57
Phumipol Aduldej, King, 31, 64, 91-2, 97, 107, 131, 140
Pibul Songkram, Field Marshal, 29, 64, 89, 96, 123, 135, 140, 151, 169, 170-171, 199, 200
Ping, River, 17, 18
Pitsanulok, 74, 159
Ploughing, Festival of, 53-4

Pnom Penh, 79, 134
Pote Sarasin, 135, 140
Poumi Nosavan, General, 137-8
Pra Chedi Klang Nam, 57
Prajadhipok, King, 88-90, 141
Pramane Ground, 95, 134
Praphass, General, 96, 141-2
Prisoner on the Kwai, 122

Q

Quaritch-Wales, H. G., 82-3, 85-6

R

Railway of Death, 30, 110-22
Railway Hotel Chiengmai, 16
Rama I, 34, 74-5
Rama II, 34, 75, 76-7, 78
Rama III, 34, 77-80
Rama IV (King Mongkut), 34, 80-82
Ramayana, 37, 179
Ram Kamhaeng, King, 26-7
Rampai, Queen, 90
Ranong, 76
Rayong, 73
Red Guards, 201
Rice, 44-9
Ronapakas, General, 132
Rotary Club, 134, 193
Rubber, 185-6
Rusk, Dean, 138
Ruth, 123, 127

S

Saffron robe, 85, 100, 104, 108, 154
Saiyoke, Waterfall, 113
Samanaris, 105
Sanan, 13, 14, 15, 19, 24
Sangha, 66
Saraburi, 174
Sarit, Field Marshal, 41, 100, 134, 135-141, 150, 160, 197
Sarn Seri, 138
Savitri, 13, 14, 15, 16, 18, 24
Schools, Monastic, 153-5
——Mission, 154, 158, 159
——Private, 158, 159
——State, 152, 156, 160, 161
S.E.A.T.O., 135, 137, 138, 139, 171, 198
Seni Pramoj, Mom, 127, 197, 200
Siam Rath, 138
Silas, 195
Singapore, 114, 117

Silver Street, 18
Sirikit, Queen, 94, 97, 107, 158
Snakes, 29, 46, 47, 59
Songkla, 90
Song Suradet, Colonel, 89
Soupanouvong, Prince, 137
Souvanna Pouma, General, 137-8
State Lottery, 140
Suez, 193-4
Sukhothai 26-8, 167
Sunanda, Queen, 85, 86
Superchai, 36
Suratthani, 185
Suriyabongse, Dr. Luang, 185
Suriyothai, Queen, 30

T

Takli, 41
Taksin, King, 17
Taiwan, 168, 169, 171, 172
Talang, 76
Tamakham, 116, 121
Taoism, 66
Tawee Bunyaket, 200
Teak, 15, 16, 19
Tennasserim Range, 185
Teochiu Association, 172
Thai Airways, 61
Thai Autonomous People's Republic in Yunnan, 170
Thai Boxing, 40
Thai-Chinese Friendship Society, 169
Thai Classical Dancing, 39-40
Thai Independence Group, 196
Thai Patriotic Front, 196
Thai Press, 199
Thai State Railways, 15, 113
Thakhek, 65
Thamassat University, 161, 162, 192, 197
Thanbyuzayat, 111, 115, 116
Thanom Kittikachorn, General, 136, 140, 141, 142
Than Poo Ying Mo, 62
Three Pagodas Pass, 30, 117
Tiang Sirrikhan, 64
Tonkin, 65
Tran Van Duong, 71
Tripitaka, 105

Tunku Abdul Rahman, 187

U

Ubol, 41, 61, 62
Udorn, 41, 71, 139
United Nations, 83, 130, 156
United States, 25, 69, 127, 137, 138, 142, 190, 191, 194-5, 201
Un-Thai Activities Act, 170
U.S.I.S., 193
U.S.O.M., 14

V

Vajiravudh, King, 34, 86-8
Vajiravudh school, 90
Valluya, 13, 14, 15, 19, 25, 28, 36, 40, 42, 107, 194
Vichit, 13, 14, 28
Vientiane, 67-8
Vietminh, 64, 65, 68
Vietnamese, 64, 65-7, 70-71, 79, 142, 194, 202
Virginia Water, 90
Visakha Puja, Festival of, 54
Vishnu, 178

W

Wang Yai, 119, 121
Wanlan Viaduct, 118
Wan Waityakorn, Prince, 170
War Graves Commission, 112
Wat Arun, 36, 57
Wat Benchamopitr, 38-9
Wat Bovornines, 98
Wat Mahathat, 75
Wat Po, 38
Wat Pra Doi Suthep, 18
Wat Pra Keo, 33, 34, 37, 38
Wat Sraket, 39
Wat Sutat, 39
Wat Traimitr, 39
Water, Festival of, 52-3
Wild Tigers, 86-7, 88

Y

Yao Tribe, 23
Yasovarman, King, 180
Yunnan, 26, 123, 195, 200